CA$H CLOUT

CA$H CLOUT

Political Money in Illinois Legislative Elections

by Kent D. Redfield

University of Illinois at Springfield
Springfield, Illinois

Printed in the United States.

Library of Congress Cataloging-in-Publication Data

Redfield, Kent.
Ca$h clout : political money in Illinois legislative elections /
by Kent D. Redfield.
p. cm.
Includes bibliographical references and index.
ISBN 0-938943-05-7
1. Campaign funds--Illinois. 2. Illinois. General Assembly-- Elections. I. Title.
JK1991.5.I3R43 1995
324.7'8'09773--dc20 95-35616
CIP

Cover design by Larz Gaydos
Cover photograph by Terry Farmer

Institute for Public Affairs
University of Illinois at Springfield
Springfield, Illinois, 62794-9243

CONTENTS

TABLES

PREFACE

In one sense, deciding to write a book about the role of money in Illinois legislative elections is an easy choice for a former participant and long-time student of Illinois politics. The rough and tumble of politics in the Land of Lincoln is legendary. The vast sums of money that fuel Illinois elections move through one of the most open systems of state regulation in the country. The action is particularly dramatic in legislative elections. Every two years, control of the General Assembly rests on the outcome of key contested races in which the legislative leaders and major interest groups orchestrate contests that rival any state legislative election in the country in cost, technical sophistication, and intensity. For both the practitioner and the student of Illinois politics, the answer to the question "Who gives how much to whom?" is vital and fascinating.

The same elements that make the role of money in Illinois legislative elections so interesting to students of Illinois politics (high costs and high stakes) also raise serious concerns among the citizens of Illinois. Surveys show they are concerned about the high cost of elections in general and the influence that campaign contributions give to interest groups in particular. These doubts and negative feelings are also reflected in the responses to national surveys of political attitudes.

However, just because a book on financing legislative elections in Illinois is potentially interesting and timely does not mean it will be easy to research or write. Prior to the 1994 election cycle, none of the data on the individual receipts and expenditures of candidates for legislative, statewide, or local offices were available to the public in any form other than paper or microfiche copies of the original pages of the reports submitted by candidates to the Illinois State Board of Elections. The state board is now engaged in a project that will produce a database of the receipts of all candidates for state office for the last six months of 1994.

The receipt and expenditure data presented here for the 1990 and 1992 legislative elections were constructed by entering thousands of records from microfiche into a database program and then identifying and classifying each receipt and expenditure. Given the long, difficult, and frustrating task of accessing these records and converting them into a useable form that can be aggregated, classified, and examined, it is not surprising that there appear to be no previous attempts to examine campaign finance in Illinois in any comprehensive, systematic way. This project will be immensely helpful to anyone researching campaign finance in the future.

What follows is a book about the financing of legislative elections in Illinois during the 1990 and 1992 election cycles. The history and mechanics of the regulation of campaign finance in Illinois are addressed first. The main body of the book examines the role of the legislative leaders, interest groups, and state political parties in raising and spending money in legislative elections, along with the dynamics of the financing of key legislative races in 1992. Finally, some thoughts and modest suggestions are offered on changing the system used to regulate campaign finance in Illinois.

The research for this book was conducted under the auspices of the Illinois Legislative Studies Center at the University of Illinois at Springfield (UIS), formerly Sangamon State University. Without the support and guidance of Jack Van Der Slik, director of the center, the success achieved to date in studying campaign finance in Illinois would have been impossible. An extremely talented and dedicated group of graduate assistants participated in the design and building of the database and the seemingly endless task of entering, classifying, and analyzing the data. They are David Hobby, Dennis Johnson, Deryl Sequeria, and Pusparaj Mohanty. Ann Aldrich of the center staff also spent many long hours entering the data.

Three readers gave freely of their time and advice in trying to make the text more accurate, accessible, and interesting: Ronald Michaelson, executive director of the Illinois State Board of Elections and a nationally respected expert on the administration and regulation of state elections; Charlie Wheeler, director of the Public Affairs Reporting intern program at UIS and formerly a longtime statehouse reporter for the *Chicago Sun-Times*; and Kathy Best, the political reporter who covers Illinois politics for the *St. Louis Post-Dispatch*. While I tried to respond to their many useful suggestions and insightful questions, responsibility for the content, along with any errors or omissions, rests solely with me.

The Publication Unit of the Institute for Public Affairs at UIS, directed by Marilyn A. Huff, was responsible for both the editing and the publishing of the book. Sharon Johnson-Dietsch shouldered the monumental task of turning a mountain of data and academic prose into a book that is accessible not just to the political junkie or the dedicated scholar, but also to the interested observer of Illinois politics. Assistance was provided by Jackie Wright and Valerie Nifong. Any success in that transformation is attributable to their efforts. A special thank you is due Brenda Suhling of the Publication Unit, whose role it was to take multiple copies of the text and tables with multiple changes and translate them into a single manuscript.

Finally, the Joyce Foundation provided both financial support for publishing and marketing the book and invaluable moral support through the encouragement and wise counsel of Larry Hansen, who is directing the foundation's initiative on the role of money in politics.

The joy and satisfaction of producing a book are private matters that are difficult to share with your family, while the stress, strain, and frustration are all too easy to share. Jan, Jenny, Alicia, and Renee endured these with grace and understanding, and I am grateful for their support.

"Money is the mother's milk of politics."

Jesse Unruh, speaker of the house (1960-1970)
California Legislature

CHAPTER 1
MONEY IN ILLINOIS LEGISLATIVE ELECTIONS

Illinois legislators make a base salary of $39,420 a year. In 1990 Patrick Welch, the incumbent senator from the 38th Senate District, spent $371,000 to retain his seat in the legislature. His opponent, Nancy Beasley, spent $452,000 to defeat him. The combined total spending topped $823,000. All of this for a job that paid $39,420. While still a record, that kind of spending in Illinois legislative elections is not rare. In 1992 the incumbent and the challenger for a state senate seat in the rural, southern Illinois 55th Senate District spent $763,000 between them, while the incumbent and the challenger in the nearby 58th Senate District spent $653,000. These are just the most extreme examples of what has become a regular cycle of ever-increasing costs for state legislative elections in Illinois.

Historical information about the cost of legislative elections in Illinois is hard to come by, primarily because of weaknesses in the reporting system, which has been in effect since 1974. Data before 1974 are virtually nonexistent. Nationally, all of the studies of the cost of state legislative elections point to significant increases in cost. Inflation-adjusted increases of 20 percent to 100 percent every two years during the 1980s were found in almost every state where aggregate data are available (Alexander 1991). An examination of spending by the major interest groups in Illinois on legislative elections over the past 10 years suggests that we have at least matched national trends. In 1982 the top five groups in contributions to legislative campaigns gave $775,000 to candidates for house and senate seats (Michaelson 1987). In 1992 those same five groups gave $3.48 million to candidates for state legislative seats, an increase of more than 400 percent in 10 years.

In all, candidates for the Illinois General Assembly spent $12.4 million in the general election in 1990 (Illinois State Board of Elections 1992). In 1992 general election spending by General Assembly candidates almost doubled, to $22.3 (Illinois State Board of Elections 1993).

That is a dramatic increase, even allowing for the difference in open seats and opportunities for change between 1990, the last election under an existing legislative map, and 1992, the first election under a new map. In 1990, with 20 senate seats up for reelection, only 2 senate races had total combined spending of more than $300,000. In 1992 all 59 senate seats were up for election because of redistricting. That year there were 5 senate races where the two candidates, combined, spent more than $500,000 and the top 10 most expensive senate races cost slightly more than $5 million.

The dramatic increase in spending between 1990 and 1992 can be seen most clearly in a comparison of the most expensive house races in 1990 and 1992 (table 1.1). All 118 house seats were up both years. In 1990 there were 7 house races with combined spending exceeding $200,000 with a top of $322,000. The 20 most expensive races account for $3.7 million in spending. In 1992 there were 17 house races with combined spending of more than $200,000 and a top of $433,000. The 20 most expensive house races accounted for $5.4 million in spending.

Table 1.1
Cost of Running for a Seat in the Illinois House

	1990	1992
Number of races where combined spending exceeded $200,000	7	17
Most expensive race	$322,000	$433,000
Total cost of 20 most expensive races	$3.7 million	$5.4 million

By any measure, legislative elections in Illinois are expensive. Are they too expensive? Just knowing how expensive Illinois legislative elections are does not tell us much. Compared to the amount of money in the Illinois state budget, $823,000 for a single race and $22.4 million for one election doesn't seem like a lot of money. The Illinois legislature appropriates funds for a state budget, which was approximately $30 billion for the 1994-95 fiscal year. The state agency with the largest individual budget is the Department of Public Aid. Every 90 minutes that agency spends more than the total spent by both sides in the most expensive legislative race in Illinois history. Every 36 hours Public Aid spends more than the amount spent by every legislative candidate in the 1992 general election.

While the average house race in Wisconsin cost only half of the average house race in Illinois, the average house race in California was five times more expensive than the average Illinois house race (Sorauf 1988). Given the size and wealth of the population of Illinois, the makeup of the state's economy and political system, and the stakes involved in the policy decisions made by state government, the cost of Illinois legislative elections is probably in line with what has been going on in other states over the past decade.

Is the high cost bad for the state? Without knowing who contributes, how much they contribute, who controls the use of the resources in legislative campaigns, and the eventual impact of the current system on the makeup of the state legislature and on the policy decisions that legislators make, it is impossible to make a judgment about whether the current system is good or bad or too costly. Once we have a clearer picture of the way we finance legislative elections in Illinois we can return to questions of strengths and weaknesses and alternatives.

Researching Campaign Finance in Illinois

"Follow the money" is one of the basic rules of detectives in mystery novels. It is also good advice for those who want to understand the nature and dynamics of legislative elections in Illinois and the impact of those elections on the legislative process. But largely because of the time and expense involved in obtaining information about contributions and expenditures in legislative campaigns, questions such as, Who contributes money? How much money is contributed? What strategies are used by those who contribute? and How is campaign money spent? have been a mystery to all but a small group of insiders and a few diligent academic researchers and news reporters.

Elections in Illinois take place under a campaign finance law that places virtually no restrictions on contributions and expenditures, but does require complete disclosure and reporting. All candidate and political action committees that exceed a certain dollar threshold are required to file campaign finance reports with the State Board of Elections. What makes the research of campaign finance in Illinois state elections so difficult is that the only data from those reports entered into a database by the State Board of Elections are certain aggregate totals and committee officers' filing histories. The detailed information from the reports is placed in raw form on microfiche and made available in the board's Springfield and Chicago offices for inspection or purchase as unprocessed data. In order to analyze and crosscheck the reports, the information (name, amount, and date for each contributor to a campaign or each vendor selling services to a campaign) must be typed into a computerized database. Once that task is completed, each record must be coded and sorted into categories. A company, political action committee, or individual name listed in a report does not tell you what interest is being represented. It takes a good deal of time and hard work to enter these data and then determine the nature or identity of each contributor or vendor.

A comprehensive picture of the campaign finance process for the 1990 and 1992 legislative elections in Illinois is now available as a result of an ongoing campaign finance project conducted by the Illinois Legislative Studies Center, which is part of the Institute for Public Affairs at the University of Illinois at Springfield. With the exception of some information gathered from examining the campaign finance reports from candidates in selected house and senate races from 1990 and 1992, all of the data presented here come from a campaign finance database on the 1990 and 1992 election cycles created for the project by the Illinois Legislative Studies Center. It was built from the annual and semiannual reports of Campaign Contributions and Expenditures (D-2s*) filed with the State Board of Elections by the following: the 65 interest groups and corporations that contributed the most to legislative elections during the 1990 and 1992 election cycles, the political committees of the four legislative leaders during that time, the four chamber political committees (formed by the four legislative caucuses, e.g., the House Republican Campaign Committee), and the two state political parties. Receipts or expenditures from January 1, 1989, to December 31, 1990, were considered part of the 1990 election cycle, and receipts or expenditures from January 1, 1991, to December 31, 1992, were considered part of the 1992 election cycle. Receipts and expenditures were classified using a coding system developed for the project.

The Illinois Legislative Studies Center's campaign finance database contains over 82,000 records. Each of those records had to be typed into the database and then classified. The effort required to create and maintain this database makes it easy to understand why so little systematic research has been conducted in Illinois on state-level campaign finance.

Articles based on the early findings of this ongoing campaign finance study have been published in *Illinois Issues* (Redfield 1991, 1992, 1993)

---

* See appendix A, p. 177 for a copy of this form.

magazine on the role of legislative leaders in the 1990 elections, the role of money in targeted house races in the 1992 legislative elections, and the role of the state political parties in the 1990 legislative elections. An article on interest group campaign contribution strategies in the 1992 legislative elections was published in the 1994 *Almanac of Illinois Politics*.

An Overview of the Illinois Campaign Finance System

Regulating Campaign Finance. Campaign finance in Illinois is regulated by a law passed in 1974. That law has remained remarkably unchanged over the past two decades. Compared to the campaign contribution and spending regulations that govern federal elections and those in effect in most states, Illinois has a very wide-open, unrestricted, campaign finance system. Candidates for public office, including the state legislature, who spend more than $1,000 in support of their campaigns, and groups that spend more than $1,000 in support of a candidate are required by law to file periodic reports with the State Board of Elections. In those reports, all receipts and expenditures must be reported in the aggregate. Individual receipts and expenditures that exceed $150 must be itemized and identified: who gave the money or who received the money. Those reports are filed with the state board and are available for public inspection.

Beyond the requirement for full reporting and full disclosure, there are very few restrictions on the actions of contributors or candidates. No individuals, public officials, political parties, interest groups, or corporate entities are currently prohibited from contributing to legislative campaigns. There are no limits on how much an individual, public official, political party, interest group, or corporate entity can contribute to a candidate or spend on behalf of a candidate. While industries that are regulated by the state, such as horse racing, have been prohibited from contributing to candidates for state office, those restrictions were removed from the law in the early 1980s. There are no limits on how much a candidate can spend on a political campaign and virtually no limits on what a candidate for political office can spend campaigns funds for. Individuals are not to use campaign funds for personal purposes, but what constitutes *personal use* is undefined. Many of these activities are prohibited or severely restricted in campaigns for federal office and prohibited or restricted in most state-level campaigns. And in contrast to presidential elections and some gubernatorial and state legislative elections, there is no public funding of political campaigns at any level in Illinois. Chapter 2 will present the history and an analysis of Illinois' campaign finance law.

The Two Worlds of Legislative Elections. The story of the financing of legislative elections in Illinois is really the story of two very different elections. The first is the world of very expensive, strongly contested elections. These contests are dominated by support from the legislative leaders and powerful interest groups with large amounts of resources to direct into political campaigns. This is a relatively small world. In 1992 only 13 senate races (22 percent) and 48 house races (40 percent) could be classified as competitive, contested races in terms of the amount of money the candidates spent. These were races where the losing candidate spent more than $20,000 and received more than 40 percent of the vote.

The larger world of Illinois legislative elections is one where the well-financed winning candidates, often incumbents, run unopposed or run against weak opponents who spend little or no money. In 1992 more than 44 percent of the senators elected (26 candidates) had no opponent in the general election, and an additional 34 percent (20 candidates) had opponents who spent less than $20,000 and received less than 40 percent of the vote. In the house, 31 percent of the candidates elected in the general election (37 candidates) had no opposition, while an additional 29 percent (33 candidates) had opponents who spent less than $20,000 and received less than 40 percent of the vote.

Why do legislative elections in Illinois split into two groups in terms of campaign spending: contested and uncontested? The answer lies in the way the legislative district maps are drawn. Every 10 years it is the legislature's responsibility to create a new set of legislative districts that take into account population changes in the state over the past decade. Legislative districts must be drawn that are equal in population, compact, contiguous, and do not dilute the voting strength of minority populations. If the legislature fails to pass a new legislative map, or if the governor refuses to approve a map passed by the legislature prior to June 30 of the second year after a new federal census, then the responsibility for drawing a new map shifts to a commission of eight members, two appointed by each of the four legislative leaders. This results in a commission with four members from each political party. If no compromise is reached, control of that committee is determined by placing the name of one Republican and one Democrat in a "hat" and drawing out one name. Whoever is elected becomes the ninth member of the committee, thereby giving one party a 5-to-4 majority. This happened in 1981 when a Democrat was chosen and in 1991 when a Republican was chosen (Van Der Slik and Redfield 1989).*

Faced with the broad options of drawing as many competitive districts as possible or as many safe districts as possible, the general strategy in 1981 and 1991 was for the legislative leaders of the party in control to draw as many safe districts as possible for both parties, while structuring the competitive districts to favor the party that controlled the process. Given the political geography of the state, this strategy makes sense. It is unlikely that Republican candidates will win, or even run, in overwhelmingly Democratic districts in the heart of Chicago. The same is true for Democratic candidates in heavily Republican districts in DuPage County. It is even more unlikely that legislative leaders or interest groups will contribute to or spend money in support of those candidates. In other areas where the partisan division among voters is more even, who controls the map can be the major factor in determining which party is successful in winning the subsequent elections. In 1981 the Democrats drew largely urban house districts around Springfield, Decatur, and Champaign-Urbana. These districts elected Democrats throughout the 10-year existence of the map. In 1991 the Republicans eliminated these downstate, urban house districts, splitting the urban areas into three districts that contain substantial rural territory. These new districts were expected to favor Republican candidates. In 1992 the house Democrats held all three. In the national and state Republican landslide of 1994, two of the three districts elected Republicans. Under both maps, there are large portions of the state that are made up of safe districts for one or the other of the two political parties. Under both maps, there are also natural battlegrounds where candidates from either party might win. The essence of good mapmaking from a partisan standpoint is to draw districts in those competitive areas that give your party an advantage in terms of the partisan makeup of the districts.

Illinois has single-member senate districts, which cover the same territory as two single-member house districts. This creates a conflict during redistricting within the party that controls the process: those representing the senate side want to create a set of 59 senate districts that are most favorable to their interests and then divide each of those 59

---

* In 1981 the hat used for the drawing was one that had been worn by Abraham Lincoln.

senate districts into two house districts. Those representing the house side want to create a set of 118 house districts that give them the most electoral advantage and then combine them into 59 senate districts. Each of the four legislative leaders and chamber groups is primarily concerned with partisan control of his/her chamber.

This focus on gaining control of districts affects how legislative elections are financed. It results in a legislative election process in which there are (1) a small number of very expensive races where the two candidates are competitive in terms of the amount of money expended and (2) a large number of inexpensive races in which one candidate faces no opposition or a well-financed candidate faces a poorly funded opponent. This context will be important in describing and evaluating the participation of legislative leaders, interest groups, and political parties in the financing of legislative elections in Illinois.

The Role of Legislative Leaders, Interest Groups, and Political Parties. Nationally we are in an era of candidate-centered elections. Candidates at all levels run primarily as individuals rather than as members of the Republican or Democratic party. However, an important change has taken place in legislative elections in many states: the growing influence of legislative leaders (Gierzynski 1992; Loftus 1994). In Illinois, competitive legislative elections are dominated by the four legislative leaders and the chamber political committees they control. The leaders recruit candidates for open seats and to challenge incumbents, organize and run the campaigns of incumbents and challengers, and, most important, finance those campaigns. More than one-third of *all* resources expended in Illinois legislative elections are controlled by the legislative leaders; in the general election the percentage rises to 40 percent. And in elections that are targeted by the leaders, they control over half of the spending. The dominance of legislative leaders in legislative elections in Illinois has increased steadily over the past decade, mirroring the trends in many state legislatures. This leader dominance has strong implications for both the electoral process and policymaking in the legislature, which will be addressed in chapter 3.

At the same time, the role of state and local political parties in legislative elections has been steadily decreasing. State political parties, never big players in state legislative races, function primarily as conduits for the transfer of funds and as bulk purchasers of services, which are financed and distributed under the direction of the legislative leaders. At the local level, even the vaunted Cook County Democratic Party no longer dominates legislative races in Chicago, having fragmented into warring factions. Chapter 4 will take up the role of political parties in Illinois legislative elections.

In contrast to political parties, interest groups are important players in legislative elections in Illinois. One interest group, the Illinois State Medical Society, spent almost $1.5 million on legislative elections during the 1992 election cycle, and the top 20 interest groups accounted for $6.42 million in spending during the same cycle. How specific interest groups participate in legislative elections is a function of how they relate to the complex environment of elections and legislative process in Illinois.

The combination of a large number of safe seats for both parties, a number of competitive districts with competitive elections, the strong influence of the four legislative leaders in competitive elections, and a closely divided legislature dominated by the four legislative leaders presents a number of strategic options to interest groups that want to contribute to legislative candidates and legislative leaders. Most interest groups, seeking to establish goodwill with and access to those in power, will contribute to all four legislative leaders and key incumbents from both parties during the first year of the two-year legislative cycle when there are no elections. Some interest groups are high-risk, partisan players in legislative elections, working closely with the legislative leaders in targeted races in both the primary and general elections. Other interest groups are partisan in their giving, but pursue a lower-risk strategy, giving primarily to incumbents and the leaders of the party they favor. Most interest groups pursue a bipartisan, low-risk approach, contributing to the incumbents and leaders of both parties in both chambers on an equal basis during the election year. How interest groups participate in legislative elections in Illinois will be taken up in chapter 5.

Targets and Surprises. The configuration of high-profile, targeted races and low-profile, untargeted races in Illinois legislative elections has continued from election cycle to election cycle over the past decade. In addition, legislative elections are essentially two separate elections: a battle for control of the house and a battle for control of the senate. The individual leaders view each election as a set of house races or a set of senate races rather than as a unified legislative election. Historically there is very little coordination or cooperation between house and senate leaders of the same party during legislative elections. The senate Republican caucus did provide assistance with some house races in 1994, but it is too early to tell if this is a trend. Interest groups that are partisan and electorally active may think in more comprehensive terms when they develop strategy for a particular election or they may choose to focus primarily on house or senate elections.

The overall configuration of legislative elections in Illinois (targeted and untargeted races in house elections and senate elections under a given map) is predictable. The outcomes of those elections are not. While the legislative map provides an initial advantage to one partisan side, legislative elections seldom produce all of the results that would be predicted by the voting patterns in each district from previous partisan elections. Particular elections are determined by the candidates that run and how they present themselves, the issues raised, and the financing available to each candidate.

Occasionally, national or statewide political trends will affect state elections. In 1994 the national and state landslide for Republican candidates certainly played a role in the Republican takeover of the Illinois house. Each election produces its share of miscalculations and surprises. Untargeted races are sometimes closer than expected, occasionally producing upsets. Large expenditures by both sides in targeted races may only reinforce the existing partisan distribution of votes in a district, and targeted spending against incumbents who have built a solid basis of support in a district is often ineffective. Money is important and necessary, but it is rarely the sole factor in determining who wins. Using the role of money in targeted and untargeted legislative races in the 1992 legislative elections as a case study, the importance of the various actors and the impact of money on elections and policy outcomes will be examined in chapter 6.

Alternatives and Outcomes

The system of financing legislative campaigns in Illinois and the law that regulates it reflect the Illinois political system as much as they shape it. Measures such as imposing severe limitations on contributions by interest groups and restrictions on transfers by legislative leaders or adopting a system of public financing would not produce the same results in Illinois as they would in Wisconsin. Nor would such restrictions necessarily produce the results intended by those who advocated their adoption. Students of political reform often refer to the "law of unintended consequences." The proper response to the question, How am I doing? is always, Compared to what?

There are two broad options for restricting the way money is raised and spent in political campaigns. The first is the "sunshine" option: maximum reporting and disclosure and minimum restrictions. The underlying assumption is that it is difficult to restrict the flow of campaign money and that many restrictions do not accomplish their intended results. Hence, advocates of a sunshine system prefer a law designed to place as much information in the hands of the voters as possible, relying on candidates to avoid behaviors and appearances that could become campaign issues. The second is the regulation option: limitations on who can contribute and how much they can contribute. These contribution limits are sometimes combined with a system of public financing, which is provided as an inducement for candidates to accept voluntary spending limits. The underlying assumption is that given free rein, money will have a corrupting influence on elections and the legislative process. Only by placing severe limitations on contributions and promoting spending limits and public financing of campaigns can legislative elections be kept free from the influence of money.

In Illinois, the existing campaign finance law is not a complete sunshine law, but it could be. The requirements for who reports and what they must report provide an adequate amount of information; however, there should be a process that shines light on the data that are collected. Requiring the occupation or employer of individuals making itemized contributions would make the law stronger and analysis easier. Putting campaign reports in an electronic database and making that database easily accessible to everyone would go a long way toward making the law operate as a sunshine law.

Choosing the regulation option in Illinois would be much more complicated. Limits on who can contribute and how much they can contribute to a candidate have been widely adopted at the federal and state level and are clearly constitutional under existing judicial rulings. However, placing statutory limits on how much a person or group can spend on behalf of a candidate or statutory limits on how much a candidate can spend on a campaign would clearly be unconstitutional under the same judicial rulings. Offering the carrot of public financing is the way most states try to induce candidates to agree to spending limits, and most of these programs apply only to statewide office, not legislative elections. Options for restricting or managing the role of money in legislative elections in Illinois will be the focus of the concluding chapter.

"I happened to be listening to WBBM this morning and they were featuring in one of their articles a lady named Baby Doll, 70 years old, a madam from Peoria. And she said when she came to Peoria it was a $1 town and now it is a $10 town. I think we've established what we are, we're merely dickering for a price."

State senator John Knuppel during the floor debate on the 1974 Illinois campaign finance law, commenting on an amendment to raise the threshold for an itemized reporting of a contribution from $150 to $500.

Senate Debates, Illinois General Assembly, June 6, 1974, p. 187.

CHAPTER 2
REGULATING CAMPAIGN CONTRIBUTIONS AND EXPENDITURES IN ILLINOIS

The modern era of state regulation of campaign contributions and expenditures is rooted in the Watergate scandal. The primary focus of the congressional and media investigations on Watergate was the question of obstruction of justice and abuse of power by President Nixon. But revelations about the amount of money raised for Nixon's 1972 reelection campaign, and the way money was raised and spent, sparked renewed interest in establishing a tough federal law regulating contributions and expenditures in federal elections. That law (the 1974 amendments to the Federal Election Campaign Act) provided for strict limits on campaign contributions and expenditures in federal elections and a system of public funding for presidential elections.

At the same time there was a flurry of activity at the state level as state legislators reacted to criticism of the role of money in the electoral process from the public and the news media. During the period of 1973 to 1975 most states either strengthened existing laws regulating campaign finance or enacted them for the first time. Many of these laws mirrored the federal law in providing limits on who could contribute to candidates and how much they could contribute and limits on how much a candidate could spend or how much could be spent by others in support of a candidate (Alexander 1991; Sorauf 1988).

While the Watergate scandal provided strong impetus for enacting or strengthening campaign finance laws at the state and federal level, the momentum was short lived. In 1976 the United States Supreme Court invalidated large portions of the 1974 amendments to the federal election law with their ruling in *Buckley v. Valeo* (1976). The Court ruled that requirements that campaign contributions be reported and disclosed and that limits on how much a person or group can contribute to a candidate are constitutional. But the Court also held that limits on how much a candidate can spend or on how much a person or group can spend independently on behalf of a candidate are unconstitutional violations of free speech.

Congress was forced to revise the federal election law to bring it into compliance with *Buckley*. Since the Supreme Court's ruling also extended to the states through the Fourteenth Amendment, the decision also defined what states can and cannot do in restricting the flow of money into political campaigns and in restricting spending by candidates and others in support of candidates. Many states had to adopt significant changes in their campaign finance laws to bring them into compliance with the ruling in *Buckley*. Nineteen years later the constitutional framework for regulating campaign finance at the federal and state level remains almost completely unchanged.

Constitutional Limits on Regulating Campaign Finance

Prior to the *Buckley* decision, it was widely assumed that laws regulating campaign contributions and expenditures represented a legitimate governmental interest in protecting the integrity of the electoral process. United States Supreme Court rulings upholding federal election laws had relied on arguments to that effect. The major decision prior to *Buckley*, *Burroughs v. U.S.*, was decided in 1934. When the 1974 changes in the federal election law were challenged in court in 1975, the United States Court of Appeals upheld the changes. The lower courts accepted the arguments of the proponents of the law that this was an area that could be regulated by legislative action because of the need to protect the electoral process from the corrupting and distorting impact of money (Sorauf 1988).

In deciding *Buckley*, the Supreme Court held that giving a campaign contribution to a candidate and campaign spending by a candidate or on behalf of a candidate is political speech, a form of free speech protected by the First Amendment to the U.S. Constitution. Having held that campaign contributions and expenditures are protected speech, the Court then considered what, if any, restrictions Congress might legitimately place on them. The Court rejected the idea that there was a legitimate legislative interest in preserving the integrity of the electoral process that would justify placing limits on the rights of individuals to engage in political speech through campaign expenditures. As such, the Court held that there was no legitimate legislative interest in limiting expenditures on political campaigns, either by candidates themselves or by others acting independently of the candidate they support. Following that logic, the Court struck down federal limits on campaign expenditures by candidates and by others acting in support of candidates as unconstitutional limits on free speech. They did uphold limits on spending by political party committees on behalf of candidates.

The Court did find that there was a legitimate legislative interest in preventing corruption or the appearance of corruption of the political process. By corruption, they were referring to the exchange of a campaign contribution for a favorable action by a public official or a candidate once elected, a quid pro quo. As such, the Court upheld limits on how much an individual, group, or political party committee can contribute to a candidate for public office.

Because reporting and disclosure are essential to determining what relationship exists between contributors and candidates, the Court also upheld requirements that candidates report the sources and amounts of the contributions they accept and the expenditures they make and that those reports be disclosed to the general public.

Finally, on the issue of public funding and voluntary spending limits, the Court upheld public funding of presidential campaigns and the requirement that candidates accept voluntary spending limits as a condition for receiving public funds.

Only two other significant campaign finance decisions have been handed down by the Supreme Court since 1976 (Sorauf 1988). In *First National Bank of Boston v. Bellotti* (1978), the Supreme Court examined the question of what limits can be placed on contributions in support of state public policy referendums and initiatives, elections where there are no candidates. The Court held that prohibitions on participation by corporate entities were unconstitutional because the absence of a candidate for a public office eliminated any possibility of a quid pro quo. In *Federal Election Commission v. Massachusetts Citizens for Life* (1986) the court invalidated a federal prohibition on direct corporate activities in elections as they applied to nonstock corporations formed entirely to pursue policy goals, while leaving the general prohibition on direct corporate activity in elections in place.

In light of these Supreme Court decisions, it seems clear that states can limit the amount of money that individuals, groups, and corporate entities can contribute to state campaigns. They can require candidates to report the amount and source of campaign contributions and the amount and recipient of campaign expenditures and make those reports public. They can prohibit certain groups (such as labor unions) or corporate entities (such as insurance companies) from contributing to state campaigns. But states cannot prohibit individual members or employees of groups or corporations from contributing to state campaigns. They can provide for public funding and make acceptance of voluntary spending limits a condition for receiving public funds. They can limit the amount that political party committees can spend on behalf of candidates. But they cannot limit how much a candidate spends or how much a group or individual spends independently on behalf of a candidate.

Illinois Enacts a Campaign Finance Law

Prior to 1974 no comprehensive state law existed in Illinois to regulate campaign contributions or expenditures by candidates for public office. Reacting to public and news media pressure and to activity in other states, the legislature considered but did not pass campaign finance legislation in 1973. Facing both fall legislative elections and continued public and news media attention on the issue, the legislative leaders agreed to work on a bill that could be passed with bipartisan support during the 1974 legislative session. Bills were introduced in the house and senate with the cosponsorship of the legislative leaders in each chamber.

What emerged was legislation that would require the reporting and disclosure of amounts and sources of campaign contributions and expenditures. The General Assembly debated and rejected expenditure limits for legislative and statewide campaigns. Never seriously considered were limits on how much individuals or groups could contribute or limits on the activity of political party committees, general prohibitions against contributions by certain groups or corporate entities, and restrictions on the purposes for which campaign contributions could be spent.

State senator John B. Roe outlined what he felt were the major points of the bill that was later passed and signed into law when he presented the conference committee report on SB1568 to the senate for a final vote:

Senator Roe: I will indicate what the major provisions of the Conference Report are....The threshold on disclosure for political committees and candidates contained in the conference report is 150 dollars (for itemized reporting). There is a provision in the report indicating that contributions and expenditures of 20 dollars and under need not be accounted for in the sense of keeping records...but they must be kept in the aggregate. A knowing violation of the Act as far as filing is concerned or as far as what is filed by a political committee or a candidate is a Class B misdemeanor subjecting the person or parties to imprisonment for up to six months and/or a fine of 500 dollars. There are five reporting dates in the Act....Notice is covered in the Act both by certified mail to everyone who would be or may be subject to the Act as well as at the time of the filing of nominating petitions....There is a 1000 dollar threshold in the bill for state and local candidates and for local ballot issues indicating that those who take in less than 1000 dollars or spend less than 1000 dollars in a calendar year are not subject to the provisions of the Act. The State Board of Elections administers the Act as far as candidates who are presently required to file with the Secretary of State under the State Ethics Act....The statute of limitations is 18 months and records must be maintained by the candidate, committee, and State Board of Elections for 24 months (*Senate Debates*, 30 June 1974, 142-3).

The dominant impression from reading the house and senate debates on SB1568 is a sense of resolution that a bill regulating campaign finance would have to be passed. There was little enthusiasm for the task and some reluctance to accept even a bill dealing only with disclosure and reporting. The following exchange in the senate when SB1568 was on second reading is illustrative:

Senator Hudson Sours: What is the purpose of reporting, Senator Roe? What effect do you expect that will have when it is a published fact that you can identify everybody who made a contribution? I say to you then, so what, what happens then?

Senator Roe: Senator, I certainly think it will have a healthy effect as far as the public of this state is concerned, I think that the public has indicated that it is interested in knowing where campaign contributions come from and in what amounts. I think you only have to look at the proposition that passed in California by a 2 to 1 vote with many business and labor interests opposed to it. It passed by 2 to 1, a much more stringent proposition than is presented in this bill...(*Senate Debates*, 6 June 1974, 187).

Rep. Philip W. Collins stated the case more positively during the floor debate in the house:

> Representative Collins: It's high time that we enact such legislation to show the people of the State of Illinois that, in the main, candidates for public office have nothing to hide, as a matter of fact, [we] welcome the opportunity to open their books and show that we are running campaigns in good faith...(*House Debates*, 20 June 1974).

The floor debate in both chambers also shows a strong concern that candidates would be penalized for unintentional violations, particularly since the General Assembly had recently passed emergency legislation extending the deadline for filing statements of economic interest for a number of legislators and other public officials who had failed to comply with the filing deadline in the Illinois Governmental Ethics Act. Rep. Gerald W. Shea's comments are representative of this concern:

> Representative Shea: We are passing a bill with criminal penalties in it that are going to subject a lot of people, to put them in a position where they could go to jail, not through any negligence, not through any willful intent. But because they are not aware of the provisions of this bill...(*House Debates*, 20 June 1974, 222-23).

The unsuccessful floor amendments that received the most attention and received the most votes in both chambers were those that sought to limit to whom the bill applied or to increase the dollar threshold necessary for identifying contributors. Amendments limiting total expenditures in legislative and statewide races according to formulas based on population were offered, but were easily defeated.

A partisan battle in the house over an attempt to apply the bill to Cook County elections in the fall of 1974, while delaying its application to local elections in the rest of Illinois until 1975, resulted in SB1568 failing in the first attempt at final passage in the house. The final bill that emerged from a house-senate conference committee passed both chambers easily, but with little enthusiasm. The last two speakers before the final vote in the senate were Sen. John L. Knuppel and Sen. Cecil A. Partee:

> Senator Knuppel: I just want to say one thing. Garbage. Everything everybody's said here is garbage. But I will vote for this bill and some of the goody two-shoes who want it. It won't make anybody a more honest candidate.

> SENATOR PARTEE: Everybody's anxious for a roll call. This is a personal decision. Roll call (*Senate Debates,* 30 June 1974, 142).

The final vote was 52 yeas and 0 nays in the senate and 146 yeas, 2 nays, and 5 present in the house. Senate Bill 1568 was signed into law on September 3, 1974, as Public Act 78-1183. The basic structure of the law—who has to report and what has to be reported—has been modified only slightly over the past 20 years.

Illinois' Campaign Finance Law

The only state law regulating campaign finance in Illinois is the campaign finance law passed in 1974 (an Act in Relation to Campaign Finance 10 ILCS 5/9 - 1 et seq: hereafter referred to as the Illinois campaign finance law). It applies to candidates for public office and groups and individuals who support or oppose candidates for public office or support or oppose questions of public policy and whose receipts and expenditures exceed certain dollar thresholds. It requires them to keep records of their receipts and expenditures and to file reports at regularly specified intervals. Disclosure reports relating to campaigns for local public offices or local referendum questions within a single county are filed with the county clerk, with copies to the State Board of Elections. Disclosure reports relating to candidates for statewide office or the state legislature or campaigns for statewide ballot questions are filed with the State Board of Elections. The board or county clerk receives the disclosure reports and makes them available for public inspection. The State Board of Elections also has the power to investigate complaints and to assess civil penalties for willful violations of the disclosure law. Those who willfully violate the disclosure law may also be subject to the criminal penalties provided by the law.

General Scope and Application of the Law. The Illinois Supreme Court addressed the question of the general intent and applicability of the Illinois campaign finance law in a case brought by former governor Daniel Walker (*Walker v. State Board of Elections* 1979). He challenged the State Board of Elections' finding that a committee formed to pay off campaign debts from his 1972 gubernatorial campaign was required to report its receipts and expenditures to the board. In ruling in favor of the position taken by the State Board of Elections, the court held:

> The Act is designed to preserve the integrity of the electoral process by requiring full public disclosure of the sources and amounts of campaign contributions and expenditures and the regulation of practices incident to political campaigns. The legislature wished the public to be informed of the total contributions received and expended by a political committee, the names of significant contributors, and of individuals to whom a political committee is indebted.

The court went on to conclude:

> Nothing in the Act compels the conclusion that it was to be limited in application only to political committees for declared candidates and nominees for public office. Rather, the Act was designed to cover a broad range of campaign activity and we believe that it requires the filing of all campaign reports by state political committees in existence after the effective date of the Act.

Still, the law is almost exclusively a disclosure law. It does not prohibit any person or group from contributing to political campaigns. It does not limit the amount that anyone can contribute or the amount that may be spent by or on behalf of a candidate. It does not provide for the public funding of any campaigns as an inducement for accepting voluntary expenditure limits. Nor does the law attempt to define what is a proper or improper expenditure of campaign funds or to authorize the board to inquire into the propriety of any expenditure made by any political committee. The United States Supreme Court's finding in *Buckley v. Valeo* required no modification in Illinois law.

Who Must File Campaign Disclosure Reports? The Illinois campaign finance law provides that every candidate for public office who accepts contributions or makes expenditures in an aggregate amount exceeding $1,000 in a 12-month period must form a political committee, file a statement of organization report, and file periodic campaign disclosure reports as set forth by the State Board of Elections schedule. Every individual, trust, partnership, committee, association, corporation, or any organization or group of persons that accepts contributions or makes expenditures during any 12-month period in an aggregate amount exceeding $1,000 on behalf of or in opposition to a candidate for public office must form a political committee, file a statement of organization report, and file periodic campaign disclosure reports as set forth by the State Board of Elections schedule. Every individual, trust, partnership, committee, association, corporation, or any organization or group of persons that accepts contributions or makes expenditures during any 12-month period in support or opposition to any question of public policy to be submitted to the electors of an area encompassing no more than one county must form a political committee and file a statement of organization report and file periodic campaign disclosure reports as set forth by the State Board of Elections schedule. For questions of public policy to be submitted to the electors of more than one county the aggregate threshold amount is $3,000.

The act also provides that political committees that operate with respect to elections within a single county are designated local political committees and file their organization statements and disclosure reports with the county clerk. Political committees that operate with respect to legislative, statewide, and multicounty judicial elections are designated as state political committees and file their organization statements and disclosure reports with the State Board of Elections. Political committees that operate as both state and local political committees must also file their organization statement and disclosure reports with the State Board of Elections.

The forms provided by the state board for organizing a political committee are called D-1s and those for reporting campaign contributions and expenditures are called D-2s. (See appendix A, pp. 175-77, for copies of these forms.)

What this means is that candidates for local public offices (county board, county offices, school board, mayor, council member, park board member, etc.) and local political party groups must form political committees if their campaign receives or spends more than $1,000 in a 12-month period. The officers of the political committee must file reports of receipts and expenditures with the clerk of the county in which they are seeking office. A local group formed to support or oppose a policy question being voted on in a local election, such as a referendum on a tax increase for a school district, is required to form a political committee if it receives or expends more than $1,000 in a campaign to influence the outcome. The officers of that committee must file reports of receipts and expenditures with the clerk of the county in which the election is being held, with copies to the State Board of Elections.

Candidates for statewide office, the state legislature, and most judicial offices and state and legislative political party groups must form a political committee if their campaign receives or spends more than $1,000 in a 12-month period. The officers of the political committee must file reports of receipts and expenditures with the State Board of Elections. A group formed to support or oppose a question of public policy to be decided by the voters of the state, such as a constitutional amendment, must form a political committee if they receive or expend more than $3,000 in a 12-month period. The officers of that political committee must file reports of receipts and expenditures with the State Board of Elections.

The application of the law to individuals who are not candidates and to groups (other than political party groups) that contribute to candidates or spend resources on behalf of candidates is somewhat ambiguous. Administrative rules adopted by the State Board of Elections provide that individuals or corporate entities that contribute to a candidate solely from personal income or profits do not automatically qualify as a political committee regardless of the amount they contribute or spend on behalf of a candidate. Neither an individual who gives $25,000 to a candidate nor a company such as Philip Morris that gives $25,000 to a candidate is required to organize as a political committee and file disclosure reports with the State Board of Elections. These contributions would be reported by the candidates receiving them.

State and local political parties and campaign committees formed by legislative chamber groups (e.g., house Republicans, senate Democrats) all organize as political committees and file disclosure reports with the State Board of Elections. However, township, precinct, and ward committeemen do not have to file reports. Legislation requiring them to file has routinely been defeated by the Illinois General Assembly. It appears that all statewide professional associations that contribute to candidates for local and state office (e.g., Illinois Realtors Association, the Illinois State Bar Association, the Illinois Hospital Association) organize as political committees and file disclosure reports with the State Board of Elections. The same is true for the employee political action committees of corporations such as Illinois Power or Central Illinois Public Service, statewide public employee unions, and state and regional trade union associations. Groups formed to influence the outcome of statewide policy elections also organize as political committees and file disclosure reports. Many of the local, regional, and state associations of individual trade unions organize as political committees and file disclosure reports with the State Board of Elections, but some do not. The same is true for voluntary associations formed to promote political or ideological causes. Some corporations that contribute to candidates for public office in Illinois organize as political committees and file disclosure reports with the State Board of Elections, but most do not. The same is true for national labor unions and national voluntary associations, such as the National Rifle Association, which contribute to candidates running for state or local office in Illinois; some file, but most do not.

While the reporting status of noncandidate groups and individuals could be made more consistent by a change in the law or in the board's interpretation of the law, any contributions that are made by nonfiling groups and corporations should be reported by the candidates receiving them. If all corporations, associations, and groups that contribute to candidates or spend resources on behalf of candidates were required to organize as political committees and file disclosure reports, it would be easier for the public to know the relationships that exist between candidates and their financial supporters and would increase public understanding of the process. Such disclosure would also simplify the work of researchers. However, faced with scarce resources, the state board has chosen to focus on ensuring that candidates and political party groups comply with the disclosure provisions of the law. Contributions by nonfilers can be gleaned from individual candidate reports, but even though such information is available it is difficult to access.

Because the threshold amounts in the act were not indexed for inflation, in relative terms the act now requires more individuals to file reports and requires more contributions and expenditures to be itemized than was the case in 1974. If the $1,000 threshold for forming a political committee and the $150 threshold for itemizing a contribution or expenditure had been indexed for inflation, in 1994 only candidates and groups that received or spent more than $3,150 during a 12-month period would have to form a political committee and file disclosure reports, and only those contributions and expenditures that exceeded $475 would have to be reported separately. Legislation increasing these thresholds was passed by the General Assembly in 1985, but vetoed by then governor James R. Thompson.

When Must Campaign Disclosure Reports be Filed? All political committees must file preelection reports of campaign contributions on D-2 forms no later than 15 days preceding each election (including primary elections) in which the committee has or is accepting contributions or has or is making expenditures. Such reports shall be complete as of the 30th day preceding the election. Any contribution of $500 or more received by the committee between the last date covered in their preelection campaign report and the date of the election shall be reported within 2 business days after its receipt on a Schedule A-1 (see appendix A, p. 179). The intention of requiring preelection reports and the reporting of large contributions received during the last month of the campaign is to provide information to the voters when it is most useful: prior to the election.

All political committees must file two semiannual reports of campaign contributions and expenditures each calendar year on D-2 forms. A report covering the period of January 1 to June 30 shall be filed no later than July 31, and a report covering the period of July 1 to December 31 shall be filed no later than January 31 of the following year. Shifting from annual reports filed at the end of June to semiannual, six-month reports is one of the few substantive changes made in the act since it became law. The intention was to provide a more timely accounting of the receipts and expenditures of candidates. It also provides reports that follow the election cycle, particularly in the even-numbered years when a statewide primary takes place in the first six months of the year and a general election occurs during the last six months of the year.

Reports of expenditures and receipts should be filed in a timely manner according to the schedules set out by the campaign disclosure law. Amended reports are often filed to correct omissions and errors. However, some ambiguity seems to exist as to whether expenditures officially occur when the services are rendered, when the billing takes place, or when the bill is paid. For example, in the report filed for the first six months of 1993, the Senate Republican Campaign Committee reported over $250,000 in expenditures on behalf of successful and unsuccessful senate candidates in the 1992 general election. One of those expenditures was over $50,000 in support for the one incumbent Republican senator defeated in 1992. While these expenditures were reported as 1993 expenditures, the services were rendered prior to the 1992 general election. In order to get an accurate picture of the total amount of spending that took place in support of a candidate's general election campaign, it may be necessary to examine reports from the first 6 months of the year following the election.

What Must Campaign Disclosure Reports Contain? The reports of campaign contributions filed by political committees prior to each election must contain aggregate information for the reporting period on the beginning balance of the committee; the total amount of funds from contributions, transfers to and from other political committees, and loans; the total amount of in-kind contributions of goods and services received by the committee; and the total of all receipts by the committee for the reporting period. All contributions, transfers, loans, and in-kind contributions that exceed $150 for the reporting period from a single source must be itemized. Subtotals for itemized and not-itemized contributions, in-kind contributions, loans, and transfers to the committee must also be reported.

The semiannual reports filed by political committees must contain the same aggregate and itemized contribution information contained in the campaign contribution reports filed before each election. In addition they must contain expenditure information in aggregate and itemized form. All expenditures to a single recipient that exceed $150 in the aggregate for the reporting period and all expenditures made on behalf of a candidate or with regard to a public policy issue that exceed $150 must be itemized. The ending balance reflects the beginning balance, total receipts, and total expenditures, but not outstanding debts or expenditures made by other political committees on behalf of the candidate.

Itemized reports of receipts and expenditures over $150 must list the name and mailing address of the source of the receipt or the recipient of the expenditure, the amount of the receipt or expenditure, the date it was made, and the aggregate total from the source or to the recipient for the reporting period. Political committees are required to keep records of all receipts and expenditures that exceed $20, but only those that exceed $150 in the aggregate for the reporting period have to be reported individually. All reports are cumulative and comprehensive for the period covered. Political committees must keep their records for a period of 24 months.

Inspection of Statements and Reports. All statements and reports filed with the State Board of Elections or the county clerk are available for examination and copying by the public during business hours. Reports filed with the State Board of Elections are copied onto microfiche and may be examined in the board offices. Persons who want a copy of a report may purchase microfiche containing the report or purchase copies of all or part of a report.

Anyone examining a report or statement or purchasing copies of a report or statement must fill out a D-3 form (see appendix A, p. 183), which contains the name, occupation, address, and telephone number of the person examining the report and the date and reason for examining or purchasing the report. That form also contains a statement of the criminal penalties for altering or falsifying information contained in the report with the intent of misrepresenting the information and the criminal penalties for using the information in the report for soliciting contributions or business solicitations. The state board or county clerk is required to promptly send a copy of the D-3 form, filled out by the person examining a report, to the political committee that filed the report. Illinois is alone among all 50 states in imposing this type of requirement.

Violations of the Law: Procedures and Penalties. In one of the few Illinois court cases dealing with the law, the Appellate Court of Illinois for the First District considered whether the State Board of Elections had acted properly when it dismissed a complaint contending that a political committee formed to support the candidacy of William Scott, the Illinois attorney general, had improperly diverted funds for personal use. The court held that

> the Act is a disclosure statute with sanctions for failure to account accurately for funds designated by the statute as contributions and expenditures and for noncompliance with organizational, advertising, and accounting provisions....None of the above provisions give the Board the authority to question the propriety of disbursals (*Troy v. State Board of Elections*, 1980).

As a result, the state board has authority to require record keeping, reporting, and disclosure of campaign contributions and campaign expenditures, but it does not have any authority to question where money comes from or how money is spent. If a candidate were to file a report that listed a receipt from an international terrorist organization or an expenditure of campaign funds to hire a hit man to eliminate the opposition candidate, the only official concern of the state board would be whether the receipt and expenditure were listed in proper form and filed in a timely manner. However, the concerns of federal and state criminal justice officials would not be so limited. While such a scenario is unlikely, it is possible under the current law for political committees to spend funds for purposes that appear to be largely or completely unrelated to running for public office. This problem will be examined in the concluding chapter.

Given the highly restricted scope of the Illinois campaign finance law, many of the potential violations that might occur under more stringent laws are not issues in Illinois. The most common violations of the reporting requirements of the law are failure to file reports, late filing of reports, and filing incomplete or inaccurate reports. Such violations are usually not intentional. Errors and omissions in reports are usually brought to the attention of the board or the county clerk when the political committee files a corrected report on its own initiative. Serious violations of reporting requirements of the law involve refusal to file reports and intentionally filing false or incomplete reports. All complaints of violations of the law must be filed within 18 months of the alleged violation.

The State Board of Elections is authorized by the law to hold investigations, inquiries, and hearings concerning any matter covered by the law, including violations of the reporting requirements. The board is authorized to take sworn testimony, subpoena witnesses, and compel the production of documents. The law provides for a timetable for reviewing and resolving complaints. An expedited schedule is provided for complaints filed 30 days or less prior to an election, requiring the board to make a finding before the election if possible. The board has the authority to impose civil penalties for violations of the law (up to $1,000 per violation) and to forward its findings to the attorney general or the appropriate state's attorney for possible criminal prosecution under the criminal penalties provided by the law (up to six months in jail or a $500 fine as a Class B misdemeanor).

In discharging its duties, the board has adopted administrative procedures that first attempt to obtain voluntary compliance. The staff of the board reviews all filing of reports and notifies political committees when it appears they have failed to file a required report or have filed an incomplete or inaccurate report. The notice also includes the date, time, and place for a compliance conference. At that conference, the political committee is given the opportunity to come into compliance with the law and to dispose of all matters in dispute by stipulation or agreed settlement. If the political committee had not previously failed to comply with the law, the board's approval of any agreement is not required. If the matter cannot be resolved by a compliance conference, then a complaint is filed against the political committee by the board.

When dealing with a sworn, written complaint from a third party or a complaint brought by the board, the board acts through a hearing examiner system to discharge its responsibilities under the law. The opportunity always exists to dispose of the case at any time during the proceedings through a written stipulation, agreed settlement, or consent order. Such a resolution of a case must be reviewed and approved by the board. If the case is contested, the process would generally proceed as follows: The first step is a closed preliminary hearing in which the hearing examiner appointed by the board decides if the complaint is justified. Both the person bringing the complaint and the person against whom the complaint has been filed have the opportunity to testify at the preliminary hearing. Next, the finding and recommendation of the hearing examiner are forwarded to the general counsel for the board, who reviews the finding and recommendation and forwards them to the board, along with his recommendations or comments. The board then decides whether to dismiss the complaint or to proceed. If the complaint is not dismissed, the board will order a public hearing conducted by a hearing examiner.

The public hearing of a complaint is adjudicative in nature, with provisions for discovery, subpoenas, transcripts, and an official record. The hearing officer makes recommendations in a written report to the board, which is also reviewed for the board by the general counsel. The board then makes a judgment on the case. If the board finds a party in violation of the law, it directs the person to comply with the requirements of the law. If any party is ordered by the board to comply with the law or has agreed to comply with the law through a stipulation, agreed settlement, or consent decree, and subsequently fails to comply with the law, that party is subject to civil penalties. If the board determines that willful violations of law have occurred, then its findings are forwarded to the attorney general or the appropriate state's attorney for possible criminal prosecution.

Language encouraging consultation and facilitating voluntary compliance and language providing for civil penalties were added in the early 1980s. These types of substantive changes have been very rare in the 20 years since the act became law. Proposals for major changes rarely make it out of legislative committees. Two notable exceptions are legislation providing public funding for state political parties, which passed in 1985, and legislation providing public funding for candidates for governor, which passed the legislature in 1988. Both were vetoed by then governor James R. Thompson.

Public Knowledge of Campaign Finance Information: The Unfulfilled Promise

In the case of *Walker v. State Board of Elections* (see p. 19) the Illinois Supreme Court held that information about campaign contributions and expenditures should be disclosed and reported because "The legislature wished the public to be informed" about how much was being spent on political campaigns and who was financing them. While the Illinois campaign finance law has been successful in compelling the disclosing and reporting of campaign contributions and expenditures, the wish that the public be informed has gone largely unfulfilled.

Campaign disclosure reports from political committees throughout the state flow into the offices of the State Board of Elections prior to every election and twice a year during January and July. The staff of the board copy those reports onto microfiche and store them. For most of the general public, that is the end of the story. Except for frequent inspections by the opponents of the candidates filing the reports, occasional inspections by journalists, and infrequent inspections by academic researchers, the mountain of data on file at the state board goes undisturbed, year after year.

Currently, individuals or groups wishing to analyze campaign contributions and expenditures for statewide, legislative, or judicial candidates face a major obstacle: they have to deal with raw reports that must be entered into a database and coded before any analysis can take place. The recent investigative report by the *State Journal-Register* on the relationship between contributions to state officials and the awarding of contracts for services by those officials may be the first time a news organization has used a database of campaign contributions as the basis for an in-depth look at the role of money in the political process (McDermott and others 1993, 1994). And in order to do their story they created their own database from microfiche copies of campaign disclosure reports from the State Board of Elections. The irony is that in any serious political campaign in Illinois the names and addresses and amounts of all contributions are stored on a database on a computer. The campaign then generates a written report from the database, which the State Board of Elections copies onto microfiche and makes available to the public. Going from a computer database to paper to microfiche is not progress.

Part of the reason for the lack of campaign finance information available to the general public is financial. While creation of a State Board of Elections is mandated by the 1970 Illinois State Constitution, the board has shared the same financial history as most state campaign watchdog/disclosure agencies. As one observer noted in a 1992 article in *Governing*:

> They are treated like poor stepchildren. They rarely have the staff or resources to analyze what is happening to the campaign finance system as a whole, to perform specific audits of candidates' returns or even to make the data available in a form that allows people to figure out, say, how much the dairy industry has contributed to a particular candidate (Gurwitt 1992).

The Illinois State Board of Elections' budget has been slow to grow, even in good fiscal times. The major budget cut suffered by the board in fiscal year 1992 was only the most recent hit absorbed by the board. A lack of staff, equipment, and contractual money has severely limited the computerization of the board's record keeping and retrieval activities. Not having even aggregate information on a database prior to 1990 has made it very difficult for the board's staff to prepare even basic reports on campaign contribution and expenditure activity. The aggregate receipts and expenditures by candidates for statewide office and for the legislature in the 1990 election cycle were published in the 1992 report, the first such general report issued by the board in its history. A similar report was published on the 1992 election cycle. If the board is successful in putting campaign receipt information from candidates for statewide office for the 1994 elections into a database, it will be the first time that any information, other than committee names and identification numbers for political committees, has been stored in a database by the state board.

The lack of resources provided by the governor and legislature through the appropriation process is one manifestation of the primary reason information about campaign finance in Illinois is so hard to obtain: a political climate that discourages public dissemination of campaign finance information. In 1974 state senator John J. Nimrod offered an amendment to SB1568 to eliminate the authority of the board to prepare and publish reports on the information contained in the disclosure reports. In arguing for his amendment, he contended:

> The information is still available to anyone who wants to take it, who wants to get it, but it does eliminate the expenditure of possibly millions of dollars to publish and distribute these records, which are available to anyone who wants copies of this information....Now I'm sure that we do not want to prohibit or restrict any of this information from reaching the persons who are interested in getting it, but it certainly is not a responsibility of (the legislature to pay) to publish this information (*Senate Debates*, 6 June 1974, 173).

His amendment failed, but it was evident in the floor debates over SB1568 that the general lack of enthusiasm for disclosing and reporting campaign finance information extended to disseminating the information, and 20 years later little has changed.

The requirement that persons who want to examine a campaign disclosure report must identify themselves, their occupation, place of work, and their reason for examining the report and the requirement that a copy of the request form be sent to the treasurer of the political committee serve little purpose except to make the process of examining a report cumbersome and intimidating. Efforts to modify or eliminate the requirement over the past 20 years have been unsuccessful. In contrast, efforts in the 1994 spring legislative session to amend the recently strengthened lobbying registration and reporting law to require a similar procedure for examining the reports filed by lobbyists were met with strong objections from the news media and the proponents of the law. They contended that such procedures would limit public access and thwart the intent of the law to make the information generally available to the public. The passage of a strengthened lobbying registration and reporting law and the recent efforts of the state board to publish information and computerize campaign finance records do give some hope that attitudes about access to and dissemination of campaign finance information may be changing. But experience argues against expecting a complete reversal of past attitudes and practices in the near future.

"Yeah, we dropped about a half a mil to turn out the base vote."

Senate Republican staffer commenting on their unsuccessful efforts in 1990 to unseat incumbent Democratic senator Patrick Welch

CHAPTER 3
FINANCING LEGISLATIVE ELECTIONS IN ILLINOIS: THE ROLE OF LEGISLATIVE LEADERS

The old pattern of Illinois governors (usually Republican) sitting down with the Democratic mayor of Chicago to decide state policy is gone. It was replaced in the early 1980s by negotiations among the four legislative leaders, the governor, and on certain issues, the mayor of Chicago. In an era of declining political parties and fragmented, individualized politics, it may seem surprising that legislative leaders of the Illinois General Assembly have increasingly become stronger and more independent. State and local political parties, the traditional sources of power and control for the legislative leaders, have steadily declined since the early 1970s. In spite of that decline, by the end of the 1980s, the four legislative leaders, house speaker Michael Madigan, house minority leader Lee Daniels, senate president Philip Rock, and senate minority leader James "Pate" Philip, all had consolidated their control over their chamber party delegations.

How have the legislative leaders been able to build independent power bases within their respective legislative chambers? While a number of factors are important, a key to the increased influence and control of the legislative leaders over their chamber party delegations has been their use of the power and resources of their offices to build large, highly effective, centralized fundraising and campaign organizations. Prior to the start of the 1990 election cycle, each of the four legislative leaders controlled an extensive campaign organization devoted to winning legislative elections.

Party-centered Campaigns and Candidate-centered Campaigns

Historically, political parties were at the center of the American electoral process. They recruited the candidates. They raised the money. They ran the campaigns. They got out the vote. The model of a post-World War II, party-centered electoral process in Illinois has always been

Cook County elections as orchestrated by the political machine of the late Chicago mayor Richard J. Daley. Those days are gone. Most observers of Illinois politics acknowledge the decline of power of state and local political parties over the past two decades; some will even lament it. While state and local political parties did play a role in the 1990 and 1992 legislative elections, they are no longer the key players. The role of state political parties in legislative elections will be examined in chapter 5.

Politics, like nature, abhors a vacuum. Candidate-centered electoral processes have been both the beneficiary and partial cause of the declining role of parties in elections. Open primaries; modern media campaigns; computer-based campaign technology including polling, targeting, and direct mail; and political action committees have all contributed to a shift away from parties and toward candidates as the focus of elections. All have been factors in Illinois except open primaries. The shift away from party-centered campaigns at the state level in Illinois is symbolized by Dan Walker's 1972 victory over Paul Simon (the candidate of Chicago mayor Richard J. Daley and the state Democratic Party) in the Democratic gubernatorial primary and Walker's subsequent victory in the general election. Walker recruited himself, raised his own money, formed his own campaign organization, and made himself the focus of a modern, media-oriented campaign. The power of a party-centered campaign can be seen in the 1976 Democratic primary in which Mayor Daley used the Cook County Democratic machine to turn out enough votes to deny Governor Walker renomination. Michael Howlett, the popular secretary of state, was nominated in his place. The triumph was short lived. Turning Howlett's long career in politics and his ties to the Cook County Democratic Party against him, the Republican candidate, James R. Thompson, ran as a crusading former federal prosecutor, ready to sweep out the old Illinois politics. Howlett suffered a humiliating defeat, illustrating the limitations of a party-centered campaign in the era of candidate-centered politics.

Candidate-centered campaigns—self recruitment, personal campaign organization, computerized campaign technology, direct mail and media-oriented focus on the candidates, and interest group campaign contributions—were critical factors in the outcome of the 1990 and 1992 legislative elections. Of these factors, the rise of interest groups as the major, often primary, sources of campaign funds has been particularly important. The role of interest group campaign contributions in legislative elections will be examined in chapter 4.

Legislative-leader Directed Campaigns

At the same time that party-centered elections have been on the decline and candidate-centered elections on the rise, a third factor in Illinois legislative elections has been steadily growing in importance: the role of legislative leaders. Beginning in the late 1970s, legislative leaders have become increasingly involved in recruiting candidates, raising money, running campaigns, and getting out the vote. In the 1990 election cycle the legislative leaders' political committees and their chamber political committees raised over $7.1 million, more than double the $3.3 million they raised for the 1984 election cycle (Johnson, 1987). In the 1992 election cycle, legislative leader and chamber political committee fundraising topped $11.5 million, an increase of $4.4 million in just two years. Prior to the late 1970s it was rare for a partisan legislative staff person to take a leave of absence from the state payroll and move full time to a legislative campaign payroll, even during the last few weeks before an election. In 1990 and 1992, staff members from all four of the partisan legislative staffs started going onto campaign payrolls as soon as the spring session adjourned. By the first of October only skeleton partisan legislative staffs were left at the statehouse.

The raising and spending of this large amount of money by the legislative leaders have given organization and focus to legislative elections that has elements of the old party-centered process. It has also greatly increased the influence of the four legislative leaders. A legislature populated by members who independently control their own elections is a legislature of free agents. Members who get elected and reelected with substantial help from their legislative leaders tend to be much more easily led than those who do not.

Legislative-leader and Legislative-chamber Political Committees

As explained in chapter 2, all candidate and political action committees that exceed a certain dollar threshold are required to file campaign finance reports with the State Board of Elections. Each of the four legislative leaders serving during the 1990 and 1992 election cycles—Madigan, Daniels, Rock, and Philip—had political committees. Each of the four legislative chamber groups—house Democrats, house Republicans, senate Democrats, and senate Republicans—had political committees. These four committees are: the House Democratic Majority

Committee, the Senate Republican Campaign Committee, the Committee to Reelect the Democratic Senate, and the Republican State Senate Campaign Committee. In addition, the senate Republicans used a separate fundraising committee, the "Dinner Committee," which was created each year for the sole purpose of raising money for the senate Republican chamber political committee. In the research reported here, the individual receipts and expenditures of the Dinner Committee are treated as individual receipts and expenditures of the senate Republican chamber committee.

For purposes of this analysis, the receipts and expenditures of each set of leader and chamber political committees were combined into a legislative leader/chamber political committee. For example, the receipts reported for Madigan/house Democrats are the combined receipts of the Friends of Michael J. Madigan committee and the House Democratic Majority Committee. In comparing the data from the house and the senate, it is important to note that all 118 house seats were up in 1990, while only 19 of the 59 senate seats were up that year. In 1992, the first election under the new legislative district map, all senate and all house seats were up for reelection. In looking at the receipts and expenditures for the senate Democrats in 1992, it is also important to take into account that the senate president, Philip Rock, announced in the fall of 1991 he would not seek reelection. He remained senate president until leaving office in January of 1993. While he did make contributions from funds in his political committee to the campaigns of Democrats running for the senate, the financial role of his political committee in the 1992 legislative elections was less significant than that of the other three legislative leaders.

Total Contributions: Who Raised the Most? Who Gave the Most?

During the 1990 election cycle, the four legislative leader/chamber political committees raised a total of $7.13 million (tables 3.1 and 3.2, pp. 40 and 41). In 1992 the figure was $11.5 million. Of that total, the house Democrats and house speaker Madigan raised the most money, $2.45 million during the 1990 election cycle and $4.15 million during the 1992 election cycle. Those totals gave the house Democrats a substantial advantage over the house Republicans and house minority leader Daniels, who raised $1.67 million during the 1990 election cycle and $3.01 million during the 1992 election cycle. On the senate side, the senate

Republicans and senate minority leader Philip raised only slightly more than the senate Democrats and senate president Rock during the 1990 election cycle ($1.53 million to $1.47 million). In the 1992 election cycle, the senate Republicans' advantage over the senate Democrats was substantial ($2.5 million to $1.87 million).

Contributions to the four legislative leader/chamber political committees come primarily from three general sources: (1) candidate* political committees and state and local parties, (2) interest groups and corporations, and (3) individuals and small contributions (under $150) that are not itemized. On tables 3.1 and 3.2 (pp. 40 and 41) contributions from candidate political committees and state and local parties are listed in a single category (candidate/party), as are contributions from individuals and not-itemized contributions. Contributions from interest groups and corporations are broken out into 11 sectors. Interest income from the investment funds and contributions that could not be categorized are listed in a separate category, miscellaneous/interest.

While contributions from individuals and from candidates and parties are significant, the vast majority of the money contributed in both election cycles came from the interest group sectors ($5.36 million in 1990 and $7.01 million in 1992—see tables 3.1 and 3.2). Among the interest groups, the most significant sector is the financial sector (financial institutions, insurance companies, real estate firms, CPAs) and the lawyer sector (law firms, bar associations, attorneys). On the second tier of total contributions are the manufacturing sector (firms, associations) and the union sector (state and national trade unions, public employee unions, labor associations). At a somewhat lower level are the health sector (health providers and facilities), retail sales sector (firms and associations), construction/engineering/architecture sector (firms and associations), service industry sector (hotels, public relations and advertising firms and associations), communication sector (phone companies, cable companies, TV, radio, newspapers), and distribution sector (wholesale, transportation, storage). The least significant group in terms of total contributions is the agriculture/mining sector (firms and associations). A complete description of the contribution sectors is presented in appendix B (pp. 184-85).

While interest group contributions, contributions from individuals, and not-itemized contributions are generally straightforward transfers of

* The term *candidate*, when used in the context of campaign receipts and expenditures, refers to both incumbent and nonincumbent candidates.

resources, contributions from candidates and state and local parties are more difficult to analyze. Contributions from candidate committees to legislative chamber committees may be transfers of "surplus" money from an incumbent legislator in a safe district or a candidate for an open seat with no opponent. But they may also be a reimbursement to the legislative chamber committee for services provided to the candidate. For example, the legislative chamber committee may pay for the printing of a mailing on behalf of a candidate because the chamber committee can get a better price due to large-volume purchasing of printing for more than one campaign. The candidate receiving this "in-kind" contribution from the chamber political committee may then transfer money to the chamber political committee in an amount equal to the cost of printing. The chamber political committee in this case is operating as a purchasing agent for the candidate. What is itemized as a contribution from a candidate to the leader or chamber political committee and what is itemized as "pass back" for services provided has to be determined on a case-by-case basis. This issue will be addressed later in this chapter when analyzing legislative chamber committee receipts and expenditures and in chapter 6, when the receipts and expenditures of candidates in targeted races are examined.

The totals in tables 3.1 and 3.2 (pp. 40 and 41) do not represent all of the money that the interest groups and corporations, political parties and candidates, and individuals contributed to legislative elections. They represent only contributions to the legislative leader/chamber political committees. While some groups and individuals make most of their contributions to legislative races through the legislative leaders, others make most of their contributions directly to legislative candidates. A complete picture of the dynamics of financing legislative elections also requires an examination of the election activities of state and local parties and political action groups and an analysis of the receipts and expenditures for legislative races targeted by legislative leaders, parties, or interest groups. These will be taken up in chapters 4, 5, and 6.

Contribution Patterns: Who Gave to Whom?

More important than total contributions is, Which groups gave to which leaders? A breakout of the receipts of each of the four legislative leader/chamber political committees by source yields a number of interesting patterns (tables 3.1 and 3.2). The patterns of giving are not uniform, nor are they random. They suggest several variations of bipartisan and partisan contribution strategies.

The contributions of some groups appear to be largely bipartisan and status quo oriented. In 1990 the groups represented in the financial sector (financial institutions, insurance companies, real estate firms, CPAs) gave approximately the same amount of money to the house and senate Republicans and the senate Democrats and gave in excess of $100,000 more to the house Democrats (table 3.1, p. 40). In 1992 the same groups gave the most to the house Democrats, $75,000 to $100,000 less to the two Republican groups, and $236,000 less to the senate Democrats (table 3.2, p. 41). The pattern in 1990 and 1992 suggests both a desire by groups in the financial sector category to have general influence in the process and an acknowledgment that the Democratic speaker of the house was the most powerful legislative leader at the time. The decline in contributions by the groups in the financial sector to the senate Democrats in 1992 may reflect a judgment that fortunes of the senate Democrats were declining due to both the retirement of senate president Rock and adoption of a legislative map favoring the Republicans. Contribution patterns for the groups in the communication, distribution, and agriculture/mining sectors indicate similar bipartisan strategies.

Other contribution patterns are intensely partisan. Contributions from lawyers favor the Democrats over the Republicans by a margin of over 8 to 1 in the house for both election cycles and 3 to 1 in the senate for the 1990 election cycle. The continuing controversy over the issue of tort reform in Illinois accounts, in large portion, for both the magnitude and the partisan nature of the contributions from the lawyer sector. Tort reform has been a legislative objective for the Illinois State Medical Society, the Illinois Manufacturers' Association, and other corporate groups throughout the 1980s and into the 1990s. The Illinois Trial Lawyers Association has battled for more than a decade against tort reform. The Democrats in the legislature have tended to favor the trial lawyers' position, while Republicans in the legislature have tended to favor the manufacturers' association and medical society's position. The heavy concentration of lawyer contributions to the house Democrats reflects both the fact that a group needs to win at one point only in the process to defeat a bill and a judgment that focusing on the house is the best strategy.

The patterns of contributions by the union, manufacturing, and retail sales sectors also reflect traditional political alliances. In 1990 union contributions favored the Democrats over the Republicans by almost a

Table 3.1
Receipts from Contributions and Transfers - 1990 Election Cycle
Legislative Leader and Chamber Political Committees
(Excludes transfers between leader and chamber committees)
(Amounts in units of $1,000)

Source:	Total	HouseDem Madigan	HouseRep Daniels	SenDem Rock	SenRep Philip
Candidate/Party	479	83	145	115	136
Interest Group and Corporation Sectors:					
Union	502	237	25	196	44
Lawyer	1,129	765	70	222	72
Financial	1,229	413	293	268	255
Manufacturing	676	146	217	123	190
Retail Sales	369	83	156	52	78
Distribution	173	47	47	36	43
Service Industry	274	112	52	27	83
Construct/Engr/Archit.	320	94	103	35	88
Agriculture/Mining	35	9	7	8	11
Health	380	93	90	77	120
Communication	271	70	80	58	63
Individuals/Not-itemized	796	165	200	205	226
Misc./Interest	492	136	185	46	125
TOTAL	7,125	2,453	1,670	1,468	1,534

10-to-1 margin in the house and more than a 4-to-1 margin in the senate. In 1992 the margins were 7 to 1 in the house and almost 3 to 1 in the senate. While the margins were smaller (3 to 2 in 1990 and less than 2 to 1 in 1992), contributions from the manufacturing and retail sales sectors strongly favored the Republicans. Healthcare contributions were bipartisan during the 1990 cycle, but clearly favored the Republicans in 1992. The smaller margins favoring the Republicans for the manufacturing, retail sales, and healthcare sectors reflected the fact that the Democrats held majorities in both legislative chambers during the two election cycles. The shift of control in the senate to the Republicans after the 1992 elections should result in a modest increase in lawyer and union sector contributions to the senate Republicans and a more significant decrease in the manufacturing and retail sales sector contributions to the senate Democrats.

The degree of control exercised by a legislative leader in his chamber has an impact on contribution patterns. In 1992, contributions from the construction/engineering/architecture sector strongly favor the Republicans in the senate, but are equal in the house. One explanation is that the

Table 3.2
Receipts from Contributions and Transfers - 1992 Election Cycle
Legislative Leader and Chamber Political Committees
(Excludes transfers between leader and chamber committees)
(Amounts in units of $1,000)

Source:	Total	HouseDem Madigan	HouseRep Daniels	SenDem Rock	SenRep Philip
Candidate/Party	1965	423	774	513	255
Interest Group and Corporation Sectors:					
Union	934	485	66	280	103
Lawyer	1,175	844	93	122	116
Financial	1,478	474	367	238	399
Manufacturing	930	247	288	112	283
Retail Sales	320	92	104	41	83
Distribution	333	113	90	52	78
Service Industry	345	108	72	45	120
Construction/Engr/Archit.	376	116	116	42	102
Agriculture/Mining	61	20	16	8	17
Health	789	183	305	93	208
Communication	272	90	64	60	58
Individuals/Not-itemized	1,730	747	416	157	410
Misc./Interest	816	211	234	105	266
TOTAL	11,524	4,153	3,005	1,868	2,498

general tendency of some groups to favor Republican candidates was neutralized in the house because of the extraordinary influence of the Democratic speaker. Contribution patterns for the service sector may also reflect this dynamic. The question of interest group contribution strategies will be examined in detail in the next chapter.

House Democratic Receipts Profile. The contribution patterns presented in tables 3.1 and 3.2 (pp. 40 and 41) give each of the legislative leader/chamber political committees a distinct profile of receipts. The house Democrats' interest group profile was dominated by contributions from the lawyer and financial sectors. Contributions from the lawyer sector dwarfed those from any other group to any of the leaders. The house Democrats also received greater union and financial sector contributions than any of the other three leader/chamber committees. The scale of the contributions to the house Democrats overwhelms those to the other three leaders. The manufacturing and retail sales sectors are the only interest group sectors from which the house Democrats receive significantly smaller contributions than do the two Republican legislative leaders in both election cycles. As previously noted, the contribution patterns involving the lawyer, union, manufacturing, and retail sales sectors reflect partisan policy differences, while the contributions from the financial sector reflect a desire for general access or influence.

In the area of contributions from parties and candidate committees, the house Democrats generally received smaller total amounts than did the other three groups. In 1990 and 1992 their receipts from this category amounted to approximately 60 percent of the total received by the house Republicans. While the house Democrats had contributions from individuals and not-itemized receipts that were of the same magnitude as the other leaders in 1990, in 1992 they led the other leaders in this category by a large margin, particularly in relation to the senate Democrats.

House Republican Receipts Profile. In contrast to the house Democrats, the house Republicans' interest group receipts profile (tables 3.1 and 3.2, pp. 40 and 41) is shaped by contributions from the finance, manufacturing, healthcare, retail sales, and construction/engineering/architecture sectors. Only the manufacturing and retail sales sectors contributed more to the house Republicans than to the house Democrats in both election cycles. In the areas of union, lawyer, manufacturing, and retail sales sector contributions, the house Republicans' receipts profile is the direct opposite of the house Democrats, with unions and lawyers favoring the Democrats and manufacturing and retail sales groups favoring the Republicans.

Due to the large amount of pass back from legislative candidates, the house Republicans had the largest total of receipts from candidates and parties of any of the leaders in 1990 and 1992.

Senate Democratic Receipts Profile. The interest group receipts profile of the senate Democrats (tables 3.1 and 3.2) is shaped primarily by contributions from the financial, lawyer, union, and manufacturing sectors for both election cycles. Although the scale is less, the profile is the same as that of the house Democrats.

In 1990 the senate Democrats received contributions from individuals and candidate/party groups in amounts similar to the other leader/chamber committee profiles. In 1992 the senate Democratic chamber committee had significantly smaller individual contributions than did the other three groups and the second largest amount of candidate/party contributions. A substantial portion of candidate contributions came from incumbent Democratic senators with safe races, many of whom were hopeful of becoming the new leader in the 1993 legislative session. By transferring surplus campaign funds to the chamber committee, these senators hoped to demonstrate their leadership and fundraising ability to their colleagues who would be voting for a new senate Democratic leader in 1994. The smaller amount of individual contributions may reflect a shift of large individual Democratic contributors to the house Democrats prompted by an assessment that the Democrats had a much better chance to retain control of the house than the senate under the new legislative district map.

Senate Republican Receipts Profile. The senate Republicans' interest group receipt profile is primarily shaped by contributions from the financial, manufacturing, and health sectors (tables 3.1 and 3.2, pp. 40 and 41). While quite similar to the house Republicans' profile, contributions from the retail sales sector are less significant for the senate Republicans. The union and lawyer sector contributions (low) and the manufacturing sector contributions (high) mirror those of the house Republicans. For the house and senate Democrats the pattern is the opposite, with high union and lawyer contributions and low manufacturing contributions.

While the amounts received from candidate/party groups in 1990 were fairly equitable for each leader, the senate Republicans had the smallest amount of the four leaders in 1992. The senate Republicans' receipts from individuals were similar to the house Republicans for both 1990 and 1992.

Total Expenditures: How Much Was Spent? Where Did It Go?

Together, the four legislative leader/chamber political committees spent $6.74 million during the 1990 election cycle and $11.06 million during the 1992 election cycle (tables 3.3 and 3.4, pp. 44 and 45). As with contributions, house Democrats legislative leader/chamber political committee had a significant expenditure advantage over the other three leader/chamber political committees. The house Democrats spent a total of $2.44 million in 1990 and $3.86 million in 1992; the house Republicans, $1.88 million in 1990 and $2.90 million in 1992; the senate Democrats, $1.04 million in 1990 and $1.93 million in 1992; and the senate Republicans, $1.38 million in 1990 and $2.37 million in 1992. The

Table 3.3
All Expenditures - 1990 Election Cycle
Legislative Leader and Chamber Political Committees
(Excludes transfers between leader and chamber committees)
(Amounts in units of $1,000)

	Total	Madigan HouseDem	Daniels HouseRep	Rock SenDem	Philip SenRep
Legislative Elections	5,536	1,948	1,609	758	1,221
Direct Support	(4,921)	(1,948)	(1,331)	(758)	(884)
State Party Pass Back	(615)	--	(278)	--	(337)
State Party	273	256	0	17	0
Local Parties	160	97	15	36	12
Nonlegislative Candidates	156	37	60	32	27
Nonelection Expenditures	613	105	195	193	120
TOTAL	6,738	2,443	1,879	1,036	1,380

house Democrats outspent the house Republicans by $556,000 in 1990 and $959,000 in 1992. The senate Republicans advantage in total spending over the senate Democrats was $344,000 in 1990 and $435,000 in 1992.

Of the total expenditures made by the four leader/chamber political committees, the vast majority in each election cycle went to direct support of candidates for the legislature. Those expenditures, totaling $5,563,000 in 1990 and $9,617,000 in 1992, will be examined in detail in the next section. After legislative elections, the most significant expenditure category in both election cycles was *nonelection* expenditures. In the 1990 election cycle $613,000 in expenditures was classified as nonelection expenditures, while the figure in the 1992 election cycle was $1,177,000. Most of these nonelection expenditures were for items such as office and overhead expenses and staff, meeting, and travel expenses, but they also included donations to charitable causes, contributions to interest groups, gifts, flowers, staff Christmas parties, group meals for legislators during evening legislative sessions, membership dues for private clubs, and tickets for sporting and cultural events. The vast majority of the expenditures classified as nonelection were made from the legislative leader political committees rather than from the chamber political committees.

If money transferred from the legislative leader and chamber political committees to the state Democratic and Republican parties were classified as contributions, it would rank as the second largest area of expenditures after direct expenditures on legislative elections. However,

Table 3.4
All Expenditures - 1992 Election Cycle
Legislative Leader and Chamber Political Committees
(Excludes transfers between leader and chamber committees)
(Amounts in units of $1,000)

	Total	Madigan HouseDem	Daniels HouseRep	Rock SenDem	Philip SenRep
Legislative Elections	9,617	3,526	2,481	1,517	2,093
Direct	--	(3,526)	(1,537)	(1,517)	(1,671)
State Party Pass Back	--	--	(944)	--	(422)
State Party	90	35	17	15	23
Local Parties	104	50	14	21	19
Nonlegislative Candidates	78	8	7	34	29
Nonelection Expenditures	1,177	242	383	347	205
TOTAL	11,066	3,861	2,902	1,934	2,369

the reality is that most transfers by the Republican chamber political committees to the state Republican Party were not contributions aimed at providing resources for state party activities. Instead, the state Republication Party took that money and paid for mailings in support of Republican legislative candidates. They took the money from the leaders and passed it back to them in the form of services. These transactions are labeled as state party pass back in tables 3.3 and 3.4 (pp. 44 and 45). The amount the state Republican Party paid for printing and mailing direct-mail pieces for Republican candidates for the house and senate (table 3.5, p. 46) was equal to the amount transferred to the party by the house and senate Republicans in 1992 and exceeded the amounts transferred in 1990 (table 5.3, p. 118). As a result, transfers of money by the house and senate Republicans to the state Republican Party in 1990 and 1992 were counted as expenditures by the leaders on legislative elections, not as contributions to the party. These pass-back expenditures by the house and senate Republicans totaled $615,000 in 1990 (table 3.3) and $1.36 million in 1992 (table 3.4). Because of the way the state Democratic Party reported expenditures, it is not possible to determine how much was spent by the Democratic Party to support legislative candidates. For this reason, while it is probably safe to assume the amount exceeded the amounts transferred by the house and senate Democrats to the state Democratic Party in 1990 and 1992, it was not counted as legislative election expenditures. Except for the transfer from the house Democrats in 1990, nonpass-back transfers by leader or chamber political committees to the state parties were small, a total of $273,000 in 1990 (table 3.3) and $90,000 in 1992 (table 3.4).

Table 3.5
Legislative Election Expenditures - 1990 Election Cycle
Legislative Leader and Chamber Political Committees
(Amounts in units of $1,000)

	Total	Madigan HouseDem	Daniels HouseRep	Rock SenDem	Philip SenRep
Transfers to Candidates	472	197	99	48	128
Media	456	29	125	97	205
Targeting/Direct Mail (incl. party pass back)	2,791	1,154	655	372	610
Campaign Staff	810	308	273	130	99
Fundraising	696	195	290	83	128
Misc. & Unclassified.	311	65	167	28	51
TOTAL	5,536	1,948	1,609	758	1,221

Contributions by the leader/chamber committees to local political parties ($160,000 in 1990 and $104,000 in 1992) and nonlegislative candidates ($156,000 in 1990 and $78,000 in 1992) made up only a small portion of the total expenditures for either election cycle (see tables 3.3 and 3.4, pp. 44 and 45). The only difference of note is that the house and senate Democratic leader/chamber political committees gave significantly more to local political parties than did the Republicans in both election cycles.

Total Legislative Campaign Expenditures: Where Did the Money Go?

The breakout of expenditures on legislative elections into detailed categories reveals a number of interesting patterns (tables 3.5 and 3.6, pp. 46 and 47). In terms of total expenditures, the most significant category is targeting and direct mail, which accounts for 50 percent of total legislative election expenditures in both election cycles. Included in this category are payments to political consulting firms for polling, identifying voters in particular categories, and designing, printing, and mailing campaign literature to targeted groups. The next most significant category is expenditures on campaign staff, accounting for 15 percent of total legislative election spending in 1990 and 12 percent in 1992. This category includes both legislative staff paid by campaign payrolls and staff hired for a campaign. The third most important category is transfers of money to legislative candidates, accounting for 9 percent of total legislative election spending in 1990 and 14 percent in 1992. Except for fundraising expenditures in 1990, none of the other categories exceeds 8 percent of the total.

Table 3.6
Legislative Election Expenditures - 1992 Election Cycle
Legislative Leader and Chamber Political Committees
(Amounts in units of $1,000)

	Total	Madigan HouseDem	Daniels HouseRep	Rock SenDem	Philip SenRep
Transfers to Candidates	1,376	622	191	131	432
Media	422	161	126	95	40
Targeting/Direct Mail (incl. party pass back)	4,805	1,727	1,346	860	872
Campaign Staff	1,184	554	160	253	217
Fundraising	495	202	262	9	22
General Consulting	576	61	144	12	359
Phone/Telemarket.	318	146	51	102	19
Misc. & Unclassified.	441	53	201	55	132
TOTAL	9,617	3,526	2,481	1,517	2,093

Direct contributions of money to legislative candidates, while significant, are less important than expenditures on staff hired by the leaders to work on campaigns and are far less important than the targeting and direct-mail services provided by the leaders to candidates. Rather than just providing candidates in key targeted races with money to spend, the legislative leaders and their staffs are directly involved in the operation of those campaigns, providing experienced campaign staff and purchasing and coordinating polling, targeting, direct mail, and media services. The degree of control in individual races will vary, but the influence of the legislative leaders and their staff is there.

What is particularly striking about the expenditure data for the four leader/chamber groups is their overwhelming commitment to direct contact with individual voters through computerized targeting techniques and polling and the heavy emphasis on the use of direct-mail pieces designed for the targeted groups. All four make extensive use of nationally known political consulting firms to generate sophisticated profiles of the voters in legislative districts. The amount of money spent on less focused, more indirect voter-contact techniques (e.g., media spots or billboards and yard signs) by the leader/chamber groups is very small in comparison. However, most TV and radio expenditures are made by the candidate's campaign committee. The amounts spent by the four leader/chamber groups on paid campaign staff clearly indicate that both experienced management and face-to-face contact through working the precincts and get-out-the-vote efforts are important parts of the overall strategy. Any final conclusions about the use of various campaign techniques cannot be drawn without looking at the expenditure reports of the candidates. While leadership expenditures are very important, the data in chapter 7 will show that leadership expenditures rarely account for more than half of the expenditures made in races that are targeted by the legislative leaders.

The data in tables 3.5 and 3.6 (pp. 46 and 47) should not be interpreted to mean that legislative campaigns spend little on television and radio. Rather, it means that media expenditures tend to be made directly by the local campaigns rather than purchased by the leaders. If a campaign for a downstate Democrat purchases a TV spot on the local station, it looks better to local media for the check to come from Citizens for Smith than from a committee controlled by a legislative leader from Chicago.

The detailed expenditure categories in table 3.5 differ from those in 3.6 because the way expenditures are reported varies between committees and varies from one election cycle to the next for the same committee. The purposes listed for a large expenditure to a political consulting firm may be broken out as direct-mail design, postage, and consulting in one report, while in another report the purpose may be listed as just *political consulting*. The problem of incomplete and inconsistent reporting makes coding the data for both receipts and expenditures difficult. It is impossible to accurately code an expenditure simply listed as a payment to a credit card company with no specific purpose or with three or four unrelated purposes.

Chamber/Legislative Leader Expenditures over the 1992 Election Cycle

The distribution of spending by legislative leaders and chamber political committees in the off-year, primary, and general election periods for the 1992 election cycle is presented in table 3.7 (p. 49). There appear to be a number of differences between the legislative leaders and chamber committees and between the house and senate committees. As might be expected, the legislative leaders concentrate a greater percentage of their spending in the primaries than do the chamber committees. The portion of legislative election expenditures made by the leaders in the 1992 primary ranged from 20 to 59 percent, while the portion of legislative election expenditures made by the chamber committees ranged from 4 to 14 percent.

Questions are more likely to be raised about the chamber committees being involved in intraparty conflicts than legislative leaders, particularly

Table 3.7
Legislative Election Expenditures - 1992 Election Cycle
Off-year, Primary, and General Election Breakout
Leader and Chamber Political Committees
(Amounts in units of $1,000)

	Off-year	Primary	General	Total
Madigan	112 (12%)	562 (59%)	286 (30%)	960 (100%)
HouseDem	60 (2%)	225 (9%)	2,281 (89%)	2,566 (100%)
Madigan/HouseDem	172 (5%)	787 (22%)	2,567 (73%)	3,526 (100%)
Daniels	154 (33%)	124 (26%)	190 (41%)	468 (100%)
HouseRep	198 (10%)	277 (14%)	1,538 (76%0	2,013 (100%)
Daniels/House Rep	353 (14%)	401 (16%)	1,728 (70%)	2,481 (100%)
Rock	34 (42%)	17 (21%)	30 (37%)	81 (100%)
SenDem	99 (7%)	60 (4%)	1,278 (89%)	1,437 (100%)
Rock/SenDem	133 (9%)	77 (5%)	1,308 (86%)	1,518 (100%)
Philip	79 (19%)	82 (20%)	249 (61%)	410 (100%)
SenRep	31 (5%)	64 (4%)	1,588 (94%)	1,683 (100%)
Philip/SenRep	110 (5%)	146 (7%)	1,837 (88%)	2,093 (100%)

in cases where an incumbent is being challenged in the primary. The leaders are expected to protect their members, even in primary fights, while the chamber committees are expected to be more concerned with supporting candidates in the general election. The leaders also generally have greater flexibility in directing spending from their own political committees. The expenditures of house speaker Madigan in the 1992 primary stand out, both in terms of the amount spent and as a percentage of total spending.

The greater expenditures in the primary by both house leaders and house chamber committees over those of the senate leaders and senate chamber committees are largely a function of the larger number of seats up for election in the house. The greater number of house seats being contested makes recruitment by the leaders more difficult and independent challengers more likely than is the case with senate seats.

Leadership Expenditure Patterns: Who Spent How Much on What?

The legislative election expenditure patterns for the four legislative leader/chamber political committees indicate differences between house and senate and Democratic and Republican approaches. In particular, each of the four leader/chamber political committees has a distinct expenditure profile (tables 3.5 and 3.6, pp. 46 and 47).

House Democratic Expenditure Profile. The Madigan/house Democratic expenditure profile (tables 3.5 and 3.6) shows a commitment to a targeting and direct-mail strategy with almost 60 percent of legislative election expenditures devoted to that category in the 1990 election cycle and almost 50 percent in 1992. Expenditures for campaign staff are the next most significant (16 percent in both 1990 and 1992), followed closely by expenditures for money transfers to legislative candidates (10 percent in 1990 and 18 percent in 1992). With the exception of fundraising in 1990, no other category exceeds 6 percent in either election cycle. Expenditures on media are very small but, as previously noted, most media buys are paid from the candidates' campaign committees. The most striking feature of the Madigan/house Democratic profile over both election cycles is the overwhelming dominance of expenditures on targeting and direct mail, the strong use of paid campaign staff, and the relatively large amount of money transfers to candidates. The way the legislative leaders and chamber committees filed their reports in 1992 made it easier to identify phone and telemarketing activity than in previous reports. The differences between tables 3.5 and 3.6 in this area are primarily a function of the lack of consistency and uniformity in how campaign expenditures are reported.

House Republican Expenditure Profile. Like the Madigan/house Democrats, the Daniels/house Republicans expenditure profile (tables 3.5 and 3.6) is dominated by expenditures on targeting and direct mail (41 percent in 1990 and 54 percent in 1992). In contrast to the house Democrats, the second largest expenditure category for house Republicans is fundraising (18 percent in 1990 and 11 percent in 1992). That is followed by campaign staff (17 percent in 1990 and 6 percent in 1992). Part of the difference between 1990 and 1992 in resources spent on staff is a reflection of what payrolls individuals are placed on and how those expenditures are reported. As noted above, a complete picture requires an examination of the reports of individual candidates. Compared to the profile for the house Democrats, direct contributions of money to legislative candidates are significantly smaller for the house Republicans. Over the two election cycles, the dominant features are spending on targeting and direct mail, relatively heavy expenditures on fundraising, and a significant commitment to campaign staff.

Senate Democratic Expenditure Profile. Like the Madigan/house Democratic profile, the Rock/senate Democratic expenditure profile (tables 3.5 and 3.6, pp. 46 and 47) shows the greatest portion of election expenses on targeting and direct mail (49 percent in 1990 and 57 percent in 1992) and the next largest portion on campaign staff (17 percent in 1990 and 1992). In sharp contrast to the house Democratic and Republican committees, the senate Democrats spent 13 percent of their resources on media in 1990 (table 3.5). However, with only two competitive races among the 19 senate seats up for reelection that year, no long-term conclusions should be drawn. In 1992 the percentage of electoral expenditures that went to media was only 6 percent, which was similar to the other three leadership expenditure profiles (table 3.6). The third-largest expenditure category in 1992 was money transfers to candidates, but at 9 percent it was less than half that of the house Democrats or the senate Republicans. None of the other expenditure categories exceeded 7 percent. The two consistent features over the two election cycles are the dominance of expenditures on targeting and direct mail and the strong commitment to paid campaign staff.

Senate Republican Expenditure Profile. The largest portion of campaign expenditures by Philip/senate Republicans (tables 3.5 and 3.6), like that for the other three groups, was on targeting and direct mail (50 percent in 1990 and 42 percent in 1992), although their 1992 percentage of spending in this category is the lowest of the four leader/chamber groups. The next largest expenditure categories for the Philip/senate Republicans were media in 1990 (17 percent) and money transfers to candidates in 1992 (21 percent). Both the senate Republicans and the house Democrats spent more on this category in 1990 and 1992 than did the house Republicans and the senate Democrats. Like the senate Democrats, the senate Republicans spent a much higher percentage on media in 1990 than did either house group. Also, like the senate Democrats, the percentage in 1992 dropped to a level (2 percent) more in line with the house groups. The large percentage of expenditures in 1992 on general consulting for the senate Republicans was a function of how they reported their expenditures on their 1992 second semiannual report. Expenditures to consultants for services such as media and targeting/direct mail were broken out into specific categories in 1990. On the 1992 reports, many of these were reported as general consulting services. The amount of spending on campaign staff by the senate Republicans was lower, but still comparable to the other three leader/chamber groups. The two consistent features of the senate Republican expenditure profiles are the dominance of expenditures on targeting and direct mail and the large amount of money transfers to legislative candidates in the 1990 and 1992 election cycles.

The Electoral Success of the Madigan/Chamber Political Committee

Prior to the 1990 elections, all four of the legislative leaders had been in office for at least eight years. Each had built highly successful fundraising and campaign organizations. Each had talented staff people with vast campaign experience. Still, looking back over the 1980s and early 1990s, it is hard to argue with the fundraising success or the electoral success of Speaker Madigan and the house Democrats. That record of success ended in 1994 when the Republicans gained control of the Illinois house by a 64-to-54 margin. Data on the 1994 election are not yet available, so it is impossible to determine what role national trends played and what role the leaders played in determining the outcome. While the senate Democrats and the senate Republicans battled on relatively even terms during the last decade, the house Democrats increased both their fundraising advantage and their legislative majority. The count of 72 Democratic seats in the house after the 1990 election was the high-water mark for the decade. A favorable map resulting from Democratic control of the 1982 redistricting process was a key factor in the success of the house Democrats. But in 1992, facing a map drawn by the Republicans, the senate Republicans took control of the senate, while the house Democrats held control of the house by a comfortable margin.

Factors other than the fundraising advantage and political skill of the house Democrats were certainly in play. On the senate side, the announced retirement of senate president Rock and loss of key Democratic staff, including the election of Rock's longtime chief of staff to the post of auditor general in the spring of 1992, left the senate Democrats with a lame-duck leader and a less-experienced campaign staff than in previous elections. On the house side, the lack of a strong Republican presidential campaign in Illinois in 1990 probably had a negative impact on all Republican candidates. The house Democrats benefited from

Table 3.8
Legislative Leader Expenditures - 1990 Election Cycle
(Amounts in units of $1,000)

	Madigan	Daniels	Rock	Philip
Direct Expenditures on Legislative Elections	347	276	48	51
Transfers to Chamber Political Committee	1,060	0	5	75

strong women candidates in a number of key races in a year when women candidates did well in races across the country.

In assessing the success of the house Democrats, a number of factors are relevant. The speaker's political committee and the house Democrats' political committee appear to be better integrated than those of the other three chamber groups. Treating the legislative leader political committee and the chamber political committee as parts of an integrated whole is a somewhat artificial construction for the other three chamber groups; for the house Democrats, it is a reflection of reality. A comparison of expenditures on legislative elections made by the four leader political committees shows a clear dominance of Speaker Madigan over the other three leaders (tables 3.8 and 3.9, pp. 53 and 54). Even more important, Speaker Madigan provided a large percentage of the total receipts of the house Democratic chamber political committee through transfers of funds, slightly more than $1 million in 1990 and $1.67 million in 1992 (tables 3.8 and 3.9). In contrast to the other three chamber political committees, the house Democrats' political committee is more a mechanism for campaign expenditures than a vehicle for fundraising. The concentration on fundraising in the speaker's political committee gives him a greater degree of control over expenditures than is the case with the other three legislative leaders. It also focuses attention on him as the source of assistance.

Better integration between legislative leader and chamber political committees and a greater concentration of power in the hands of the legislative leader can facilitate raising money and winning elections. It also helps to have experienced staff and effective campaign strategies. In 1990 Speaker Madigan's chief of staff and his issues-development staff director each had been directing legislative election campaigns for the house Democrats continually for 9 years, beginning when Madigan was elected house minority leader in 1981. (Neither is still with the house Democratic staff. The chief of staff was elected chairman of the state Democratic Party in 1991 and elected to the state senate in 1992, while the issues-development staff director took a position with an association

Table 3.9
Legislative Leader Expenditures - 1992 Election Cycle
(Amounts in units of $1,000)

	Madigan	Daniels	Rock	Philip
Direct Expenditures on Legislative Elections	960	468	81	410
Transfers to Chamber Political Committee	1,672	0	20	208

in Washington, D.C.) The political staff assembled by Speaker Madigan was the first group organized to give a leader a staff that could support individual members when they were in session and then move off the state payroll during the election periods to form the basis of a statewide legislative campaign organization.

Finally, the legislative election expenditure data from the 1990 and 1992 election cycles show a house Democratic campaign strategy built around targeting and direct mail and providing candidates with paid, experienced campaign staff (tables 3.5 and 3.6, pp. 46 and 47). Both of these require the commitment of large sums of money. The development and refinement of this approach since 1980 was a key element in the electoral success of the house Democrats in 1990 and 1992.

The house Democrats' political organization served as a model during the 1980s for those developed by the other three leader/chamber groups. Whether the house Democrats will be as successful in the 1990s under a legislative map favoring the Republicans remains to be seen.

Looking to Legislative Elections in the 1990s

History teaches us that Illinois legislative maps do not always produce the results intended by their drafters. The legislative map that house speaker Robert Blair helped draft in 1971 was supposed to guarantee Republican control of the Illinois house for the decade. It worked well in 1972. In 1974 the outrage of suburban voters over the creation of the Regional Transit Authority helped end Speaker Blair's legislative career in the primary election, and the general outrage of voters over the Watergate scandal helped end the Republicans' control of the Illinois House of Representatives in the general election. The 101 Democrats elected to the house that year provided a majority that the Republicans were unable to overcome until 1980.

Because of the volatility of the electorate and the decline of political parties, the key elements in any election—recruiting good candidates, raising sufficient money to mount a serious race, running an effective campaign, and getting out the vote—will be even more important in legislative elections through the rest of the decade. More than ever, it will be important for the legislative leaders to have effective organizations for raising money and running campaigns. It is clear that many of the legislative races will be determined by the outcome of battles between the powerful campaign organizations that the legislative leaders have built over the past decade. The detailed look at the funding of key legislative races in 1992 presented in chapter 6 illustrates the continuing role that legislative leaders play in determining the outcomes of legislative elections.

"I'd like to remain the people's representative. The trouble is that the people don't have any money."

An Illinois legislator commenting on the need to raise large sums of money in order to win reelection

CHAPTER 4
INTEREST GROUPS AND LEGISLATIVE ELECTIONS

For awhile during the spring of 1993 it appeared that the General Assembly, for the first time in four years, would pass a bill dealing with abortion. The right-to-life supporters went head-to-head with the pro-choice supporters over a parental notification bill. The right-to-life forces won in the house and again in the senate when the bill came up for votes on third reading. It seemed certain that a bill requiring women under the age of 18 to notify one of their parents prior to obtaining an abortion would reach the governor's desk. Instead, the bill lost in the house when it came back for the approval of changes made in the senate. The bill failed because of objections raised at the last minute by one of the most powerful interest groups in Illinois, the Illinois State Medical Society.* After the medical society signaled its opposition, 13 legislators who voted for the bill in the house on the first roll call changed their votes to *no* or *present* on its final vote. The medical society's opposition was based on concerns about the penalty provisions in the bill that would have applied to doctors who knowingly violated the law.

Why was the medical society successful in defeating the bill? The sources of interest group influence are many: large memberships, strong grassroots organizations, expert knowledge, persuasive representatives, and powerful emotional appeals. But the most effective currency of influence in the legislature is currency. As noted earlier, legislative elections in Illinois are very expensive and are becoming more expensive with each election cycle. With very few exceptions, influential interest groups in Illinois politics are those that contribute large sums of money to the campaign committees of legislative leaders, incumbent legislators, and candidates for legislative office.

In raising and spending money on legislative campaigns, the medical

---

* See appendix C, p. 186 for an alphabetical listing of the top 20 interest group contributors to legislative campaigns.

society stands head and shoulders above all other interest groups. During the 1992 election cycle (calendar years 1991 and 1992), the society contributed $1.48 million to the political committees of candidates for the legislature and those of legislative leaders and their chamber political committees. The next largest amount contributed by a single interest group was $639,000, contributed by the Illinois Education Association's (IEA) Political Action Committee, IPACE. While the IEA is also able to influence legislative elections by directing local volunteers and local education association money in targeted races, the medical society's advantage is still substantial. The medical society was also the largest contributor to legislative elections during the 1990 election cycle (tables 4.1 and 4.2, pp. 87 and 88).

Do those who contribute the most money always win in the legislature? If that were true, then legislation raising the state tax on cigarettes would have remained buried in committee in the 1993 spring session, just as it had in previous sessions. Most of the groups supporting a cigarette tax increase are not-for-profit or public-interest groups, such as the Illinois Cancer Society, that have little or no money to contribute to political campaigns. In contrast, the tobacco interests have a long history of contributing large amounts of money to legislative leaders and members and, until 1985, an equally long history of successfully opposing attempts to increase the tax on cigarettes. A review of the campaign reports of legislative candidates and leaders for the last six months of 1992 shows that two corporations (Philip Morris, Inc. and R. J. Reynolds Company) and one group representing tobacco interests (Tobacco Institute) contributed more than $240,000 to legislative campaigns during the period. But all of that money did not prevent the governor and the legislature from incorporating both a cigarette tax increase and a new tax on other tobacco products as key pieces in the budget agreement passed in early July of 1993 (Gherardini 1993, 48-49).

The Major Players

Who is on and who is not on a list of the top interest group and corporate contributors to the 1990 and 1992 legislative elections says a lot about Illinois politics. See tables 4.1 and 4.2 for lists of the top 20 interest group contributors to legislative campaigns during the 1990 and 1992 election cycles. These lists are dominated by healthcare provider and facility groups, public employee and trade labor unions, lawyer associations, and business and financial associations.*

The totals in these two tables do not account for all of the funds that are contributed to legislative candidates on behalf of the interests that the groups and corporations represent. Depending on the candidates, a review of the campaign finance reports filed in strongly contested legislative races will also disclose contributions from a wide variety of individual entities including law, manufacturing, and retail firms; local public employee and trade unions; financial institutions; public utilities; real estate and insurance companies; and physicians groups and healthcare facilities. The tables do accurately reflect the composition and relative strength of the major players in legislative elections in Illinois. To determine the total amount of money contributed to legislative elections from any one category, it would be necessary to classify and total all of the contributions made to all of the legislative candidates.

Missing from the list of major contributors are environmental groups, consumer groups, and social service organizations representing children, the poor, the physically or mentally disabled, and others. Also absent are groups representing single issues or ideological positions with the exception of Personal PAC, a group advocating a pro-choice position on abortion. It is a paradox that very large categories of people with common interests, such as the consumers of electricity or healthcare patients, do not organize and raise money for campaign contributions precisely because they are so large. The communication and organizational costs are too great, and the incentives for any individual to act are too small. Raising a large amount of money for campaign contributions is almost always the result of the individual actions of corporations, the cooperative actions of a relatively small number of private corporations, or the collective actions of members of professional associations or compulsory labor unions (Olson 1965).

Looking at the list of the largest contributors from the 1990 and 1992 election cycles, it is clear that the total amount of money increased dramatically from 1990 to 1992. The top 10 groups in 1992 (table 4.2, p. 88) gave almost $2 million more than the top 10 in 1990 (table 4.1, p. 87). Two factors were at work here. In 1990 there were statewide campaigns for governor, secretary of state, state attorney general, state treasurer, and state comptroller. All of these races were competing with legislative races for campaign contribution dollars. Second, in 1990 there

* See appendix D.1 (pp. 187-89) and D.2 (p. 190-92) for an overview/breakdown of intererst groups and corporations making campaign contributions in excess of $50,000 for the 1992 election cycle (*Almanac of Illinois Politics—1994*, 408-13).

were only 20 state senate seats up for reelection, and it was the last election under the 1981 redistricting map. Only two senate races generated much attention, and the house Democrats appeared to be in firm control of that chamber. In contrast, in 1992 there were no statewide races to compete with the legislative races, and every legislative seat in the house and senate was up. Of equal importance, the new legislative map had been drawn by the Republicans. The result was a large number of open seats and competitive races with political control of both chambers in doubt. As a result the flow of money from interest groups and corporations into state legislative races increased dramatically in 1992.

While all 20 of the top contributors to legislative elections in 1992 increased their contributions from two years earlier, the percentage of increases varied widely. At the top of the scale were Personal PAC (242 percent), UAW (119 percent), Illinois State Medical Society (131 percent), and Illinois Hospital and Healthsystems Association (92 percent), while the smallest percentage increases came from Philip Morris, Inc. (5 percent), Illinois Trial Lawyers Association (16 percent), Illinois State Dental Society (18 percent), and Illinois Bankers Association (19 percent). The large percentage increases can reflect either aggressive fundraising in anticipation of a significant election (e.g., medical society and UAW) or natural growth for groups whose roles in legislative elections have been increasing rapidly over previous election cycles (e.g., hospitals/healthsystems and Personal PAC). Smaller percentage increases may indicate either a nonaggressive approach to the 1992 elections (e.g., Philip Morris, dentists, bankers) or a strategic decision to put more emphasis on contributions by individual members to legislative candidates and less emphasis on organizational contributions to the legislative leaders (e.g., trial lawyers). Even at this aggregate level there are patterns that suggest the kinds of decisions that lie at the heart of the contribution strategies pursued by the groups that contribute to legislative campaigns in Illinois.

Contribution Strategies

While all of the groups and corporations listed in tables 4.1 and 4.2 (pp. 87 and 88) contributed significant amounts of money to legislative campaigns, they did not pursue identical contribution strategies. The data from the 1990 and 1992 election cycles show that interest groups varied significantly in (1) their emphasis on giving to leaders and members, (2) their partisanship in giving, (3) the amount of risk-taking they engaged in, and (4) their commitment to changing or preserving the status quo.

Leader-oriented v. Member-oriented Contribution Strategies. Interest groups may seek to influence legislative elections or to improve their access to the legislative process by (1) primarily contributing directly to candidates, (2) primarily contributing to legislative leaders and their chamber PACs, which then provides resources for candidates, or (3) splitting contributions between members and leaders. The 1990 and 1992 contribution patterns of the Illinois Education Association (IEA) through its political committee, IPACE, and Personal PAC (tables 4.1 and 4.2, pp. 87 and 88) clearly show a candidate-oriented contribution strategy. In contrast the 1990 and 1992 contribution patterns of the Teamsters Joint Council No. 25 and Philip Morris indicate a more legislative leader-oriented strategy. While there is a good deal of continuity in the contribution patterns for the two election cycles, the large shift from leader contributions to member contributions for the trial lawyers suggests that strategic considerations for a particular election may override a group's established pattern.

Contribution strategy in relation to the legislative leaders rests on a number of considerations. Because the General Assembly is dominated by the four legislative leaders, it is usually important for interest groups to build good relationships with legislative leaders from both parties in both chambers of the legislature through campaign contributions. Groups without strong grassroots ties to the state in terms of members or jobs and who are primarily interested in preserving the status quo, such as Philip Morris, or groups with relatively limited resources, may decide that their most effective strategy is to work primarily through the leaders.

However, a contribution made directly to a candidate insures that the interest group controls where the money goes and that the candidate knows where the money comes from. The contribution pattern of the IEA suggests they do not want any question in candidates' minds about the source of contributions, and they believe they can be effective without contributing to the leaders and chamber committees. The IEA is an interest group with a long-standing practice of working directly in the campaigns of candidates in races they target. While they tend to give to Democratic candidates and to work closely with legislative leadership in campaigns, their effectiveness and independence results in a contribution pattern somewhat different from most influential interest groups.

Contributing directly to a candidate also insures that anyone reading the candidate's report to the State Board of Elections knows where the money came from. In contrast, the original source of money given to a legislative leader or chamber PAC, which is then given by the leader to a candidate in the form of money or services, is impossible to trace. This may be viewed by interest groups or candidates as an advantage. If the source of a contribution might be politically embarrassing to a candidate, then the group may route the contribution through a friendly leader or chamber committee. For example, it makes good sense for groups such as Chicago-based labor unions to work through the Democratic legislative leaders to provide support for Democratic candidates in areas where neither Chicago nor organized labor is very popular.

In contrast, if the interest being promoted by a group is controversial and largely nonpartisan, such as the pro-choice Personal PAC, contributions to legislative leaders would be ineffective and probably unwelcome. In such a case, the legislative leaders would not want to be identified as favoring one particular side in the controversy and some candidates would not want to take money from leaders that could be characterized as having been provided in part by pro-choice groups. Identifying specific candidates who support their position and concentrating exclusively on them is a more effective and appropriate strategy for such groups.

Partisan or Bipartisan Contribution Strategies. The General Assembly is an intensely partisan place. Members are elected as Republicans or Democrats and the chambers are organized along party lines. However, only 10 of the 20 groups and corporations listed in tables 4.1 and 4.2 (pp. 87 and 88) clearly directed their contributions to legislative candidates and leaders from one party regardless of incumbency or leadership control. As will be demonstrated below, many interest groups try to play it safe with their contributions by giving primarily to incumbents and to the legislative leaders. Groups pursuing this kind of bipartisan strategy would have tended to give more money to the Democratic side prior to the 1990 and 1992 elections because the Democrats controlled both the house (67 to 51 in 1990 and 72 to 46 in 1992) and the senate (31 to 28 both years). Groups that consistently favored Republican leaders and Republican candidates in spite of the Democratic control of the legislature during that time can be safely regarded as partisan-Republican in their orientation.

There are 10 groups (tables 4.1 and 4.2) that clearly pursued a partisan strategy. Identified as partisan-Republican are those that favored the Republicans in their contributions in both 1990 and 1992: medical society, manufacturers, and insurance agents. Identified as partisan-Democratic are those that averaged more than 80 percent in contributions to Democratic candidates and leaders for the two cycles combined: trial lawyers, IEA, Teamsters, AFSCME, UAW, AFL-CIO, and Personal PAC. These 10 groups were clearly pursuing a partisan strategy. In contrast, there were eight groups (tables 4.1 and 4.2, pp. 87 and 88) that averaged between 50 and 65 percent in contributions to Democratic candidates for the two cycles: realtors, bankers, beer distributors, CPAs, dentists, Philip Morris, cable TV, and car/truck dealers. These eight groups appear to be pursuing a bipartisan approach. The distinction between the bipartisan and partisan approaches of interest groups is also evident when only contributions to leaders are examined (tables 4.3 and 4.4, pp. 89 and 90).

Two groups do not fall within these categories: bar association and hospitals. Over the two election cycles the percentage of their contributions to Democratic candidates ranged between 63 and 72 percent. This placed them between the bipartisan and partisan-Democratic categories. The more detailed analysis of the contribution behavior of the 20 groups that follow will help clarify the exact nature of their orientation.

Groups following a bipartisan approach are primarily interested in giving to candidates who were incumbent members and to the leaders who controlled the process. The resulting advantage to the Democrats in 1990 and 1992 was based on strategic rather than partisan considerations. The intensity and uncertainty of the struggle for partisan control of the General Assembly actually contribute to groups taking a bipartisan approach to contributions. Most interest groups want to have good relationships with those in power, which means maintaining good relationships with both sides. They also realize that active involvement in primaries and contested races is much more expensive and is riskier than a bipartisan approach.

A bipartisan approach to campaign contributions makes good sense for groups pursuing interests that are not generally partisan (CPA or beer distributor issues) and for groups with a strong stake in the status quo (in areas such as real estate or banking). Bipartisan strategies are also usually incumbent and status quo oriented because the objective is to keep things as they are and to maintain access to those in power. These types of groups have been successful in dealing with members and leaders already in office and are not interested in enacting major policy changes into law.

Partisan campaign contribution strategies require both a desire to affect the partisan control of the process and the resources to carry out that strategy. Interest groups such as those representing the medical society, the IEA, the trial lawyers, the manufacturers, public employee and private trade unions, and the independent insurance agents may adopt partisan contribution strategies as the result of traditional political alliances (e.g., Democrats and big labor, Republicans and big business) or issue-conflicts that have developed in Illinois along partisan lines (the Democrats and the trial lawyers vs. the Republicans and the state medical society over tort reform). These same groups also have the resources to pursue more expensive, partisan contribution strategies.

Contribution Patterns over an Election Cycle

The political axiom that "timing is everything" also applies to campaign contributions. The timing of interest group contributions during the two calendar years of an election cycle reveals a good deal about contribution strategies. There are no elections during the first year of a cycle; in the second year there is a primary during the first six months and the general election in the last six months. Differences in contribution patterns within and between election cycles indicate the broad outline of a group's contribution strategy. A complete picture of each group's strategy develops from a more detailed examination of each group's contributions at different times in the election cycle.

At the beginning of the 1990 and 1992 election cycles, the prospects for changes in control of the legislature appeared significantly different. The 1990 election cycle came at the end of a decade of elections under the legislative district map drawn by the Democrats in 1981. While all 118 house members were up for reelection, the Democrats were in firm control of that chamber (67 to 51). The Democrats' control of the senate was less firm (31 to 28), but only 19 senate seats were up for reelection and only one contested race presented a realistic opportunity for the Republicans to pick up a seat. With the incumbent governor's retirement, there was an open race and the outcome was expected to be close. In contrast, 1992 was the first election held under the map drawn by the Republicans after the 1990 census. Retirements and the changes in district boundaries had created many open seats and many competitive races involving incumbents. A change in partisan control appeared likely in the senate and possible in the house.

How the major interest groups split their contributions to legislative candidates between the off-year, primary, and general election periods for the 1990 and 1992 election cycles is shown in tables 4.5 and 4.6 (pp. 91 and 92). The patterns in the data suggest that the 20 groups differ in their involvement in elections and their response to increased opportunities for change.

Four groups (Teamsters, Personal PAC, UAW, bar association) had a low level of participation in 1989 and 1991, the off-years. They made the vast majority of their contributions in the election years. Five other groups (medical society, IEA, trial lawyers, independent insurance agents, AFL-CIO) gave a much smaller portion of their election cycle contributions in 1991 than in 1989. This allowed them to focus a greater portion of their resources on the 1992 election. These 9 groups appear to be more electorally oriented than the other 11. At the other end of the spectrum, five groups (bankers, hospitals, CPA, dentists, and new car/truck dealers) all gave between 38 percent and 51 percent of their total contribution during the off year in both cycles. These five groups appear to be less election oriented and potentially more status quo oriented than the nine groups identified above. The patterns for the remaining six groups (manufacturers, realtors, beer distributors, Philip Morris, AFSCME, cable operators) are indeterminate at this level of analysis. A more detailed look at each portion of the election cycle reveals a more complex set of contribution patterns.

Off-year Contributions. Off-year contributions go, by definition, to incumbents. Beyond that, they flow most heavily to legislative leaders and chairpersons and members of committees that are important to the interest groups. A comparison of the contributions to legislative leaders shows that a much greater percentage of total contributions from interest groups goes to legislative leaders in the off years than during the primary or general election time periods. Most groups gave approximately the same amounts to leaders from both parties during the 1990 and 1992 off years. Among groups that contributed more than a total of $20,000 to legislative leaders in either 1989 or 1991, two groups, the medical society and the manufacturers, strongly favored the Republicans, while four groups, the trial lawyers, the UAW, Philip Morris, and the hospitals, strongly favored the Democrats (tables 4.3 and 4.4, pp. 89 and 90). If the contributions by Philip Morris and the hospitals were strategic rather than partisan, then the change in control of the Illinois senate after the 1992 elections should result in a shift for these groups toward more balanced contributions to the legislative leaders. This is one of a number of interesting questions to be resolved when data from the 1994 election cycle become available.

Table 4.7 (p. 93) shows the total legislative campaign contributions for the 20 interest groups during 1989, the first year of the 1990 election cycle, while table 4.8 (p. 94) shows the same information for 1991, the first year of the 1992 election cycle. The groups in tables 4.7 and 4.8 that focus the largest percentage of their contributions in the off years (the CPAs, bankers, dentists, hospitals, and new car dealers in both 1989 and 1991) are likely to be pursuing a low-risk, status quo, and incumbent-oriented strategy, although that cannot be confirmed without looking at their contributions in the primary and the general elections. The magnitude of the medical society's campaign effort can be seen in the fact that the total they contributed in the 1989 off year exceeded that of the next largest contributor by $130,000, while during the 1991 off year, the margin was more than $100,000.

Primary Election Contribution Strategies. The 1992 primary and general legislative elections in Illinois were held after a new legislative map was approved through the redistricting process. The new legislative districts resulted in a large number of primary challenges and open seats compared to normal primary elections. While Democratic senators seeking reelection outnumbered Republican senators by a small margin (22 to 19), there were significantly more house Democrats seeking reelection than house Republicans (58 to 33). Many incumbent legislators were faced with strong opponents in new districts, and some house members were forced either to move or to run against each other. While all 118 house seats are up for election every two years, the 1992 election was the only one during the 10-year life of the new legislative map in which all 59 senate seats were up for reelection. The combination of these factors created more competition and uncertainty than is usually present in legislative primary elections in Illinois. In contrast, with an established legislative map and only 20 senate seats up for reelection in 1990 and few open house seats, the 1990 primary generated only a few competitive contests.

The amounts contributed by groups during the 1990 and 1992 primaries drop rapidly after the top few groups. In order to have numbers large enough to make the analysis meaningful, the eight groups that ranked the highest in the amount of primary contributions to members for the two election cycles were selected for a detailed examination. Tables

4.9, 4.10, 4.11, 4.12, 4.13, 4.14, 4.15, and 4.16 (pp. 95-99) present a breakout of the contribution activity of those eight interest groups in the primary portions of the two election cycles.

Low-risk, Bipartisan Contribution Strategies. While some groups were virtual nonparticipants in the two primaries, the beer distributor, realtor, banker, and hospital groups were all active players in the primaries and all shared a low-risk, status quo, incumbent-oriented, and bipartisan contribution strategy. Their contributions went primarily to incumbents and the legislative leaders and the chamber committees of both parties (tables 4.9 and 4.10, pp. 95 and 96). In 1990 these four groups made 93 to 100 percent of their primary contributions to incumbents (table 4.13, p. 98). In 1992, with many more open seats and many incumbents facing serious challenges, they still gave 70 to 80 percent of their primary contributions to incumbents (table 4.14, p. 98). Because of the Democratic majorities going into each election and the larger number of Democratic incumbents, the incumbent orientation of these four groups resulted in greater contributions to Democratic candidates than to Republican candidates. In 1990 these four groups favored Democratic candidates by percentages from 53 to 70, while in 1992 they favored Democratic candidates in the primary by percentages of 51 to 64 (tables 4.11 and 4.12, pp. 97). The bankers, realtors, and beer distributors all gave approximately the same amounts to the legislative leaders and chamber committees of both parties, while the hospitals favored the Democrats, although not overwhelmingly (tables 4.3 and 4.4, pp. 89 and 90). These groups made 98 to 100 percent of their primary contributions to winning candidates in 1990 (tables 4.11 and 4.13, pp. 97 and 98). In the more volatile and uncertain political year of 1992, their percentage of contributions to winning candidates still ranged from 85 to 90 (tables 4.12 and 4.14, pp. 97 and 98). While contributing to winning candidates may be a sign of either accurate forecasting or successful activity in contested races, the primary election contribution patterns for the bankers, realtors, beer distributors, and hospitals are largely the result of backing sure winners.

Groups pursuing status quo and incumbent-oriented strategies do not take risks. They make moderate contributions to all the legislative leaders and small-to-moderate contributions to as many candidates as possible, trying to create access to the members and the leaders (tables 4.9 and 4.10, pp. 95 and 96, and tables 4.3 and 4.4, pp.89 and 90). They make larger contributions to those they consider to be strong supporters or key legislators for their issues, but do not have the resources or the desire to become heavily involved in contested races. The average contribution to legislative candidates in the primaries for the beer distributor, realtor, banker, and hospital groups was between $375 and $970 in 1990 (table 4.15, p. 99) and between $575 and $740 in 1992 (table 4.16, p. 99). No candidate received more than $5,000 from any of the four groups. Given a choice, these groups made medium-sized contributions to a large number of candidates rather than large contributions to a smaller number of candidates, all of which is consistent with a low-risk, status quo oriented strategy for contributing to legislative campaigns.

Risk-taking, Partisan Contribution Strategies. The contribution patterns during the 1990 and 1992 primaries for the medical society, IEA, trial lawyers, and manufacturers are more complex. While there are significant differences among their contribution strategies in and between the two primaries, the data suggest that they pursued strategies that were more high-risk and partisan and more sensitive to changes in the electoral environment in contrast to the more stable, low-risk, status quo oriented strategies of the beer distributor, realtor, banker, and hospital groups.

Moderate-risk, Partisan Strategy: The Manufacturers' Association. The manufacturers pursued a partisan-Republican and incumbent-oriented strategy in the two primaries. Overall, the manufacturers contributed to 88 candidates in the 1990 primary with an average contribution of $925 and 96 candidates with an average contribution of $1,075 in 1992. No candidate received more than $5,000 (tables 4.15 and 4.16). All of the contributions were in the form of money, none were in the form of in-kind contributions.

In the 1990 primary, facing a Democratic map and limited prospects for change, the manufacturers' contribution patterns are largely indistinguishable from those of the realtor, banker, beer distributor, and hospital groups, except for favoring Republican candidates and strongly favoring the Republican leaders (tables 4.3, 4.9, 4.11, 4.13, pp. 89, 95, 97, and 98). But presented with the opportunities in the 1992 election cycle, a different picture emerges. While the percentage of total contributions from the manufacturers that went to leaders did not change, the percentage they contributed to nonincumbents (challengers to incumbents or candidates for open seats with no incumbent seeking reelection) increased significantly over the 1990 primary (tables 4.9 and 4.10, pp. 95 and 96) as did the percentage of contributions to Republican candidates (tables 4.11 and 4.12, p. 97) and Republican leaders (tables

4.3 and 4.4, p. 89 and 90). Most of the contributions to nonincumbents were to Republican candidates in safe races. More significantly from the standpoint of risk taking, the percentage of the manufacturers' contributions to losing candidates also increased, with most of those contributions going to losing incumbents (tables 4.13 and 4.14, p. 98). These patterns suggest a relatively moderate level of risk taking, but a very partisan approach to contributions to legislative candidates in the primary. The manufacturers' approach to primary elections is more sensitive to changes in the election environment, more partisan, and less status quo oriented than the approaches of the banker, realtor, beer distributor, and hospital groups, but not as risk oriented as those of the medical society, trial lawyers, and IEA.

Medium-risk, Partisan Strategy: Trial Lawyers Association and IEA. The patterns of primary contributions by the trial lawyers and the IEA are quite similar: sensitive to the election environment, partisan-Democratic, and change oriented with moderate risk taking. Both groups contributed primarily to Democratic candidates in both primaries (71 percent in 1990 and 67 percent in 1992 for the trial lawyers; 67 percent in 1990 and 79 percent in 1992 for the IEA—tables 4.11 and 4.12, p. 97). While the IEA gave almost no money to legislative leaders, the trial lawyers were overwhelmingly Democratic in their leadership contributions (tables 4.3 and 4.4, pp. 89 and 90). In 1990 the trial lawyers contributed to 34 candidates in the primary with an average contribution of $2,235, while in 1992 they contributed to 66 legislative candidates in the primary with an average contribution of $2,850 (tables 4.15 and 4.16, p. 99). No candidate received more than $8,500. The contributions of the IEA were less concentrated. In 1990 they gave an average of $1,655 to 64 candidates, and in 1992 they gave an average of $1,275 to 87 candidates. In contrast to the trial lawyers, the IEA did invest heavily in a few primary races, with one candidate in 1990 receiving $24,700 and one candidate in 1992 receiving $17,100 (tables 4.15 and 4.16). While the majority of their contributions were transfers of money, both groups made in-kind contributions to candidates in the form of mailings and research.

Operating with a Democratic map and large numbers of Democratic incumbents, the 1990 election presented Democratic-leaning groups with opportunities to take risks by backing challengers in contested primaries on both the Democratic and Republican sides. The IEA and the trial lawyers were the only two groups out of the top eight that made significant contributions to nonincumbents in the 1990 primary. The IEA gave 35 percent of its primary contributions to winning nonincumbents and 16 percent to losing nonincumbents, while the trial lawyers gave 20 percent to winning nonincumbents and 17 percent to losing nonincumbents (table 4.13, p. 98). All of the IEA contributions to losing nonincumbents went to Republican candidates, while over half of the contributions of the trial lawyers to losing nonincumbents went to Republican candidates (table 4.11, p. 97).

In 1992, with a Republican map that created many open seats and placed many Democratic incumbents at risk, the primary contribution patterns of the IEA and trial lawyers were different from 1990. Both increased the percentage of their contributions to incumbents and both ended up contributing heavily to losing incumbents (tables 4.13 and 4.14, p. 98). The losing incumbents backed by the IEA were primarily Democratic while the losing incumbents backed by the trial lawyers were evenly divided between Democrats and Republicans (tables 4.11 and 4.12, p. 97). The fact that the Democrats had significantly more incumbents running for reelection than the Republicans, and more incumbents at risk, contributed to the trial lawyers and IEA shifting to more primary support for incumbents in 1992 in comparison to 1990. The IEA has long stressed loyalty to their friends in making contribution decisions, always rewarding "performance over a promise." That strategy is evident in the pattern of primary contributions for both the IEA and the trial lawyers with both groups actively involved in contested races involving incumbents. The trial lawyers, for example, contributed more to losing incumbents than to winning incumbents, which also reflects the fact that the new legislative map was drawn by the Republicans (table 4.14, p. 98). Compared to 1990, the amounts contributed by both groups in 1992 to nonincumbents decreased, and the percentage of those nonincumbent contributions going to losing candidates also decreased sharply (tables 4.13 and 4.14, p. 98). Faced with an unfavorable map and the prospect of the Democrats losing control of one or both chambers of the legislature, the IEA and trial lawyers focused on retaining Democratic incumbents and backing strong Democratic candidates for open seats.

Compared to the bankers, realtors, beer distributors, and hospitals, the amount of risk taking by the IEA and trial lawyers in 1992 was still high, but the context provided by the prospects for the upcoming election resulted in a more defensive, incumbent-oriented approach. The picture that emerges from the data on primary contributions for the IEA and trial lawyers is one of a medium risk-taking, highly partisan approach, which is sensitive to changes in the electoral environment.

High-risk, Partisan Contribution Strategy: The Medical Society. The contribution strategy pursued by the medical society in the 1990 and 1992 primaries shows both a sensitivity to changes in the election context and a willingness to engage in high-risk, change-oriented behavior. In 1990, faced with a Democratic map, few opportunities for change, and the prospect of continued Democratic control of the legislature, the medical society gave the majority of their contributions in the primary to leaders and incumbents, giving only 5 percent of their total contributions to nonincumbents (table 4.9, p. 95). While their overall contribution pattern is strongly Republican, they gave 58 percent of their primary contributions to Democrats, all of them incumbents (table 4.11, p. 97). Their contribution to leaders is a better reflection of their partisanship. More than 60 percent of their contributions to leaders during the 1990 primary went to Republicans. An overwhelming 95 percent of their contributions went to winners. The only contributions they made to losing candidates went to Republican incumbents who lost in the primary (tables 4.11 and 4.13, pp. 97 and 98). Overall, the medical society contributed an average of $1,725 to 80 candidates in 1990, with one candidate receiving a total of $19,700 (table 4.15, p. 99). The picture is one of maintaining access and accepting the limited opportunities presented by the 1990 election.

The medical society's contribution behavior in the 1992 primary stands in stark contrast to 1990 and to the other groups examined. The large majority of their contributions to legislative leaders went to Republicans (table 4.4, p. 90). But, as in 1990, the medical society contributed more money to Democratic candidates than to Republican candidates during the primary (59 percent to 41 percent—table 4.12, p. 97). The medical society allocated 59 percent of their primary contributions to nonincumbents, more than twice that of any other group in the top eight in primary spending (table 4.10, p. 96). The percentage of contributions that went to losing candidates in the primary (42 percent) was second only to that of the trial lawyers (table 4.14, p. 98). The medical society also spent nearly three times as much in the 1992 primary as did the next highest-ranking interest group (table 4.10, p. 96). The magnitude of the resources available allowed the medical society to provide support for incumbent friends and friendly nonincumbents with safe races and still look for additional opportunities to build influence in the legislature in both the Democratic and Republican primaries.

A more detailed breakout of the medical society's pattern of contributions to legislative candidates in the 1992 primary shows the complexity of their primary strategy (table 4.17, p. 100). They contributed heavily to a few candidates running in contested races and moderately to both a large number of incumbents with little opposition and nonincumbents running largely unopposed for open seats. The society also provided token support for a few candidates with little chance of winning. The result was an aggressive, high-risk strategy that went beyond the moderate risk taking of the trial lawyers and the IEA to include active participation in contested races in both the Republican and Democratic primaries.

The medical society contributed an average of $1,465 to 40 incumbent Republican senate and house members, none of whom faced serious opposition (table 4.17). They contributed an average of $2,545 to 27 nonincumbent Republican candidates seeking open senate and house seats, who were also without serious opposition. All of these 67 Republican candidates won easily in the primary. The medical society also contributed an average of $1,355 to 33 Democratic incumbents seeking reelection and an average of $1,660 to 5 Democratic nonincumbents seeking open seats, all of whom faced little or no opposition. All 38 of these candidates also won easily in the primary. In all, the medical society contributed to 105 candidates in the primary who were in the *sure-winner* category. The medical society also made small contributions to 13 candidates who lost in the primary, most by large margins.

The medical society also contributed heavily to a few candidates in contested primaries. A total of five Republican candidates running in hotly contested, open house seats received contributions that averaged $16,380 (table 4.17). Two of the candidates won and three lost.

The medical society's contributions to candidates in contested races in the 1992 Democratic primary were concentrated in a handful of races. They spent over $192,000 on six candidates for open seats where no incumbent was running for reelection (table 4.17). All six of the districts were strongly Democratic and located in Chicago. One of the candidates they supported won by 25 votes, another won by 520 votes; one won by over 5,500 votes, while the other three lost, one by less than 400 votes. One of the losing candidates received over $61,000 in support and lost by 1,290 votes. The three primary winners easily won election to the General Assembly in the fall. The medical society also spent $72,000 on two incumbent Democratic house members who were in contested primaries. Both lost by wide margins. The average total contribution in these eight races was slightly over $33,000, and five of the eight candidates lost. While the potential payoff in access and influence is great, the risks in participating heavily in contested races are also great.

The total amount of money the medical society invested in primary elections and their willingness to invest large amounts in contested races in both Republican and Democratic primaries set them apart from any other interest group in Illinois politics.

General Election Contribution Strategies. Like the data from the primary periods, interest group contribution data for the general election periods in 1990 and 1992 indicate the same general split between groups pursuing bipartisan, status quo oriented, low-risk strategies and partisan, change-oriented, high-risk strategies. Most groups fall into these two broad categories for both election cycles, but some do not. Some groups appear to be primarily access or status quo oriented, but secondarily partisan, while others seem election oriented and willing to take some risks, but not strongly partisan. With only two election cycles and with the differences in the election environment in the two cycles, it is difficult to know conclusively what is *normal* campaign contribution behavior for any one group. Another factor that makes analysis difficult is the differences in the amount of money that groups have available. When considering the patterns for the groups at the bottom of the top 20 list where the amounts are relatively small, a single contribution can dramatically shift the appearance. Behavior is also a function of inclination, resources, and opportunity. A lack of resources or opportunity may constrain one group from pursuing desired outcomes. Groups with comparatively few resources may be forced to make tradeoffs that those with resources never face.

Finally, the outcome of the 1990 and 1992 legislative elections must also be taken into account. In 1990 the only two contested senate races resulted in the two incumbents (one Republican and one Democratic) being reelected and no change in the partisan makeup of the senate. In the house, four Republican incumbents were defeated and one open seat previously held by a Republican was won by a Democrat. It would be expected that groups with strong Democratic partisan leanings that were active in contested races would have contributed more to winning challengers than other groups, and groups with strong Republican leanings would have contributed more to losing incumbents than other groups. In 1992 the partisan outcome was reversed and the dynamic was more complex. The Republicans picked up four seats and control of the senate, going from 28-31 to 32-27. Two incumbent senators were defeated, one Democrat and one Republican. In the house, the Republicans picked up five seats, erasing their losses of two years earlier, but the Democrats still retained control of the house by a 67-to-51 margin. Eight incumbent house members were defeated, three Republicans and five Democrats. It would be expected that partisan-leaning groups that were active in contested races in 1992 would contribute more to nonincumbents than would other groups and more to losing candidates than would other groups. In particular, Democratic-leaning groups should have a higher percentage of contributions to losing incumbents and losing nonincumbents than Republican-leaning groups.

Bipartisan, Status Quo, and Incumbent-oriented Contribution Strategies. Looking across the general election period for both election cycles, there are 7 groups among the 20 examined that appear to have consistently pursued bipartisan, status quo-oriented, incumbent-oriented, low-risk contribution strategies. Those 7 are the beer distributor, realtor, banker, hospital, CPA, dentist, and new car/truck groups. In so far as they participated actively in the primaries, they took the same approach to contributions to legislative candidates and leaders in the general election as they took in the primary election. First, the great majority of their contributions in 1990 and 1992 went to incumbents and the legislative leaders. While the percentage of their contributions to nonincumbents increased in 1992, they still contributed significantly less to nonincumbents than did the partisan, risk-oriented groups, such as the medical society or IEA (tables 4.18, 4.19, 4.20, and 4.21, pp. 101, 102, 103, and 104). Second, their contributions to legislative candidates and legislative leaders were divided fairly evenly between Democrats and Republicans (tables 4.3, 4.4, 4.22, and 4.23, pp. 89, 90, 105, and 106). Third, only 2 to 9 percent of their contributions in 1990 and only 10 to 15 percent of their contributions in 1992 went to losing candidates (tables 4.20, 4.21, 4.22, and 4.23, p. 103, 104, 105, and 106). Finally, as in the primary, these groups spread their contributions evenly between a large number of candidates, did not invest heavily in contested races, and did not greatly increase the size of their average contribution from 1990 to 1992. In general, they increased their total contributions in 1992 by giving the same average amount they contributed in 1990 to more candidates (table 4.24 and 4.25, pp. 107 and 108). The beer distributors and the realtors are representative of the groups in this category. In the 1990 general election the beer distributors gave an average of $515 to 144 legislative candidates (table 4.24); in 1992 they gave an average of

$695 to 176 candidates (table 4.25, p. 108). A total of 18 candidates received contributions of $1,000 or more in 1990. That number increased to 47 candidates in 1992, but no candidate received more than $2,500. The realtors in 1990 gave an average of $700 to 131 legislative candidates (table 4.24, p. 107), while in 1992 they gave 129 candidates an average of $710. The number of candidates receiving $1,000 or more dropped from 27 in 1990 to 23 in 1992. No candidate received more than $4,000 from the realtors.

These aggregate contribution patterns clearly show general election contribution strategies that are bipartisan, low risk, status quo, and incumbent oriented. While not true of these specific groups, other interest groups pursuing this kind of strategy will sometimes contribute to both candidates in close races or contribute to the winner after the election is over. The name of the game is gaining access and building relationships with those who are elected, not changing the makeup of the legislature.

Indeterminate Contribution Strategies. Three groups do not fit easily into either the bipartisan, low risk category or the partisan, high risk category: Philip Morris, Inc., the Cable Television and Communications Association of Illinois, and Illinois State Bar Association. While the state bar is consistently Democratic in its contributions to leaders and candidates, its lack of increased effort in the 1992 elections and its backing of generally safe candidates distinguish it from other strongly partisan groups. Philip Morris was also consistently Democratic in its contributions to candidates in both election cycles. However, bipartisan contributions to legislative leaders and a low level of risk taking, and lack of increased effort in 1992 put it in between the two major categories suggested by the contribution data. Finally, the cable TV group was strongly Democratic in its contributions to leaders, inconsistent in its contributions to members, and generally incumbent oriented and low risk in its contributions. The mixed patterns of campaign contributions for these three groups do not fit well with either of the two major patterns suggested by the data.

Partisan, High-risk, Change-oriented Contribution Strategies. Ten of the top 20 contributors to legislative campaigns fit into the category of partisan, high-risk, change-oriented contribution strategies for the 1990 and 1992 general election periods. Those groups are the Illinois State Medical Society, Illinois Manufacturers' Association, Illinois Trial Lawyers Association, Illinois Education Association (IEA), Teamsters

Joint Council No. 25, United Auto Workers (UAW), Personal PAC, Professional Independent Insurance Agents of Illinois, AFSCME, and AFL-CIO.

All of these groups were strongly partisan in their contributions to candidates and legislative leaders in both 1990 and 1992 (tables 4.3, 4.4, 4.22, and 4.23, pp. 89, 90, 105, and 106). Republican candidates for the legislature received from 80 to 90 percent of the contributions made by the medical society, manufacturers, and insurance agents in the 1992 general election (table 4.23) and between 56 and 82 percent in 1990 (table 4.22). The medical society and manufacturers also gave more than $20,000 to legislative leaders in both 1990 and 1992 with the large majority going to Republicans. The IEA, trial lawyers, UAW, Teamsters, Personal PAC, AFSCME, and AFL-CIO gave from 87 to 100 percent of their contributions to Democratic candidates in 1992 (table 4.23) and from 78 to 100 percent in 1990 (table 4.22). Only one of these seven partisan-Democratic groups, the Teamsters, gave more than $20,000 to legislative leaders in both 1990 and 1992 (tables 4.3 and 4.4, pp. 89 and 90). All but a very small percentage of those contributions went to Democratic leaders.

The aggregate contribution patterns of these 10 groups indicate an aggressive, change-oriented approach to general elections and a strong increase in their contribution effort in response to the uncertainty and challenges of the 1992 general election (tables 4.24 and 4.25, pp. 107 and 108). Eight of the 10 groups averaged over $1,000 per contribution in 1992, and 8 of the 10 significantly increased the average size of their contributions to candidates from 1990 to 1992. Two of the more aggressive groups were the medical society and the IEA. In 1990 the medical society gave 101 candidates in the general election an average of $1,600. Sixty-three of those candidates received contributions of $1,000 or more (table 4.24). In 1992 those numbers increased to 125 candidates receiving an average of $3,850 with 102 receiving $1,000 or more (table 4.25). In 1990 the IEA gave 111 candidates in the general election an average of $1,475 with 34 receiving $1,000 or more. In 1992 the numbers increased to 139 candidates with an average of $3,575 and 122 receiving $1,000 or more. Both groups were heavily involved with contested races in both 1990 and 1992 with their largest contributions to a single candidate jumping from $16,300 to $36,600 for the IEA and from $25,200 to $88,000 for the medical society. The aggregate contribution patterns for these groups are clearly different from the six identified earlier as pursuing status quo, low-risk contribution strategies, particularly during the 1992 general election (table 4.24, p. 107).

Finally, the medical society, IEA, trial lawyers, manufacturers, Teamsters, UAW, Personal PAC, insurance agents, AFSCME, and AFL-CIO engaged in significantly more risk taking in the general election. The willingness of these groups to take risks can be seen in their contributions to nonincumbents and to losing candidates (tables 4.18, 4.19, 4.20, 4.21, 4.22, and 4.23, pp. 101, 102, 103, 104, 105, and 106). In 1990 they contributed a significantly greater percentage of their total contributions to nonincumbents and contributed a much greater percentage of their total contributions to losing candidates than did the more status quo-oriented groups (table 4.18, p. 101). In 1992 the differences are even more stark. Eight of the 10 high-risk, change-oriented groups contributed between 34 and 65 percent of their legislative candidate contributions to nonincumbents (table 4.21, p. 104) and 8 of the 10 contributed between 24 and 57 percent of their legislative candidate contributions to losing candidates (table 4.23, p. 106). Risk taking is also evident in their willingness and ability to focus large amounts of money in specific races (tables 4.24 and 4.25, pp. 107 and 108).

The general contribution strategies of the 10 groups identified as partisan, change oriented, and high risk were similar in their risk taking and partisanship and stand in sharp contrast to the bipartisan, status quo-oriented, low-risk strategies of other groups. However, a more detailed breakout of the contribution patterns of the two most active Republican groups (medical society and manufacturers) and the two most active Democratic groups (IEA and trial lawyers) reveals significant differences in how the four groups approached the 1992 general election.

While the trial lawyers and the manufacturers were both partisan and both gave to candidates in contested races, their contributions to the candidates they favored in contested races showed only moderate risk taking (tables 4.26 and 4.27, p. 109). No candidate received a total of more than $10,000 from either group, and only 15 candidates received $5,000 or more from either group. In contrast, the medical society and the IEA invested heavily in contested races, contributing $5,000 or more to 43 candidates with top contributions to single candidates of $36,600 and $88,000 respectively (tables 4.28 and 4.29, p. 110). While the contributions from the trial lawyers and manufacturers were almost exclusively in the form of money, both the IEA and the medical society provided indirect support for their candidates in targeted races through paid campaign staff, polling and targeting information, and production and mailing of direct-mail pieces. Finally, in spite of their partisanship, the

IEA contributed to 31 Republican candidates (table 4.28, p. 110) and the medical society contributed to 38 Democratic candidates (table 4.29, p. 110), using their resources to broaden their access beyond a single party. This cross-partisan activity may also be rooted in necessity: if only Republicans are going to be elected from a suburban district, then a group that seeks to have influence with suburban legislators will have to contribute to Republicans.

Medium Risk-taking, Partisan Strategies. Both the trial lawyers and the manufacturers were key players in the 1992 general election. They made large partisan contributions to candidates in both safe and contested races. They were willing to take risks on behalf of their partisan and policy goals.

Trial Lawyers. The trial lawyers contributed to Democratic candidates in 35 senate races in 1992 (table 4.26, p. 109). Of those, eight lost. The average contribution to the 27 winning candidates was $2,000, while the average contribution to the losing candidates was $4,400 with no senate candidate receiving more than $8,000.

They also contributed to Democratic candidates in 69 house races (table 4.26). Of those candidates, eight lost. The average contribution to the eight losing house candidates was $2,800, while the average contribution to the 61 winning house candidates was $1,900. No house candidate received more than $8,000.

The trial lawyers also contributed to eight Republican candidates, all of whom won (table 4.26). Three of these were candidates for senate seats and received an average of $3,000, and five were candidates for house seats and received an average of $1,600. The trial lawyers did not contribute to the Democratic candidates in these races.

In all, the trial lawyers participated in 38 of the 59 senate races and 74 of the 118 house races. The largest contribution to any single candidate was $8,000, and only five candidates received $5,000 or more (table 4.26).

Manufacturers. In 1992 the manufacturers contributed to Republican candidates in 58 house races (table 4.27, p. 109). Of those, 14 lost. The average contribution to losing house candidates was $2,250, and the average contribution to winning house candidates was $1,000, with no Republican candidate receiving more than $5,000.

They also contributed to Republican candidates in 26 senate races. Of those senate candidates, two lost. The average contribution to losing senate candidates was $3,000, and the average contribution to winning senate candidates was $2,500, with no candidate receiving more than $10,000.

The manufacturers contributed to 9 Democratic house candidates and 7 Democratic senate candidates; all were incumbents and all won easily (table 4.27, p. 109). The house candidates received an average contribution of $1,100, and the senate candidates received an average contribution of $725, with no Democratic candidate receiving more than $5,000. The manufacturers did not contribute to the Republican candidates in these races. In all, the manufacturers contributed to 33 of the 59 senate races and 67 of the 118 house races. Their largest contribution to a single candidate totaled $10,000, and only 10 candidates received $5,000 or more.

In the 1992 general election both the trial lawyers and the manufacturers made major partisan contributions to both safe and contested races. In the house, where the Democrats retained control, the manufacturers' average contribution to losing Republican candidates was more than twice the average contribution to winning Republican candidates (table 4.27). In the senate, where the Republicans took control, the trial lawyers' average contribution to losing Democratic candidates was more than twice the average contribution to Democratic candidates who won (table 4.26, p. 109). As noted earlier, these data do not include contributions made by individual law or manufacturing firms or their principal owners and officers. The detailed examination of the most strongly contested legislative races in 1992 presented in chapter 6 shows active participation by such individuals and individual firms. As such, the amount of risk taking by trial lawyers and manufacturing interests is probably somewhat greater than is indicated here. The trial lawyers' and manufacturers' willingness to take risks, however, is only medium when compared to the IEA and the medical society's contribution activity in the 1992 legislative elections.

High-risk, Partisan Strategies. The IEA and the medical society stand out in their willingness to make large partisan contributions to candidates in contested races.

IEA. In the 1992 general election the IEA contributed to Democratic candidates in 71 house races (table 4.28, p. 110). Of these, 10 lost. The average contribution to the winning candidates was $2,500, and the average contribution to the losing candidates was $5,000. The largest contribution to a single candidate was $20,300, and a total of 10 candidates received contributions totaling $5,000 or more.

The IEA contributed to Democratic candidates in 37 senate races (table 4.28, p. 110). Of these, 11 lost. The average contribution to the winning Democratic candidates was $2,900. The average contribution to the losing candidates was $15,500. The largest contribution to a single candidate totaled $36,600, and a total of 12 candidates received $5,000 or more.

The IEA also contributed to Republican candidates in 23 house races and 8 senate races (table 4.28). Only 2 of the 31 candidates lost. The average contribution to these Republican candidates was $1,696, and no candidate received more than $3,300. The IEA did not contribute to the Democratic candidates in these 31 races.

In all, the IEA contributed to 45 of the 59 senate races and 94 of the 118 house races (table 4.28). A total of 22 candidates received contributions of $5,000 or more. Their largest contribution was $36,600; their reports on file with the State Board of Elections also show that 12 other candidates received contributions of $10,000 or more from the IEA.

The total impact of the IEA on legislative races went beyond the $496,000 they reported in direct contributions to legislative candidates and leaders. The IEA also rebated $60,000 from their political committee, IPACE, to local IEA chapters during 1992. Much of that money was subsequently spent on legislative races, but the specific amounts and targets cannot be determined from the reports filed by IPACE. In contrast to the contribution patterns of lawyers, no large contributions from individuals to candidates in targeted legislative races were identified as being from teachers.

Medical Society. In the 1992 general election the medical society contributed to Republican candidates in 57 house races (table 4.29, p. 110). Of these, 10 lost. The average contribution to the 47 winning candidates was $3,350. One of the losing candidates was an incumbent who was also a physician; he received $88,000 in support, the society's largest contribution to a single candidate. The average contribution to the 10 losing candidates was $13,100; excluding the one very large contribution, the average to losing candidates was $4,778. A total of 14 candidates received $5,000 or more.

The medical society contributed to Republican candidates in 30 senate races (table 4.29). Only one candidate lost, an incumbent senator. Their average contribution to the winning candidates was $4,350, while the losing senate candidate received $4,300. Seven candidates received $5,000 or more, with a high of $21,300.

The medical society also contributed to Democrats in 26 house races and 12 senate races, with an average contribution of $1,634 (table 4.29, p. 110). No Democratic candidate received more than $4,900. All 38 Democratic candidates won. The medical society did not contribute to Republican candidates in these races.

In all, the medical society participated in 83 house races and 42 senate races (table 4.29). They contributed $5,000 or more to 21 candidates, and their largest contribution to a single candidate totaled $88,000. A more detailed examination of their contribution records filed with the State Board of Elections shows that 7 other candidates received $14,000 or more. The reports also show they contributed heavily to Republican legislative leaders in the general election, giving $107,000 to the house Republicans and $41,000 to the senate Republicans.

The examination of contributions to candidates in targeted legislative elections in chapter 6 does reveal some large contributions from individual physicians, although the vast majority of contributions from physicians are made through the medical society. This pattern is very different from that of lawyers and law firms. Among all of the interest groups and corporations that contributed to legislative candidates in the 1992 general election, the medical society and the IEA stand out. The three factors that set them apart are the total amounts contributed, the partisan focus, and the concentration of very large contributions in contested races. More than any other group, they had the resources to make a difference and were willing to risk those resources in contested races as well as in support of friendly candidates in uncontested races. With these two groups and the other eight groups classified as partisan, risk taking, and change oriented, reasons for contributing are two fold. Like the more bipartisan, status quo-oriented groups previously identified, the medical society and IEA are interested in access and building relationships with those who are elected. But they are also committed to having an impact on who is elected and, in the case of the medical society, thereby changing the makeup of the legislature in order to advance their agendas, or, in the case of the IEA, preserving the status quo by reelecting friends in the face of serious opposition.

The Impact of Interest Groups on Legislative Elections

Interest groups' contributions play a significant role in legislative elections in Illinois. From the aggregate numbers and the profiles of the activities of specific interest groups it is clear that interest groups provide both a strong base of funding for incumbents and a pool of resources that electorally oriented groups channel to candidates who are trying to fill open seats or defeat incumbents. The larger question is, Do these contributions make a difference in who wins and who loses?

Identifying the factors that account for a particular candidate's win or loss is difficult and complex. The factors that determine the outcome of an election are numerous: quality of candidates, issues, statewide and national candidates, state and national political candidates, turnout, district makeup, funding, and campaign strategy and execution. Funding for legislative elections comes from a wide variety of sources (e.g., leaders; interest groups; party organizations; and local individuals, businesses, and organizations). Chapter 6 presents a detailed look at the funding for the candidates in key house and senate races in 1992.

What is not in doubt is the general importance of money to electoral success. Research and analysis on both state legislative races and congressional elections support the conclusion that money is a "threshold" factor. Having enough money to finance communication with voters (meeting a threshold) is a necessity, but not a sufficient condition for electoral success. There is a strong, positive correlation between the amount of funds raised by a nonincumbent and the chances of that candidate winning the election. Having enough money to mount a competitive campaign does not guarantee that a candidate will win. But not having enough money does guarantee that a candidate will remain off the radar screen of both the media and the voters (Jacobson 1987, 124). Candidates who have money are taken seriously and, therefore, can raise more money. In fundraising it is often the case that the rich get richer and the poor stay poor.

Contributions, Access, and Influence

"While the current system of financing elections does not allow you to buy a congressman, it does allow you to lease one"—this often repeated gag line, while commonly held, would be an oversimplification of the relationship between campaign contributions and influence in the Illinois General Assembly. A straight quid pro quo between an interest group and a legislator on a vote is both unusual and illegal. The only interest group representative convicted of offering a legislator money for a vote in the last 15 years was a woman lobbying for the Equal Rights Amendment. And she was probably more guilty of a lack of sophistication than of an attempt to corrupt a legislator (Farr 1980). What interest groups and corporations seek through campaign contributions, first of all, is access, a foot in the door.

Lobbying is communication. But even before lobbyists can present their positions and rationale, they must first gain access to the decision-makers. After all, if legislators won't return phone calls or meet face to face to discuss legislation, lobbyists will have little influence on their voting behavior no matter how persuasive the arguments and coherent the analyses. Campaign contributions ensure that phone calls are returned and meetings are held. They are not, however, the only means for gaining access: a strong grassroots organization, connections with a legislative member, and a reputation for good policy research or good political analysis are all ways to gain access to legislators. But most interest groups will form PACs and make campaign contributions if they have the resources. Contributions provide direct linkages to legislators and also signal that the interest group is a serious player in the legislative game.

Ultimately, groups that are organized are better able to raise money, and money helps groups organize and communicate with legislators. If voices with money want to pass a bill and those who might be affected are unorganized and silent, the outcome almost always favors the organized. The Illinois New Car/Truck Dealers Association ranked 18th on the list of the largest interest group contributors to legislative elections in 1990 and 19th in 1992. Nowhere on the list do you find the buyers or potential buyers of cars. It is not surprising that the law that makes it illegal to sell cars in Illinois on Sunday was passed at the request of the new car/truck dealers and that they have successfully resisted attempts by individual legislators to repeal the ban.

In addition to access, campaign contributions may provide leverage with a legislator for an interest group because they can be increased, decreased, withdrawn, or given to an opponent in the next election. The importance of campaign contributions was reflected in the number of newspaper stories in November of 1993 concerning the upcoming vote in Congress on the North American Free Trade Agreement (NAFTA). Many national labor unions came out strongly in opposition to NAFTA and openly threatened members of Congress with the withdrawal of support if they voted for the treaty. Many of those members struggled openly with their vote on NAFTA in the face of that threat. While the role of campaign contributions in a legislator's voting decisions is rarely on public display the way it was prior to the vote on NAFTA, the potential impact of a roll-call vote on campaign contributions is always a consideration for legislators.

The opposite outcomes of the parental notification abortion bill and the cigarette tax increase in the 1993 legislative session illustrate both the influence of campaign contributions in the General Assembly and the limit of that influence.

Access and Influence: Parental Notice of Abortion

When the Parental Notice of Abortion Act (HB1300) passed the Illinois senate in the spring of 1993 and came back to the house for concurrence in the changes made by the senate, the medical society, which had previously taken no position on the bill, signaled that they had concerns with the penalty provisions that could be applied to a physician. When the sponsors of the bill indicated they were not interested in entering into new negotiations on the bill, the medical society took a position in opposition to the bill. When the bill came up for a vote on concurrence, 13 house members who voted for the bill the first time changed their votes to *present* or *no*. The net result was that the bill received only 53 votes, down 11 from the first vote and 7 votes short of the 60 needed for passage. (While a legislator's position on abortion legislation may cost some votes in an election, it is widely believed by legislators and political observers that being identified as a person who has flip-flopped on the abortion issue can be even more politically damaging. Deciding to change a vote on an abortion bill may be all the more significant because of this.) Of those 13 legislators who changed their votes, 12 received campaign contributions from the medical society. Four legislators received contributions totaling between $10,000 and $36,000. The remaining 8 received contributions totaling between $1,250 and $3,000.

If the only consideration in voting on the bill were campaign contributions, then the seven other house members who voted for the bill on third reading who received campaign contributions of $5,000 or more from the medical society would have switched their votes when the bill came back to the house for concurrence. The medical society's campaign contributions and their reputation for aggressive involvement in legislative elections gave them access to a large number of legislators. A legislator's voting decisions are usually the result of a calculation that takes into account personal policy preferences, who is supporting and who is opposing the bill, the preferences of constituents, and the intensity of those preferences. The medical society's interest in the parental notification bill caused the process toward passage of the bill to stop as members considered the medical society's opposition and arguments against the bill.

While a parental notification abortion bill was not as important an issue in the universe of legislative decisions as school funding or a tax increase, its defeat does illustrate the ease with which the medical society can exercise political muscle in the General Assembly. The clout of the medical society in the Illinois General Assembly is legendary. A recent article in *Illinois Issues* recounting the success of the medical society in blocking legislation making the practice of acupuncture by nonphysicians legal is just the latest in a long list of examples (Wade 1994, 22-25). No one can know whether the legislators who changed their votes on the parental notification abortion bill did so on the basis of the soundness of the arguments of the medical society, concern over the resources they can bring to bear in elections, gratitude for past support, or some consideration unrelated to the medical society's opposition to the bill. What is clear is that the medical society's campaign contributions give them instant access to legislators and, with it, the opportunity and ability to influence votes.

Limits on Influence: Tobacco Tax Increase

Tobacco interests have long been a strong lobby in the Illinois General Assembly. Taking full advantage of the fact that corporations can contribute directly to candidates in Illinois, they have contributed freely to legislative members and leaders, cultivating key members as supporters. The tobacco interests have generally been successful at resisting attempts to increase the cigarette tax, even when those initiatives came from the governor. However, faced with a series of budget crises in the 1980s, then governor James R. Thompson on several occasions proposed raising cigarette taxes to finance state budgets. Two of these proposed increases passed, one in 1985 and one in 1989. Gov. Jim Edgar had a cigarette tax as part of his first budget proposal, but was not able to get it enacted. However, during the 1993 spring session, in spite of the $240,000 that tobacco interests contributed to the legislative election in the 1992 cycle, the legislature passed a large cigarette tax increase and imposed for the first time a tax on other tobacco products (SB 677 [PA88-0088]), all to help fund the state budget for the 1994 fiscal year.

While the tobacco interests' campaign contributions do give them considerable access and influence in the General Assembly, they are also limited in comparison to the most powerful interest groups in Illinois politics. Unlike the IEA or the medical society, they do not have a strong grassroots organization that is active in most legislative districts in the state. Unlike the manufacturers' association, they do not represent the employers of large numbers of Illinois workers. And unlike the beer distributors, the consumers of their products are not favorably portrayed in TV commercials every night. The continuing state budget crisis in 1993 gave the governor and the legislature few options once a general tax increase was ruled out. Once the cigarette tax increase had the backing of the governor and the four legislative leaders and became part of the budget agreement, no amount of intense lobbying by the tobacco interests was able to defeat the increase. The unified position of the governor and the leaders provided political cover for the members and left the tobacco interests with a major defeat.

In the end, legislators control their own votes. This limit on the ability of interest groups to influence legislators through campaign contributions is captured in a comment attributed to the late Jesse Unruh, who was speaker of the house in the California legislature in the 1960s. Speaking of the relationship between interest groups and legislators, he said, "If you can't take their money, eat their food, drink their booze, screw their women, and then vote against them, you don't belong here." While lobbyists' women and booze are less important in the legislature of the 90s, due in large part to changing mores, increased press scrutiny, and tougher lobbying reporting laws, the same cannot be said for the role of money. The cost of legislative campaigns in Illinois will continue to escalate because of the intense competition for control of the legislature and the absence of limits on how much can be contributed to or spent by a candidate. And legislators facing reelection will find it more difficult to "take their money and vote against them."

Table 4.1
Interest Group/Corporation Contributions to Legislative Elections
1989-90 Election Cycle

(Top 20 in total contributions, includes contributions to leader and chamber committees)
(Amounts in units of $1,000)

	Total	Amount to Candidates	Amount to Leaders	Percent to Democrats
Illinois State Medical Society	$641	$452	$189	39
Illinois Trial Lawyers Assn.	433	309	124	91
Illinois Education Assn. (IEA)	343	337	6	74
Illinois Manufacturers' Assn.	324	247	77	33
Illinois Association of Realtors	264	182	82	53
Illinois Bankers Association	261	191	70	57
Associated Beer Distrib. of Ill.	223	162	61	60
Illinois CPA Society	192	135	57	60
Philip Morris, Inc.*	183	103	80	60
Illinois State Dental Society	153	122	35	52
Ill. Hosp. and Healthsystems Assn.	139	88	51	71
Teamsters Joint Council No. 25*	137	59	76	97
Prof. Independ. Ins. Agents of Ill.	120	96	24	45
AFSCME	110	93	17	95
United Auto Workers (UAW)*	108	90	18	99
Illinois State Bar Assn.	106	77	29	69
Cable TV and Comm. Assn. of Ill.	89	68	31	54
Ill. New Car/Truck Dealers Assn.	88	75	13	58
Illinois State AFL-CIO	72	62	10	93
Personal PAC	62	62	0	88

Data for groups marked with an * are based on a review of reports filed by candidates for the General Assembly with the State Board of Elections.

Data for groups not marked with an * are based on reports filed by those groups with the State Board of Elections.

Table 4.2
Interest Group/Corporation Contributions to Legislative Elections
1991-92 Election Cycle

(Top 20 in total contributions, includes contributions to leader and chamber committees)
(Amounts in units of $1,000)

	Total	Amount to Candidates	Amount to Leader/Ch.	Percent to Democrats
Illinois State Medical Society	$1,483	$1,159	$322	34
Illinois Education Assn. (IEA)	639	633	5	87
Illinois Trial Lawyers Assn.	503	455	48	83
Illinois Manufacturers' Assn.	452	345	108	23
Illinois Association of Realtors	387	266	121	53
Associated Beer Distrib. of Ill.	345	245	100	58
Illinois Bankers Association	311	219	92	57
Ill. Hosp. and Healthsystems Assn.	267	177	90	63
Illinois CPA Society	231	178	53	56
United Auto Workers (UAW)*	236	187	49	100
Personal PAC	212	212	0	81
Teamsters Joint Council No. 25*	209	62	147	91
Philip Morris, Inc.*	192	90	102	64
Illinois State Dental Society	181	111	71	51
AFSCME	153	110	44	84
Cable TV and Comm. Assn. of Ill.	153	84	69	65
Illinois State Bar Assn.	152	119	34	72
Prof. Independ. Ins. Agents of Ill.	146	110	36	18
Ill. New Car/Truck Dealers Assn.	120	96	25	50
Illinois State AFL-CIO	115	85	31	96

Data for groups marked with an * are based on a review of reports filed by candidates for the General Assembly with the State Board of Elections.

Data for groups not marked with an * are based on reports filed by those groups with the State Board of Elections.

Table 4.3
Contributions to Legislative Leader and Chamber Committees for Each Period of the 1989-90 Election Cycle

(Top 20 in total contributions)
(Amounts in units of $1,000)

	1989 Off-year Period		1990 Primary Election		1990 General Election	
	Dem	Rep	Dem	Rep	Dem	Rep
Illinois State Medical Society	$23	$62	$15	$35	$ 8	$43
Illinois Education Assn. (IEA)	1	1	1	0	3	0
Illinois Trial Lawyers Assn.	36	3	19	0	62	4
Illinois Manufacturers' Assn.	10	14	5	18	8	23
Illinois Association of Realtors	18	11	13	11	13	17
Associated Beer Distrib. of Ill.	8	8	13	6	12	14
Illinois Bankers Association	16	14	8	11	9	12
Ill. Hosp. and Healthsystems Assn.	16	7	6	5	13	5
Illinois CPA Society	17	12	0	0	16	12
United Auto Workers (UAW)*	10	0	0	1	6	0
Personal PAC	0	0	0	0	0	0
Teamsters Joint Council No. 25*	6	1	1	0	66	2
Illinois State Dental Society	12	13	6	6	6	4
Philip Morris, Inc.*	19	2	5	12	23	21
AFSCME	12	1	7	0	16	0
Cable TV and Comm. Assn. of Ill.	6	7	5	6	11	2
Illinois State Bar Assn.	4	4	8	8	5	1
Prof. Independ. Ins. Agents of Ill.	3	8	8	5	2	1
Ill. New Car/Truck Dealers Assn.	5	3	3	2	3	2
Illinois State AFL-CIO	6	1	1	0	7	0

Data for groups marked with an * are based on a review of reports filed by candidates for the General Assembly with the State Board of Elections.

Data for groups not marked with an * are based on reports filed by those groups with the State Board of Elections.

Table 4.4
Contributions to Legislative Leader and Chamber Committees for Each Period of the 1991-92 Election Cycle

(Top 20 in total contributions)
(Amounts in units of $1,000)

	1991 Off-year Period		1992 Primary Election		1992 General Election	
	Dem	Rep	Dem	Rep	Dem	Rep
Illinois State Medical Society	$26	$85	$11	$46	$8	$148
Illinois Education Assn. (IEA)	0	0	0	0	0	0
Illinois Trial Lawyers Assn.	15	0	24	3	6	0
Illinois Manufacturers' Assn.	14	28	8	31	1	27
Illinois Association of Realtors	28	21	18	21	19	17
Associated Beer Distrib. of Ill.	25	17	19	14	14	13
Illinois Bankers Association	23	18	10	15	15	14
Ill. Hosp. and Healthsystems Assn.	30	8	20	12	13	7
Illinois CPA Society	22	18	0	0	6	8
United Auto Workers (UAW)*	21	0	18	0	11	0
Personal PAC	0	0	0	0	0	0
Teamsters Joint Council No. 25*	8	6	20	6	105	3
Illinois State Dental Society	14	15	8	12	11	13
Philip Morris, Inc.*	21	12	10	1	20	28
AFSCME	16	2	8	1	9	6
Cable TV and Comm. Assn. of Ill.	10	4	8	11	26	12
Illinois State Bar Assn.	7	6	3	3	15	0
Prof. Independ. Ins. Agents of Ill.	3	7	2	9	1	15
Ill. New Car/Truck Dealers Assn.	5	6	2	5	4	3
Illinois State AFL-CIO	8	2	8	1	13	0

Data for groups marked with an * are based on a review of reports filed by candidates for the General Assembly with the State Board of Elections.

Data for groups not marked with an * are based on reports filed by those groups with the State Board of Elections.

Table 4.5
Percentage of Total Legislative Contributions†
for Each Period in the 1989-90 Election Cycle
(Top 20 in total contributions, includes contributions to leader and chamber committees)

	1989 Off-year Period	1990 Primary Election	1990 General Election
Illinois State Medical Society	36	30	34
Illinois Education Assn. (IEA)	20	31	49
Illinois Trial Lawyers Assn.	21	22	57
Illinois Manufacturers' Assn.	28	32	40
Illinois Association of Realtors	27	26	46
Associated Beer Distrib. of Ill.	19	37	44
Illinois Bankers Association	41	33	26
Ill. Hosp. and Healthsystems Assn.	40	25	35
Illinois CPA Society	51	2	47
United Auto Workers (UAW)*	15	4	81
Personal PAC	4	16	80
Teamsters Joint Council No. 25*	9	3	88
Illinois State Dental Society	47	13	40
Philip Morris, Inc.*	27	10	63
AFSCME	23	18	59
Cable TV and Comm. Assn. of Ill.	35	29	36
Illinois State Bar Assn.	10	31	59
Prof. Independ. Ins. Agents of Ill.	33	18	48
Ill. New Car/Truck Dealers Assn.	42	33	25
Illinois State AFL-CIO	26	17	56

† Percentages may not total 100 percent due to rounding.

Data for groups marked with an * are based on a review of reports filed by candidates for the General Assembly with the State Board of Elections.

Data for groups not marked with an * are based on reports filed by those groups with the State Board of Elections.

Table 4.6
Percentage of Total Legislative Contributions†
for Each Period in the 1991-92 Election Cycle

(Top 20 in total contributions, includes contributions to leader and chamber committees)

	1991 Off-year Period	1992 Primary Election	1992 General Election
Illinois State Medical Society	16	41	43
Illinois Education Assn. (IEA)	4	17	78
Illinois Trial Lawyers Assn.	7	43	50
Illinois Manufacturers' Assn.	28	31	41
Illinois Association of Realtors	21	36	43
Associated Beer Distrib. of Ill.	34	31	35
Illinois Bankers Association	38	29	33
Ill. Hosp. and Healthsystems Assn.	43	32	26
Illinois CPA Society	51	5	44
United Auto Workers (UAW)*	12	11	76
Personal PAC	0	20	80
Teamsters Joint Council No. 25*	8	16	76
Illinois State Dental Society	43	22	35
Philip Morris, Inc.*	35	8	57
AFSCME	20	26	54
Cable TV and Comm. Assn. of Ill.	27	25	48
Illinois State Bar Assn.	12	34	54
Prof. Independ. Ins. Agents of Ill.	13	21	66
Ill. New Car/Truck Dealers Assn.	38	25	37
Illinois State AFL-CIO	17	22	61

† Percentages may not total 100 percent due to rounding.

Data for groups marked with an * are based on a review of reports filed by candidates for the General Assembly with the State Board of Elections.

Data for groups not marked with an * are based on reports filed by those groups with the State Board of Elections.

Table 4.7
1989 Off-year Contributions to Legislative Elections

(Top 20 in total contributions, includes contributions to leader and chamber committees)
(Amounts in units of $1,000)

	1989 Total	Percentage of 1989 Total to Leader/Ch.	Percentage of 1898-90 Total
Illinois State Medical Society	$236	36	36
Illinois Bankers Association	106	27	41
Illinois CPA Society	97	30	51
Illinois Trial Lawyers Assn.	92	42	21
Illinois Manufacturers' Assn.	90	27	28
Illinois Association of Realtors	73	39	27
Illinois State Dental Society	72	35	47
Illinois Education Assn. (IEA)	70	2	20
Ill. Hosp. and Healthsystems Assn.	56	39	40
Philip Morris, Inc.*	49	43	27
Associated Beer Distrib. of Ill.	42	38	19
Prof. Independ. Ins. Agents of Ill.	40	28	33
Ill. New Car/Truck Dealers Assn.	37	21	42
Cable TV and Comm. Assn. of Ill.	32	38	35
AFSCME	25	52	23
Illinois State AFL-CIO	19	42	26
United Auto Workers (UAW)*	17	59	15
Teamsters Joint Council No. 25*	13	54	9
Illinois State Bar Assn.	10	80	10
Personal PAC	4	0	3

Data for groups marked with an * are based on a review of reports filed by candidates for the General Assembly with the State Board of Elections.

Data for groups not marked with an * are based on reports filed by those groups with the State Board of Elections.

Table 4.8
1991 Off-year Contributions to Legislative Elections

(Top 20 in total contributions, includes contributions to leader and chamber committees)
(Amounts in units of $1,000)

	1991 Total	Percentage of 1991 Total to Leader/Ch.	Percentage of 1991-92 Total
Illinois State Medical Society	$235	39	16
Illinois Association of Realtors	133	37	34
Illinois Manufacturers' Assn.	127	33	28
Illinois Bankers Association	121	33	38
Illinois CPA Society	118	34	51
Ill. Hosp. and Healthsystems Assn.	115	33	43
Illinois State Dental Society	78	36	43
Associated Beer Distrib. of Ill.	73	58	21
Philip Morris, Inc.*	67	63	35
Ill. New Car/Truck Dealers Assn.	46	24	38
Cable TV and Comm. Assn. of Ill.	42	33	27
Illinois Trial Lawyers Assn.	37	47	7
AFSCME	30	62	20
United Auto Workers (UAW)*	30	69	12
Illinois Education Assn. (IEA)	28	0	4
Illinois State AFL-CIO	20	48	17
Prof. Independ. Ins. Agents of Ill.	19	54	13
Illinois State Bar Assn.	19	64	12
Teamsters Joint Council No. 25*	17	80	8
Personal PAC	0	0	0

Data for groups marked with an * are based on a review of reports filed by candidates for the General Assembly with the State Board of Elections.

Data for groups not marked with an * are based on reports filed by those groups with the State Board of Elections.

Table 4.9
Contributions to Legislative Elections[†]
1990 Primary Election

(Top 20 in total contributions, includes contributions to leader and chamber committees)
(Amounts in units of $1,000)

	Primary Total	Percent to Leader/Ch.	Percent to Incumb.	Percent to Nonincumb.	Percent of 1989-90 Total
Illinois State Medical Society	$192	28	67	5	30
Illinois Education Assn. (IEA)	107	1	49	50	31
Illinois Manufacturers' Assn.	102	23	69	8	32
Illinois Trial Lawyers Assn.	95	20	50	30	22
Illinois Bankers Association	87	21	75	4	33
Associated Beer Distrib. of Ill.	81	24	74	2	37
Illinois Association of Realtors	69	35	61	4	26
Ill. Hosp. and Healthsystems Assn.	34	33	67	0	25
Illinois State Bar Assn.	34	44	56	0	31
Ill. New Car/Truck Dealers Assn.	29	18	80	2	33
Cable TV and Comm. Assn. of Ill.	26	44	56	0	29
Prof. Independ. Ins. Agents of Ill.	22	59	36	5	18
Illinois State Dental Society	20	60	37	3	13
AFSCME	20	36	59	5	18
Philip Morris, Inc.*	18	92	3	3	10
Illinois State AFL-CIO	12	13	71	16	17
Personal PAC	10	0	50	50	16
United Auto Workers (UAW)*	4	36	62	2	4
Teamsters Joint Council No. 25*	3	25	25	50	4
Illinois CPA Society	3	0	100	0	2

[†] Percentages may not total 100 percent due to rounding.

Data for groups marked with an * are based on a review of reports filed by candidates for the General Assembly with the State Board of Elections.

Data for groups not marked with an * are based on reports filed by those groups with the State Board of Elections.

Table 4.10
Contributions to Legislative Elections†
1992 Primary Election

(Top 20 in total contributions, includes contributions to leader and chamber committees)
(Amounts in units of $1,000)

	Primary Total	Percent to Leader/Ch.	Percent to Incumb.	Percent to Nonincumb.	Percent of 1991-92 Total
Illinois State Medical Society	$601	9	31	59	41
Illinois Trial Lawyers Assn.	216	13	60	27	43
Illinois Manufacturers' Assn.	142	27	44	29	31
Associated Beer Distrib. of Ill.	126	26	61	12	36
Illinois Association of Realtors	119	33	51	16	31
Illinois Education Assn. (IEA)	111	0	77	23	17
Illinois Bankers Association	91	27	51	22	29
Ill. Hosp. and Healthsystems Assn.	85	38	49	13	32
Illinois State Bar Assn.	52	12	76	12	34
Personal PAC	42	0	26	74	20
AFSCME	40	23	34	43	26
Cable TV and Comm. Assn. of Ill.	40	45	40	15	25
Illinois State Dental Society	40	48	39	14	22
Ill. New Car/Truck Dealers Assn.	30	22	61	17	25
Teamsters Joint Council No. 25*	33	78	14	8	16
Prof. Independ. Ins. Agents of Ill.	31	34	23	43	21
United Auto Workers (UAW)*	27	65	28	7	11
Illinois State AFL-CIO	25	33	46	22	22
Philip Morris, Inc.*	15	76	17	7	8
Illinois CPA Society	12	0	83	17	5

† Percentages may not total 100 percent due to rounding.

Data for groups marked with an * are based on a review of reports filed by candidates for the General Assembly with the State Board of Elections.

Data for groups not marked with an * are based on reports filed by those groups with the State Board of Elections.

Table 4.11
Contributions to Legislative Candidates by Party†
1990 Primary Election
(Top 10 largest contributors, excludes contributions to leader and chamber committees)
(Amounts in units of $1,000)

	Total	Percent to Winning Democrats	Percent to Losing Democrats	Percent to Winning Republicans	Percent to Losing Republicans
Illinois State Medical Society	$138	58	0	37	5
Illinois Education Assn. (IEA)	107	67	0	17	16
Illinois Manufacturers' Assn.	79	45	0	55	0
Illinois Trial Lawyers Assn.	76	63	8	19	9
Illinois Bankers Association	69	61	1	37	1
Associated Beer Distrib. of Ill.	62	61	0	39	0
Illinois Association of Realtors	45	53	0	47	0
Ill. New Car/Truck Dealers Assn.	24	54	0	43	3
Ill. Hosp. and Healthsystems Assn.	23	70	0	30	0
Illinois State Bar Assn.	19	79	0	21	0

Table 4.12
Contributions to Legislative Candidates by Party†
1992 Primary Election
(Top 10 largest contributors, excludes contributions to leader and chamber committees)
(Amounts in units of $1,000)

	Total	Percent to Winning Democrats	Percent to Losing Democrats	Percent to Winning Republicans	Percent to Losing Republicans
Illinois State Medical Society	$544	27	32	31	10
Illinois Trial Lawyers Assn.	189	48	19	7	25
Illinois Education Assn. (IEA)	111	50	29	17	5
Illinois Manufacturers' Assn.	103	19	9	57	15
Associated Beer Distrib. of Ill.	93	47	5	42	5
Illinois Association of Realtors	80	45	6	41	8
Illinois Bankers Association	66	47	8	38	8
Ill. Hosp. and Healthsystems Assn.	53	58	6	32	4
Illinois State Bar Assn.	46	52	15	19	13
Personal PAC	42	18	11	21	50

† Percentages may not total 100 percent due to rounding.

Table 4.13
Contributions to Legislative Incumbents and Nonincumbents†
1990 Primary Election

(Top 10 largest contributors, excludes contributions to leader and chamber committees)
(Amounts in units of $1,000)

	Total	Percent to Winning Incumbents	Percent to Losing Incumbents	Percent to Winning Nonincumb.	Percent to Losing Nonincumb.
Illinois State Medical Society	$138	88	5	7	0
Illinois Education Assn. (IEA)	107	49	0	35	16
Illinois Manufacturers' Assn.	79	90	0	10	0
Illinois Trial Lawyers Assn.	76	63	0	20	17
Illinois Bankers Association	69	95	0	3	2
Associated Beer Distrib. of Ill.	62	97	0	3	0
Illinois Association of Realtors	45	93	0	7	0
Ill. New Car/Truck Dealers Assn.	24	94	3	3	0
Ill. Hosp. and Healthsystems Assn.	23	100	0	0	0
Illinois State Bar Assn.	19	100	0	0	0

Table 4.14
Contributions to Legislative Incumbents and Nonincumbents†
1992 Primary Election

(Top 10 largest contributors, excludes contributions to leader and chamber committees)
(Amounts in units of $1,000)

	Total	Percent to Winning Incumbents	Percent to Losing Incumbents	Percent to Winning Nonincumb.	Percent to Losing Nonincumb.
Illinois State Medical Society	$544	19	15	39	27
Illinois Trial Lawyers Assn.	189	32	37	23	7
Illinois Education Assn. (IEA)	111	54	23	14	9
Illinois Manufacturers' Assn.	103	43	18	34	6
Associated Beer Distrib. of Ill.	93	74	10	15	1
Illinois Association of Realtors	80	64	13	23	1
Illinois Bankers Association	66	55	15	30	0
Ill. Hosp. and Healthsystems Assn.	53	72	8	19	2
Illinois State Bar Assn.	46	59	26	12	2
Personal PAC	42	14	12	25	49

† Percentages may not total 100 percent due to rounding.

Table 4.15
Average Contributions to Legislative Candidates
1990 Primary Election
(Top 10 largest contributors, excludes contributions to leader and chamber committees)

	Number of Candidates	Average Contribution	Largest Contribution
Illinois Trial Lawyers Assn.	34	$2,235	$5,250
Illinois State Medical Society	80	1,725	19,700
Illinois Education Assn. (IEA)	64	1,655	24,700
Illinois Bankers Association	71	970	3,000
Illinois Manufacturers' Assn.	88	925	5,000
Illinois State Bar Assn.	33	575	2,000
Associated Beer Distrib. of Ill.	137	450	1,000
Illinois Association of Realtors	113	400	1,750
Ill. Hosp. and Healthsystems Assn.	61	375	1,000
Ill. New Car/Truck Dealers Assn.	84	295	1,500

Table 4.16
Average Contributions to Legislative Candidates
1992 Primary Election
(Top 10 largest contributors, excludes contributions to leader and chamber committees)

	Number of Candidates	Average Contribution	Largest Contribution
Ill. Hosp. and Healthsystems Assn.	92	$575	$2,000
Illinois Association of Realtors	129	620	5,000
Associated Beer Distrib. of Ill.	148	630	2,500
Illinois Bankers Association	89	740	2,000
Illinois State Bar Assn.	54	780	3,500
Illinois Manufacturers' Assn.	96	1,075	5,000
Personal PAC	38	1,100	9,500
Illinois Education Assn. (IEA)	87	1,275	17,100
Illinois Trial Lawyers Assn.	66	2,850	8,500
Illinois State Medical Society	131	4,150	61,000

Table 4.17
Illinois State Medical Society Contributions to Legislative Candidates
1992 Primary Election

	Number of Candidates	Average Contribution	Number of Winners
Safe Seats/Uncontested Primaries			
Republican Incumbents	40	$1,465	40
Republican Nonincumbents	27	2,545	27
Democratic Incumbents	33	1,355	33
Democratic Nonincumbents	5	1,660	5
Contested Primaries - Active Participation			
Republican Nonincumbents	5	$16,380	2
Democratic Incumbents	2	36,700	0
Democratic Nonincumbents	6	32,150	3
Contested Primaries - Token Participation			
Republican Incumbents	5	$1,760	0
Republican Nonincumbents	4	1,000	0
Democratic Incumbents	3	700	0
Democratic Nonincumbents	1	500	0

Table 4.18
Contributions to Legislative Elections†
1990 General Election

(Top 20 in total contributions, includes contributions to leader and chamber committees)
(Amounts in units of $1,000)

	General Election Total	Percent to Leader/Ch.	Percent to Incumbents	Percent to Nonincumb.	Percent of 1989-90 Total
Illinois Trial Lawyers Assn.	$246	20	50	30	57
Illinois State Medical Society	213	24	55	21	35
Illinois Education Assn. (IEA)	167	1	79	20	49
Illinois Manufacturers' Assn.	132	23	61	15	40
Illinois Association of Realtors	122	24	65	11	46
Teamsters Joint Council No. 25*	120	56	33	11	88
Philip Morris, Inc.*	116	36	63	1	63
Associated Beer Distrib. of Ill.	99	26	71	3	44
Illinois CPA Society	92	31	69	0	47
United Auto Workers (UAW)*	88	7	46	47	81
Illinois Bankers Association	67	33	57	7	26
AFSCME	65	25	42	32	59
Illinois State Bar Assn.	62	9	85	6	59
Illinois State Dental Society	61	16	81	3	40
Prof. Independ. Ins. Agents of Ill.	58	4	80	16	48
Ill. Hosp. and Healthsystems Assn.	49	36	62	2	35
Personal PAC	49	0	13	87	80
Illinois State AFL-CIO	41	17	34	49	56
Cable TV and Comm. Assn. of Ill.	32	39	60	1	36
Ill. New Car/Truck Dealers Assn.	22	21	61	17	25

† Percentages may not total 100 percent due to rounding.

Data for groups marked with an * are based on a review of reports filed by candidates for the General Assembly with the State Board of Elections.

Data for groups not marked with an * are based on reports filed by those groups with the State Board of Elections.

Table 4.19
Contributions to Legislative Elections†
1992 General Election

(Top 20 in total contributions, includes contributions to leader and chamber committees)
(Amounts in units of $1,000)

	General Election Total	Percent to Leader/Ch.	Percent to Incumbents	Percent to Nonincumb.	Percent of 1991-92 Total
Illinois State Medical Society	$631	24	51	26	43
Illinois Education Assn. (IEA)	496	0	52	48	78
Illinois Trial Lawyers Assn.	251	2	58	40	50
Illinois Manufacturers' Assn.	190	15	42	44	41
United Auto Workers (UAW)*	180	6	50	44	76
Personal PAC	170	0	35	65	85
Teamsters Joint Council No. 25*	159	68	22	11	76
Associated Beer Distrib. of Ill.	149	18	59	23	43
Illinois Association of Realtors	135	27	50	24	35
Philip Morris, Inc.*	110	44	38	19	57
Illinois Bankers Association	103	28	54	17	33
Illinois CPA Society	101	14	65	21	44
Prof. Independ. Ins. Agents of Ill.	97	16	39	45	66
AFSCME	82	19	33	47	54
Illinois State Bar Assn.	82	18	49	33	55
Cable TV and Comm. Assn. of Ill.	72	53	38	8	48
Ill. Hosp. and Healthsystems Assn.	69	29	45	26	26
Illinois State AFL-CIO	69	19	32	49	61
Illinois State Dental Society	64	37	48	14	35
Ill. New Car/Truck Dealers Assn.	44	15	62	23	37

† Percentages may not total 100 percent due to rounding.

Data for groups marked with an * are based on a review of reports filed by candidates for the General Assembly with the State Board of Elections.

Data for groups not marked with an * are based on reports filed by those groups with the State Board of Elections.

Table 4.20
Contributions to Legislative Incumbents and Nonincumbents†
1990 General Election

(Top 20 in total contributions, excludes contributions to leader and chamber committees)
(Amounts in units of $1,000)

	Total	Percent to Winning Incumbents	Percent to Losing Incumbents	Percent to Winning Nonincumb.	Percent to Losing Nonincumb.
Illinois Trial Lawyers Assn.	$181	73	1	15	11
Illinois Education Assn. (IEA)	164	75	5	10	10
Illinois State Medical Society	162	65	6	4	24
Illinois Manufacturers' Assn.	101	72	9	3	16
Illinois Association of Realtors	93	81	5	11	3
United Auto Workers (UAW)*	82	49	0	51	0
Associated Beer Distrib of Ill.	74	94	2	2	0
Philip Morris, Inc.*	74	98	0	1	1
Illinois CPA Society	64	98	2	0	0
Illinois State Bar Assn.	57	92	1	4	2
Prof. Independ. Ins. Agents of Ill.	56	79	4	6	10
Teamsters Joint Council No. 25*	53	75	0	19	5
Illinois State Dental Society	51	94	3	2	1
Personal PAC	49	13	0	87	0
AFSCME	49	56	8	35	1
Illinois Bankers Association	45	85	4	6	5
Ill. Hosp. and Healthsystems Assn.	32	94	2	4	0
Illinois State AFL-CIO	34	40	1	39	20
Cable TV and Comm. Assn. of Ill.	19	86	13	1	0
Ill. New Car/Truck Dealers Assn.	17	76	2	22	0

† Percentages may not total 100 percent due to rounding.

Data for groups marked with an * are based on a review of reports filed by candidates for the General Assembly with the State Board of Elections.

Data for groups not marked with an * are based on reports filed by those groups with the State Board of Elections.

Table 4.21
Contributions to Legislative Incumbents and Nonincumbents†
1992 General Election

(Top 20 in total contributions, excludes contributions to leader and chamber committees)
(Amounts in units of $1,000)

	Total	Percent to Winning Incumbents	Percent to Losing Incumbents	Percent to Winning Nonincumb.	Percent to Losing Nonincumb.
Illinois Education Assn. (IEA)	$496	41	10	15	34
Illinois State Medical Society	482	42	24	30	4
Illinois Trial Lawyers Assn.	245	52	7	25	16
Personal PAC	170	25	10	18	47
United Auto Workers (UAW)*	169	38	16	34	12
Illinois Manufacturers' Assn.	162	41	8	35	16
Associated Beer Distrib. of Ill.	122	66	7	21	7
Illinois Association of Realtors	99	59	9	28	4
Illinois CPA Society	87	69	7	21	3
Prof. Independ. Ins. Agents of Ill.	82	39	7	46	9
Illinois Bankers Association	74	65	9	22	3
Illinois State Bar Assn.	67	52	7	31	10
AFSCME	66	37	4	28	31
Philip Morris, Inc.*	62	55	13	26	7
Illinois State AFL-CIO	56	21	19	25	35
Teamsters Joint Council No. 25*	51	47	20	27	6
Ill. Hosp. and Healthsystems Assn.	49	57	6	33	4
Illinois State Dental Society	40	67	10	17	5
Ill. New Car/Truck Dealers Assn.	38	64	8	25	3
Cable TV and Comm. Assn. of Ill.	33	75	8	18	0

† Percentages may not total 100 percent due to rounding.

Data for groups marked with an * are based on a review of reports filed by candidates for the General Assembly with the State Board of Elections.

Data for groups not marked with an * are based on reports filed by those groups with the State Board of Elections.

Table 4.22
Contributions to Legislative Candidates by Party†
1990 General Election

(Top 20 in total contributions, excludes contributions to leader and chamber committees)
(Amounts in units of $1,000)

	Total	Percent to Winning Democrats	Percent to Losing Democrats	Percent to Winning Republicans	Percent to Losing Republicans
Illinois Trial Lawyers Assn.	$81	81	11	6	1
Illinois Education Assn. (IEA)	164	68	10	17	5
Illinois State Medical Society	162	32	0	37	30
Illinois Manufacturers' Assn.	101	18	0	56	25
Illinois Association of Realtors	93	46	0	49	5
United Auto Workers (UAW)*	82	100	0	0	0
Associated Beer Distrib. of Ill.	74	60	1	35	3
Philip Morris, Inc.*	74	59	0	40	1
Illinois CPA Society	64	61	0	37	2
Illinois State Bar Assn.	57	68	2	28	1
Prof. Independ. Ins. Agents of Ill.	56	44	0	42	14
Teamsters Joint Council No. 25*	53	95	5	0	0
Illinois State Dental Society	51	53	0	44	3
Personal PAC	49	100	0	0	0
AFSCME	49	87	8	4	1
Illinois Bankers Association	45	59	2	32	7
Illinois State AFL-CIO	34	78	20	1	1
Ill. Hosp. and Healthsystems Assn.	32	76	0	22	2
Cable TV and Comm. Assn. of Ill.	19	34	1	52	13
Ill. New Car/Truck Dealers Assn.	17	67	0	31	2

† Percentages may not total 100 percent due to rounding.

Data for groups marked with an * are based on a review of reports filed by candidates for the General Assembly with the State Board of Elections.

Data for groups not marked with an * are based on reports filed by those groups with the State Board of Elections.

Table 4.23
Contributions to Legislative Candidates by Party†
1992 General Election

(Top 20 in total contributions, excludes contributions to leader and chamber committees)
(Amounts in units of $1,000)

	Total	Percent to Winning Democrats	Percent to Losing Democrats	Percent to Winning Republicans	Percent to Losing Republicans
Illinois Education Assn. (IEA)	$496	46	43	10	1
Illinois State Medical Society	482	13	0	59	28
Illinois Trial Lawyers Assn.	245	70	24	6	0
Personal PAC	170	32	56	12	1
United Auto Workers (UAW)*	169	50	50	0	0
Illinois Manufacturers' Assn.	162	10	0	65	24
Associated Beer Distrib. of Ill.	122	50	9	37	4
Illinois Association of Realtors	99	40	6	46	7
Prof. Independ. Ins. Agents of Ill.	82	18	2	66	14
Illinois CPA Society	77	46	5	44	5
Illinois Bankers Association	74	50	4	38	8
Illinois State Bar Assn.	67	60	16	22	1
AFSCME	66	52	35	13	1
Philip Morris, Inc.*	62	63	19	18	1
Illinois State AFL-CIO	56	46	54	0	0
Teamsters Joint Council No. 25*	51	72	26	2	0
Ill. Hosp. and Healthsystems Assn.	49	47	6	43	4
Illinois State Dental Society	40	38	6	47	9
Ill. New Car/Truck Dealers Assn.	38	37	4	51	7
Cable TV and Comm. Assn. of Ill.	33	59	8	32	0

† Percentages may not total 100 percent due to rounding.

Data for groups marked with an * are based on a review of reports filed by candidates for the General Assembly with the State Board of Elections.

Data for groups not marked with an * are based on reports filed by those groups with the State Board of Elections.

Table 4.24
Average Contributions to Legislative Candidates
1990 General Election

(Top 20 in total contributions, excludes contributions to leader and chamber committees)

	Number of Candidates	Average Contribution	Number Receiving $1,000 or More	Largest Contribution
Illinois State Dental Society	139	$365	10	$1,500
Ill. New Car/Truck Dealers Assn.	45	375	0	500
Illinois CPA Society	164	390	9	2,000
AFSCME	103	475	11	3,750
Associated Beer Distrib. of Ill.	144	515	18	2,500
Ill. Hosp. and Healthsystems Assn.	59	525	6	2,000
Cable TV and Comm. Assn. of Ill.	33	575	5	5,250
Philip Morris, Inc.*	116	635	18	3,500
Prof. Independ. Ins. Agents of Ill.	82	680	21	2,000
Illinois Association of Realtors	131	700	27	1,000
Illinois Bankers Association	60	740	18	5,000
Illinois State AFL-CIO	44	770	14	4,000
Teamsters Joint Council No. 25*	67	790	30	3,000
Illinois State Bar Assn.	69	825	26	3,500
Illinois Manufacturers' Assn.	105	960	42	5,000
United Auto Workers (UAW)*	57	1,125	30	4,750
Illinois Education Assn. (IEA)	111	1,475	34	16,300
Illinois State Medical Society	101	1,600	63	25,200
Illinois Trial Lawyers Assn.	85	2,130	76	5,000
Personal PAC	9	5,445	4	21,100

Data for groups marked with an * are based on a review of reports filed by candidates for the General Assembly with the State Board of Elections.

Data for groups not marked with an * are based on reports filed by those groups with the State Board of Elections.

Table 4.25
Average Contributions to Legislative Candidates
1992 General Election

(Top 20 in total contributions, excludes contributions to leader and chamber committees)

	Number of Candidates	Average Contribution	Number Receiving $1,000 or More	Largest Contribution
Illinois State Dental Society	108	$370	2	$2,000
Ill. New Car/Truck Dealers Assn.	101	375	3	1,000
Illinois CPA Society	177	490	18	2,000
Ill. Hosp. and Healthsystems Assn.	93	525	18	1,750
Illinois Bankers Association	120	615	13	10,000
Cable TV and Comm. Assn. of Ill.	53	620	10	3,500
Associated Beer Distrib. of Ill.	176	695	47	2,250
Illinois Association of Realtors	129	710	23	4,000
AFSCME	93	710	9	11,000
Philip Morris, Inc*.	86	720	14	10,500
Teamsters Joint Council No. 25*	65	785	19	2,750
Illinois State Bar Assn.	68	985	62	4,000
Prof. Independ. Ins. Agents of Ill.	79	1,035	39	3,000
Illinois State AFL-CIO	45	1,245	24	3,800
Illinois Manufacturers' Assn.	100	1,620	59	10,000
United Auto Workers (UAW)*	94	1,800	55	7,000
Illinois Trial Lawyers Assn.	112	2,200	112	8,000
Illinois Education Assn. (IEA)	139	3,575	122	36,600
Illinois State Medical Society	125	3,850	102	88,000
Personal PAC	32	5,300	21	23,800

Data for groups marked with an * are based on a review of reports filed by candidates for the General Assembly with the State Board of Elections.

Data for groups not marked with an * are based on reports filed by those groups with the State Board of Elections.

Table 4.26
Illinois Trial Lawyers Assn. Contributions to Legislative Candidates
1992 General Election

	Number of Candidates	Average Contribution	Number Receiving $5,000 or More	Largest Contribution
House				
Dem. Winners	61	$1,900	1	$8,000
Dem. Losers	8	2,800	1	5,000
Rep. Winners	5	1,600	0	4,000
Senate				
Dem. Winners	27	2,000	0	3,000
Dem. Losers	8	4,400	3	8,000
Rep. Winners	3	3,000	0	3,000

Table 4.27
Illinois Manufacturers' Assn. Contributions to Legislative Candidates
1992 General Election

	Number of Candidates	Average Contribution	Number Receiving $5,000 or More	Largest Contribution
House				
Rep. Winners	44	$1,000	0	$4,000
Rep. Losers	14	2,250	1	5,000
Dem. Winners	9	1,100	1	5,000
Senate				
Rep. Winners	24	2,500	8	10,000
Rep. Losers	2	3,000	0	4,500
Dem. Winners	7	725	0	1,500

Table 4.28
Illinois Education Assn. (IEA) Contributions to Legislative Candidates
1992 General Election

	Number of Candidates	Average Contribution	Number Receiving $5,000 or more	Largest Contribution
House				
Dem. Winners	61	$2,500	6	$20,300
Dem. Losers	10	5,000	4	15,900
Rep. Winners	21	1,800	0	3,000
Rep. Losers	2	2,000	0	2,500
Senate				
Dem. Winners	26	2,900	5	14,600
Dem. Losers	11	15,500	7	36,600
Rep. Winners	8	1,350	0	3,300

Table 4.29
Illinois State Medical Society Contributions to Legislative Candidates
1992 General Election

	Number of Candidates	Average Contribution	Number Receiving $5,000 or more	Largest Contribution
House				
Rep. Winners	47	$3,350	8	$21,900
Rep. Losers	10	13,100	6	88,000
Dem. Winners	26	1,650	0	2,500
Senate				
Rep. Winners	29	4,350	7	21,300
Rep. Losers	1	4,300	0	4,300
Dem. Winners	12	1,600	0	4,900

"If you take away their bulk mail stamp, they might as well close up shop."

A former Illinois state party chairman commenting on the limited role of state political parties in legislative elections

CHAPTER 5
THE ROLE OF STATE POLITICAL PARTIES IN FINANCING LEGISLATIVE CAMPAIGNS

Look at the yard signs and bumper stickers or watch the TV commercials of candidates for the legislature in Illinois and you will learn most of what you need to know about the role of political parties in legislative elections. You will certainly learn the candidate's name and usually something about his/her qualifications, achievements, or positions on issues. You may even learn something about the opponent's issue positions or lack of achievements or qualifications. What you won't learn is the candidate's political party. Almost without exception, candidates for the legislature run as nominees of the Democratic or Republican party. And almost without exception they do not feature their party affiliation in messages directed at the general voter. Not only do candidates not run with their party affiliation, they often will run away from it, emphasizing their independence and the lack of partisan obligations. This phenomenon is not limited to state legislative elections. Political campaigns at all levels continue to be candidate- rather than party-centered. While the 1994 congressional elections featured a strong attempt to show more party identity among house Republican candidates, it is too early to tell whether voters will become more party conscious. And in spite of the efforts at the national level to strengthen party identification among voters, the public's satisfaction with political parties, Democratic and Republican, remains at an all-time high.

Despite the general impression gained from watching the campaigns, political parties are certainly not irrelevant to legislative elections. Many voters have some interest in a candidate's political party because it provides a starting point for classifying and evaluating the candidate. The party affiliation of a candidate is very important to the relatively small portion of the electorate that consider themselves strong, active party members. In addition, many state and local political parties still perform, to some degree, the traditional functions of recruiting candidates, raising money, running or assisting in political campaigns, providing voting cues to party members, and delivering voters to the polls. In these ways, political parties can still provide resources to party candidates that are helpful in winning elections. Just how much support parties can and do provide is a critical question.

The ability to raise and spend money on political campaigns is one measure of political party strength. The following examination of the role of state political parties in financing state legislative elections during the 1990 and 1992 election cycles provides a test of one aspect of party strength.

Fundraising by Illinois State Political Parties—Recent Trends

While the state Republican Party has long been the dominant Republican Party organization in Illinois, the Cook County Democratic Party organization dwarfed the state Democratic Party during the 1960s and 70s. The decline of the Cook County Democratic Party as a force at the state level after the death of Chicago mayor Richard J. Daley in 1977 created a void that the state Democratic Party was slow to fill. The 1984 and 1986 election cycles in Illinois illustrate the historical disparity in fundraising between the state Democratic and Republican parties. According to reports filed with the State Board of Elections for 1983-84, a presidential election cycle, the state Democratic Party raised slightly more than $700,000, while the state Republican Party raised $3.7 million. During 1985-86 those same reports show that the state Democratic Party raised slightly less than $900,000, while the state Republican Party raised $2.3 million.

The 1988 election cycle marked a reversal of this pattern. In 1986 the candidates endorsed by the state Democratic Party for lieutenant governor and secretary of state were defeated in the Democratic primary by candidates allied with Lyndon LaRouche, a right-wing political extremist who spent time in federal prison for income tax evasion. In response to this fiasco state senator Vince Demuzio became state Democratic chairman in 1986 with a mandate to revitalize the state party. During the 1988 election cycle the state Democratic Party raised $4.4 million, while the state Republican Party raised $4.7 million. The advances in fundraising realized under Demuzio's leadership were consolidated by Gary LaPaille, then chief of staff for house speaker Michael Madigan, who defeated Demuzio for the state party chairmanship in March 1990. In the nonpresidential election cycle of 1990 the state Democratic Party, for the first time in recent history, raised and spent more than the state Republican Party, $3.6 million to $2.7 million. That trend toward parity in fundraising continued in 1992 with the state Democratic Party raising $2.5 million and the state Republican Party raising $2.4 million.

The Electoral Context of State Party Activity

The receipts and expenditures of the state Democratic and Republican parties for the 1990 and 1992 election cycles are shown in tables 5.1 through 5.5 (pp. 114-20). In comparing the two election cycles it is important to again note that all of the statewide offices were contested in 1990. The most important race was for the governor's office, where the retirement of the longtime Republican governor James R. Thompson created the first governor's race without an incumbent since 1976 when the incumbent Democratic governor, Daniel Walker, was defeated in the primary. It was also the last election under the pro-Democratic legislative map drawn in 1981, with 19 senate seats and all 118 house seats up for reelection. In 1992 there was a presidential election, but no statewide offices were up. It was the first election under the pro-Republican legislative map adopted in 1991, and all 59 senate seats and all 118 house seats were up for reelection.

The electoral context is important because state parties in Illinois are not highly structured, independent organizations with stable resources and agendas. Rather their identity and function is dependent on who controls the party machinery and what races are being contested in a particular election. State parties are primarily concerned with statewide elections. Even there they play a secondary, support role because the candidates for statewide office form their own independent campaign organization outside any party apparatus. The governor's office is the key race from a state party perspective because it means jobs, power, and prestige, which can be translated into benefits for the officeholders and seekers as well as party members and organizations at all levels in the state. In contrast, legislative elections are more diffuse in their impact on state and local parties. But the most important difference is that legislative elections are strongly controlled by the legislative leaders who determine the targeted races, dominate the fundraising, and control many of the campaigns. The decision of the legislative leaders whether to work through the state party to support legislative election campaigns will alter

Table 5.1
State Political Parties Total Receipts and Contributions
1990 and 1992 Election Cycles
(Amounts in units of $1,000)

	1990				1992			
	Rep		Dem		Rep		Dem	
Political Sources	$1,869	68%	$1,630	45%	$1,836	77%	$981	39%
Interest Groups	187	7	1,559	43	346	14	1,106	43
Individuals/Not itemized	631	23	421	12	182	8	436	17
Misc/Unclassified	46	2	16	0	29	1	28	1
TOTAL	2,733	100	3,626	100	2,393	100	2,551	100

the receipt and expenditure profile of state parties in Illinois. The same is true of the presence or absence of a governor's race. It follows that the fundraising and expenditure profiles of state parties can vary widely between the two parties and between election cycles.

Patterns of Receipts—1990 and 1992

Looking across both election cycles, the most significant difference between the sources of support for the two state parties is a substantial advantage for the state Democrats in contributions from interest groups. The nearly $1.6 million they received from interest groups in 1990 was more than eight times as much money as the state Republican Party received. In 1992 the $1.1 million received by the state Democratic Party was slightly more than three times as much as the state Republican Party received from interest groups (table 5.1, p. 114). Looking at the breakout of interest group receipts in table 5.2 (p. 115), the state Democratic Party had an overwhelming advantage over the Republicans in the union and lawyer categories in both election cycles and in the business category in the 1990 cycle. Issue group contributions were not a factor for either party in 1990. In 1992, however, the Democrats received substantial money from issue groups, although the Republicans again received no contributions.* Only in 1992 does the state Republican Party come close to equaling the receipts of the Democrats in any category; that category is contributions from business, and the advantage to the Democrats is still

* The lawyer and union categories in table 5.2 are the same as those used in chapter 3 and detailed in appendix B, pp. 184-85. All the other interest group contributions were collapsed into a business category except those with a strong ideological focus, which were combined in an issue-group category.

Table 5.2
State Political Parties
Breakout of Interest Group Contributions
1990 and 1992 Election Cycles
(Amounts in units of $1,000)

	1990				1992			
	Rep		Dem		Rep		Dem	
Business	$163	88%	$823	53%	$304	88%	$538	49%
Union	22	12	352	22	5	1	301	27
Lawyer	1	0	384	25	37	11	157	14
Issue Group	0	0	0	0	0	0	110	10
TOTAL	186	100	1,559	100	346	100	1,106	100

more than $230,000.

While contributions from political sources dominate the receipts for the Republican Party for the two election cycles, interest group contributions are as important a source of support for the state Democratic Party as are contributions from political sources (table 5.1, p. 114). Interest group contributions provide the advantage in fundraising enjoyed by the Democrats for both election cycles.

In 1990 and 1992 these contributions accounted for 43 percent of the Democratic Party's total receipts. In contrast, the figures for the Republicans are 7 percent and 14 percent of their total receipts. Since the 1988 election cycle, the Democratic Party has pursued a fundraising strategy that emphasizes large contributions from interest groups and corporations. This strategy is similar to that of the legislative leaders and their chamber political committees. The desire to strengthen the state Democratic Party after the LaRouche fiasco in 1986 and the lack of a statewide fundraising organization, combined with the legislative experience of the two most recent Democratic Party state chairmen, all probably contributed to the adoption of this approach to raising funds.

The amount of money raised from individual and not-itemized contributions remained about the same for the Democrats over the two election cycles: $421,000 or 12 percent of total receipts in 1990 and $436,000 or 17 percent of total receipts in 1992 (table 5.1). In contrast, the amount generated from these sources drops off dramatically for the Republican Party from 1990 to 1992, a decrease from $631,000 to $182,000 and from 23 percent to 8 percent of total receipts (table 5.1). The variation on the Republican side appears to be related to contributions in support of statewide races, particularly the governor's race. The fact that there has been a Republican governor in Illinois since 1977 gives the state Republican Party a different focus from that of the Democratic Party. Over the same time period, the Democrats have controlled both houses of the legislature, except for the house in 1981-82. The state Democratic Party organization has developed a closer relationship with the legislature, particularly since house speaker Michael Madigan's chief of staff, Gary LaPaille, became party chairman. The result of these differences appears to have produced an ebb-and-flow pattern for individual/not-itemized contributions for the Republicans and a more constant pattern for the Democrats, although no conclusions should be drawn on the basis of only two election cycles.

The major source of funds for the state Republican Party over the two election cycles and a close second for the state Democratic Party is contributions from political sources: candidates, legislative leaders, and local and national party organizations. In 1990, 68 percent of total receipts of the state Republican Party came from political sources (candidates and officeholders including legislative leaders and state and local party organizations), while in 1992 the figure rose to 77 percent. For the state Democratic Party, the figures are 45 percent of total receipts in 1990 and 39 percent in 1992 (table 5.1, p. 114).

Compared to receipts from interest groups or from individuals, money received by the state parties from political sources is more difficult to analyze because of questions concerning who controls the spending of money from political sources. While money transferred from the political committees of candidates for statewide and legislative office and from the legislative leaders is counted as receipts on the forms filed with the State Board of Elections, the vast majority of these "contributions" are not gifts of money to the state parties to be used as the officers of the parties wish. Rather, they are payment for goods and services provided by the parties to the candidates under the direction of either the legislative leaders or the campaigns of candidates for statewide office. These transfers or "pass-through" expenditures are made primarily for financial reasons. By acting as a middleman in the purchase of services such as printing and mailing direct-mail pieces and providing access to targeting and polling information, the state parties help candidates get maximum return for their campaign dollars. Of particular importance are differences in bulk mailing rates, which can provide considerable savings on large mailings. However, there are limitations as to what can be classified as legitimate party activities, and both state parties had to reimburse the U.S. Postal Service for mailings sent out in 1992 under the general party rate, but which benefited only specific legislative candidates (Schoenburg 1993).

A secondary reason for passing money to support a legislative candidate through a state political party could be to obscure the amount or the source of support a candidate is receiving from outside the district. Contributions from state political parties do not carry the potentially negative baggage that contributions from a legislative leader or a company or labor union from outside the district may carry. If the spending in support of a legislative candidate is reported by the state party as part of its general party-building and party-candidate activities, then the expenditure would not be linked to the candidate in any of the reports filed with the State Board of Elections.

Legislative leaders or the candidates for statewide office, not the party officials, decide how much the party will spend and on whom. In 1990 this pass-through pattern can be seen in the receipts and expenditures of the state parties in regard to candidates for statewide office (tables 5.3 and 5.4, pp. 118 and 119). While the state Republican Party received more than $389,000 from the campaigns of Governor Edgar and other Republican candidates for statewide office, the party also reported more than $358,000 in expenditures on behalf of those candidates. The state Democratic Party reported receiving $240,000 in contributions from the campaigns of gubernatorial candidate Neil Hartigan and other Democratic candidates for statewide office while spending more than $586,000 on behalf of those candidates. While no statewide offices were contested in 1992, the state Republican Party does show the receipt of $153,000 from Governor Edgar's campaign committee and $152,000 in expenditures on behalf of Governor Edgar. This transaction took place early in 1991 and represents a bookkeeping adjustment from the 1990 campaign.

A breakout of the candidate and party contributions (table 5.3) shows that on the Republican side, the major source of funds from political sources in 1990 was legislative leaders and legislative candidates (46 percent of receipts from political sources). With statewide races being contested, contributions from statewide candidates (21 percent) and local parties and candidates (18 percent) also made up a significant portion of the receipts from political sources. In contrast, with legislative elections being the only state elections in 1992, the overwhelming majority of receipts from political sources for the state Republican Party came from the legislative leaders: $1.4 million or 77 percent. Receipts from the national Republican Party account for 11 percent in each of the two election cycles.

Table 5.3
State Political Parties
Breakout of Contributions from Political Sources
1990 and 1992 Election Cycles
(Amounts in units of $1,000)

	1990				1992			
	Rep		Dem		Rep		Dem	
Legislative Leaders	$655	35%	$376	23%	$1,410	77%	$48	5%
Legislative Candidates	212	11	287	17	23	1	67	7
Statewide Candidates	389	21	240	15	153	8	20	2
Local Party/Candidates	343	18	272	17	45	2	243	25
Judicial Candidates	35	2	14	1	10	1	119	12
National Party	201	11	393	24	195	11	452	46
Federal Candidates	34	2	48	3	0	0	32	3
TOTAL	1,869	100	1,630	100	1,836	100	981	100

The 1990 profile of receipts from political sources for the state Democratic Party is quite similar to that of the Republicans. (The following figures are in table 5.3, p. 118.) Legislative leaders and legislative candidates account for 40 percent of these receipts while statewide candidates (15 percent) and local parties and candidates (17 percent) are also significant. Receipts from the national Democratic Party are approximately the same dollar amount for both election cycles, but the drop in receipts from other political sources in 1992 raises the percentage of the total to 46 percent, up from 24 percent in 1990. The major difference between the receipt profiles from political sources for the two parties appears in 1992, when legislative-leader and candidate contributions account for only 12 percent of the Democrats' receipts from these sources compared to 78 percent of the receipts from political sources for the Republicans. While the difference in receipts from political sources reported in 1990 favored the state Republican Party by $239,000, in 1992, the drop in receipts from these sources for the state Democratic Party resulted in an advantage of $855,000 for the state Republican Party in this category. Since the great majority of this money is pass through rather than straight contributions, the difference illustrates the contrasting approaches adopted by legislative leaders in using the two state parties to support candidates in legislative elections. This difference in using the state party to pass through contributions will also be evident in the expenditure patterns presented later.

Overall, the pattern of receipts from the two election cycles shows a strong advantage for the state Democratic Party in raising money from

Table 5.4
State Political Parties
Total Expenditures
1990 and 1992 Election Cycles
(Amounts in units of $1,000)

	1990				1992			
	Rep		Dem		Rep		Dem	
Overhead, Salary & Not-itemized	$573	20%	$945	26%	$91	4%	$376	15%
Legislative Elections	859	30	19	0	1,402	58	272	11
Unspecified Elections	795	28	1,611	44	72	3	733	29
Local Elections/Parties	219	8	351	10	232	10	178	7
Judicial Elections	49	2	140	4	0	0	0	0
Statewide Elections	358	12	586	16	152	6	0	0
Internal Transfers	0	0	0	0	451	19	952	38
TOTAL	2,853	100	3,652	100	2,400	100	2,511	100

interest groups and an uneven picture of receipts from individuals. Contributions from these sources provide resources that party officials control, giving them some flexibility in their spending decisions. In contrast, most of the money received by both state political parties from party and candidate sources is pass through. Because it is linked to particular expenditures, it does not represent resources that can be used at the discretion of party leaders.

Patterns of Expenditures

At first glance, the major pattern that emerges from the breakout of expenditures for the two state political parties for 1990 and 1992 is no pattern (tables 5.4 and 5.5, pp. 119 and 120). Part of this is a function of the fluidity of state parties as organizations, while part is the result of differences between the two election cycles. For example, in the 1990 election cycle no internal transfers of funds from state to federal party accounts were listed. In 1992 more than $1.4 million in such transfers was recorded for the two state political parties (table 5.4). At the same time party-building activities for the two party organizations, such as voter registration and get-out-the-vote (GOTV) efforts dropped from a total of $166,000 in 1990 to $23,000 in 1992 (table 5.5). While party-building activities do in fact strengthen the parties as organizations, they also benefit the parties' candidates in the election. Resources and

Table 5.5
State Political Parties
Breakout of Selected Electoral Expenditures
1990 and 1992 Election Cycles
(Amounts in units of $1,000)

	1990				1992			
Legislative Elections	Rep		Dem		Rep		Dem	
Members	$859		$19		$1,370		$57	
Leaders	0		0		32		215	
	859		19		1,402		272	
Unspecified Election Expenditures:	Rep		Dem		Rep		Dem	
Direct Mail	$635	80%	$1,107	69%	$34	47%	$598	82%
Media	4	1	27	2	0	0	75	10
GOTV	66	8	100	6	23	32	0	0
Telemarketing	24	3	53	3	0	0	0	0
Fundraising	23	3	228	14	0	0	0	0
Miscellaneous	43	5	96	6	15	21	60	8
TOTAL	795	100	1,611	100	72	100	733	100

expenditures for these party-building activities to support statewide candidates that were on the state side of the ledger in 1990 were shifted to the federal side of the ledger in 1992 to support presidential candidates.

Spending on overhead (largely personnel dollars) also varies widely from one election to another. Some factors are particular to a single election cycle. For example, the higher overhead and salary expenditures for the Democrats in 1990 is a result of the cost of closing out the operations of former party chairman Vince Demuzio and starting operations under new party chairman Gary LaPaille in March and April of 1990 (table 5.4, p. 119). Other factors are cyclical in their impact. State parties as organizations are closely associated with statewide officeholders, and they function most effectively in support of statewide elections. It is not surprising to find personnel working in support of statewide candidates and the state party being paid out of state party accounts in an election cycle where statewide offices are being contested. But both the nature of legislative elections and the dominance of the legislative leaders limit the role that state party organization personnel can play in support of legislative campaigns. Given these differences, the drop-off in personnel and overhead spending from 1990 to 1992 is to be expected.

Most of the expenditures for both parties in both election cycles were direct election expenditures rather than overhead or internal transfers (table 5.4, p. 119). For the state Republican Party the figures are 80 percent of total expenditures in 1990 and 77 percent in 1992, while for the state Democratic Party, the figures are 74 percent in 1990 and 47 percent in 1992. The lower 1992 percentage of total expenditures for the state Democratic Party that went directly to elections reflects both a decrease in unspecified (no beneficiary reported) spending on state-level elections and a major increase in internal transfers to federal accounts. Unspecified election expenditures are reported as benefiting the state party or the state ticket. They may focus on generating support for all party candidates or they may highlight a specific candidate as part of the general appeal.

The differences in how the two state parties were used to support legislative candidates can be seen in a detailed look at spending on legislative elections and unspecified spending on state-level elections (table 5.5, p. 120). In 1990 the state Republican Party reported $859,000 in expenditures on legislative elections and $795,000 in unspecified election expenditures, a total of $1.65 million. The total amount received from legislative leaders and legislative candidates, $867,000, (table 5.3, p. 118) is approximately equal to the amount spent on behalf of legislative elections. Virtually all of the money received by the state Republican Party from legislative sources was pass-through money. Rather than being an independent force in legislative elections, the party served as a vehicle for the purchase of services, a means of saving money.

The state Democratic Party reported only $19,000 in specific expenditures in support of legislative candidates in 1990, but $1.61 million in unspecified election expenditures (table 5.5). Assuming the $663,000 received from legislative leaders and legislative candidates in 1990 (table 5.3) is pass-through and subtracting it from the total for unspecified election expenditures still leaves approximately $1 million in unspecified election expenditures for the state Democratic Party in 1990. While some of this money, which was reported as benefiting the state party, the state party ticket, or Democratic candidates, did benefit legislative candidates either directly or indirectly, it is impossible to know precisely who received the money, given the way the state Democratic Party reports expenditures to the State Board of Elections.

The expenditure data from the 1992 elections show a continuation of these patterns (tables 5.5). The state Republican Party reported expenditures of $1.4 million in support of legislative candidates. That figure is almost identical to the $1.4 million the state party reported in receipts from legislative leaders (table 5.3, p. 118). Only $23,000 was received from legislative candidates. In contrast to 1990, only $72,000 in unspecified election expenditures was reported, a decrease of more than $700,000. All of the money spent on legislative elections was pass-through and all of it was controlled by the Republican legislative leaders. Given the close correlation between total contributions from legislative sources and total expenditures on behalf of legislative candidates in both 1990 and 1992 and the large drop-off in unspecified election spending in 1992, it appears that the great majority of unspecified election expenditures reported in 1990 by the state Republican Party were probably made on behalf of statewide candidates rather than legislative candidates.

In contrast, the state Democratic Party reported relatively small legislative election expenditures ($272,000) and relatively large unspecified election expenditures ($733,000) in 1992 (table 5.5, p. 120). The majority of the legislative expenditures were in the form of $215,000 transferred to the Democratic legislative chamber political committees, $107,500 to each chamber committee. Subtracting the amount contributed by legislative leaders and legislative candidates (nearly $115,000, table 5.3) from the amount spent in support of legislative elections ($272,000, table 5.5) produces a net figure of nearly $157,000 in support above the amount of pass-through. Given the significant (though reduced from 1990) amount of unspecified election expenditures and the large amount of unincumbered resources generated from interest groups and individuals, it seems reasonable to assume that some portion of the unspecified election expenditures made in 1990 and 1992 was made in direct support of legislative candidates. How much is impossible to determine because the state Democratic Party did not break out these expenditures in their reports for the 1990 and 1992 elections.

A more detailed look at legislative election expenditures made by the state Republican Party shows that the pass-through expenditures for legislative candidates were made on behalf of specific legislative candidates and consisted almost entirely of payments for printing and postage for direct-mail pieces and for targeting and generating labels for the mailing (table 5.5). In contrast, the vast majority of legislative election expenditures reported by the state Democratic Party were in the form of transfers of money to the Democratic legislative chamber committees. Looking at the details for the unspecified election expenditures, the breakout in table 5.5 shows that the great majority of these expenditures for both parties paid for direct mail (e.g., printing, postage, targeting, labels).

The Impact of State Political Parties on Legislative Elections

While the state political parties do play a role in financing political campaigns in Illinois, it is a limited role. In the report *Illinois, Money and Elections*, the State Board of Elections found that $46.7 million was spent by candidates for public office in the 1990 election. Candidates for the state legislature reported spending $12.6 million; candidates for governor and other statewide offices reported spending $22.3 million; and candidates for local and judicial offices reported expenditures of $11.8 million. In the 1990 election cycle, the state Democratic Party made $2.71 million in direct expenditures (excluding overhead, salaries, etc.) on elections, while the state Republican Party's direct election expenditures totaled $2.28 million (table 5.4, p. 119). The total of $4.99 million is not a minor amount by any measure, but it accounts for only slightly more than 10 percent of the total campaign expenditures reported by candidates to the State Board of Elections for the 1990 election. If the $2.16 million received by the state political parties from candidates for statewide office and from legislative leaders and legislative candidates (table 5.3, p. 118) is counted as pass-through and subtracted from the $4.99 million, the independent impact of the state political parties on state elections in 1990 drops to $2.83 million, slightly less than 6 percent.

The impact of the state political parties on legislative elections in Illinois is even more limited. The 1992 elections, when no statewide races were being contested, clearly illustrate this. Excluding the pass-through spending from the legislative leaders from the 1992 expenditures, the independent impact of the state Republican Party on legislative elections is negligible. For the state Democratic Party, the reported expenditures on legislative elections in 1992 (table 5.5, p. 120) exceeds the contributions from legislative candidates and legislative leaders (table 5.3) by approximately $157,000, a relatively small amount. The state Democratic Party's 1992 unspecified election expenditures, which total $733,000 (table 5.5), create some uncertainty in drawing conclusions. As explained earlier, what portion of these expenditures benefited legislative candidates is impossible to determine. Still, even allowing for additional independent state party expenditures on the Democratic side in support of legislative candidates, any direct, independent impact of state parties on legislative elections in 1992 pales in comparison to the $9.62 million that the legislative leaders spent (see table 3.6, p. 47).

The difficulties faced by the two state political parties as they try to play a significant role in state politics are many: declining participation in party activities at all levels, public dissatisfaction with party politics, declining impact on the recruitment of candidates, lack of relevance to campaigns for statewide office, the awesome and growing electoral power of legislative leaders, and the general independence of office-seekers and officeholders from party organizations at all levels. As the cost and the complexity of political campaigns continue to increase, the state political parties will find it increasingly difficult to maintain a viable role in state politics. Maintaining the status quo will only contribute to the continued decline in the role of political parties in the face of the continued growth of individualistic, candidate-centered electoral politics in statewide and legislative elections, as well as the continued dominance of legislative leaders in contested legislative elections.

"Who you are and what you stand for wins elections, but without serious money from PACs or leadership no one will ever know who you are or what you stand for."

A longtime statehouse lobbyist commenting on the role of money in legislative elections

CHAPTER 6
THE ROLE OF MONEY IN THE 1992 LEGISLATIVE ELECTIONS

In early August of 1992, supporters of Vickie Moseley held a car wash in the parking lot of a small north end Springfield furniture store. Business was very slow. The homemade signs urging people to stop drew hundreds of blank stares and about two dozen customers. As the Democratic candidate for the house seat in the 99th House District, Moseley's chances of beating the well-known Republican candidate, Sangamon County sheriff Bill DeMarco, seemed nonexistent. The 99th had been carefully drawn to elect a Republican and much of the district was in Sangamon County with its powerful Republican county organization. The preelection forecast of the late summer counted the district as firmly in the Republican-win column. Three months later, Moseley had won an easy (59 percent to 41 percent) victory. Why Moseley was able to compete and win in the 99th House District illustrates the role of money and legislative leaders in contested legislative elections in Illinois.

When the Republicans won control of the redistricting process in the fall of 1991, conventional wisdom suggested that the senate would surely go Republican and Democratic control of the house was in jeopardy. District maps are important: Control over the redistricting process, which takes place every 10 years in Illinois, allows the party in charge to draw a map for maximum political advantage as long as it meets state and federal constitutional requirements as to equal population and nondiscrimination. The map drawn by the Democrats in 1981 is credited with maintaining Democratic control of the senate while facilitating Democratic dominance in the house during the 1980s. Having a favorable district is just the start; you still have to hold an election. Winning requires a good candidate, smart campaign strategy, and sufficient money to run a competitive campaign. An analysis of fundraising and spending in the districts targeted by the legislative leaders in the house and senate in 1992 indicates that while the new legislative district map was an important factor, the success of the Democrats in the house and the Republicans in the senate was directly attributable to the financial assistance provided by the legislative leaders to their candidates in those races.

In the Moseley-DeMarco race in the 99th House District, DeMarco's campaign never really took off. When the voters and the local media began focusing on the fall elections, his difficulty in articulating why he should be elected and what he would do if elected created an opportunity for his opponent. In turn, Moseley picked up some attention and some local endorsements through a more focused campaign. While polling in the fall showed that Moseley had become competitive, the advantage in money and local political organization was still overwhelmingly with DeMarco. What changed the dynamic of the election was the decision in October of the house Democratic campaign organization to put money and other resources into the race (table 6.1, p. 152). Moseley's campaign received $53,000 in direct contributions and in-kind contributions (e.g., donations of targeting and polling information, printing and mailing of direct-mail pieces, paid media spots) from the House Democratic Majority Committee and Speaker Madigan's political committee, Friends of Michael J. Madigan. While she was still outspent $97,000 to $69,000 during the general election period, the infusion of money from the speaker allowed her to mail campaign literature to households in the district and broadcast ads on TV and radio. Those ads were widely regarded as effective in portraying her as a penny-pinching outsider ready to change the system, but no matter how appealing the message, the voters had to get it if it was to have an impact.

While other targeted races were much more expensive, the race in the 99th House District is a clear example of the dominant role legislative leaders have come to play in contested legislative races in Illinois. While all 59 senate seats and all 118 house seats were up for reelection in 1992, control of the senate turned on the outcome in less than a dozen races, while control of the house rested on the outcome in less than two dozen races. The successes of the senate Republicans and the house Democrats in those elections resulted in a Republican-controlled senate and a Democratic-controlled house for 1993-94. While control of the senate shifted from a 31-to-28 Democratic majority to a 32-to-27 Republican majority, the Republicans picked up only five seats and the Democrats retained control of the house with a comfortable 67-51 majority.

Targeted Districts and Competitive, Targeted Districts

On the basis of the money received and expended by legislative candidates, house and senate districts in 1992 fall into two major groups, those that are targeted by the legislative leaders and those that are not. As the term *targeted* suggests, the four legislative leaders select districts where they believe that the infusion of money and resources will affect the outcome. The object may be to protect an incumbent from your party, to unseat an incumbent from the other party, or to win an open seat where no incumbent is running. Having selected certain districts as targets, the leaders use the money they have raised through their political committees and their chamber committees to try to influence the race. The leaders will transfer funds directly to a candidate's campaign committee. But as the data in chapter 3 show, the bulk of the assistance they give to candidates comes through in-kind contributions. In-kind contributions consist of items such as staff, polling, targeting, and direct-mail printing and postage that are paid for by the legislative leaders, but benefit the candidate. The outcome of the election may be close in a district that is targeted by one or both sides, but that is not the distinguishing feature. The salient feature of a targeted district is the commitment by the legislative leaders on one or both sides to spend resources in the district in an attempt to influence the outcome.

Because no leader has unlimited funds, decisions about whom to support and how to divide the available resources involve judgments and tradeoffs. Legislative leaders have always sought to provide financial support for their incumbents and promising challengers. What makes recent legislative elections different is that legislative leaders now have sufficient resources to develop and execute comprehensive strategies that encompass the entire election for the house or senate. Going into the 1992 elections, each of the four legislative leaders had a tentative plan and budget through which he hoped to gain or retain control of his legislative chamber. How each party group fared in the election was strongly affected by how well the legislative leaders adapted and executed those plans. Some races are chosen as targets well in advance of the election, while others are selected as the election develops.

Unlike the laws of physics, actions in politics do not always produce an equal and opposite reaction. Districts that are targeted by one leadership group may not be targeted by their opponents in the chamber. Faced with a leadership-backed challenge to one of their incumbents, the incumbent's leadership may conclude that he/she will be able to raise sufficient funds and conduct a campaign strong enough to win without any assistance. Similarly, leadership support for a candidate running for an open seat may not be met by comparable spending by the leadership of the other party on behalf of their candidate. The critical difference between these two cases is that leadership spending against an incumbent tends to mitigate the fundraising advantage of the incumbent and create a competitive election if the district does not overwhelmingly favor one party. In contrast, leadership spending on behalf of onc candidate in an open seat that is not countered by the other party's leadership tends to give a significant advantage to the candidate receiving leadership support, creating a noncompetitive election if the district is not overwhelmingly Democratic or Republican. Finally leadership spending on behalf of an incumbent who does not face a strong challenge results in making an uncompetitive situation even more uncompetitive. In looking at how the legislative leaders shaped their strategies in the 1992 elections, it is useful to further distinguish between competitive, targeted districts and noncompetitive, targeted districts.

In the 1992 general election, noncompetitive, targeted districts consisted of districts where leadership support was provided to incumbents who ultimately did not face a serious challenge and open districts where one candidate received strong leadership support and the other candidate did not. Contests for open seats where both candidates received strong leadership support are classified as competitive, targeted races, as are leadership-backed challenges to incumbents, regardless of whether leadership support was also provided to the incumbent.

In 1992 there were 9 senate districts that fit the competitive, targeted category (table 6.2, p. 153) In the house there were 21 house districts that fit the competitive, targeted category (table 6.3, p. 154). These numbers mean that there were 50 senate districts and 97 house districts that were either not targeted by the chamber groups or where leadership involvement was one-sided. Most of these nontargeted or noncompetitive, targeted districts strongly favored one party (based on past voting behavior) and/or had a popular incumbent running for reelection. Financing a candidate would have been a bad investment for the legislative leader of the party that was at a disadvantage in such a district.

Spending by Challengers in Targeted and Nontargeted Legislative Districts

A comparison of fundraising by the losing candidate or the challenger in targeted races to those in nontargeted races shows the impact of targeting by legislative leaders on the cost of legislative elections and the ability of candidates, particularly challengers, to raise money. In the 118 house races there were 40 districts where the winning candidate had no opponent and 43 districts where the losing candidate spent less than $25,000, with an average of less than $10,000 per losing candidate. In the remaining 35 house districts the losing candidate spent more than $25,000. However, the average amount spent by the losing candidate in the 14 contested districts that were not targeted was $38,000. In the 21 districts targeted by the legislative leaders, the losing candidate spent an average of $116,000. The same spending pattern existed in elections for the senate. Of the 59 senate races, there were 32 districts where the winning candidate had no opponent and 16 districts where the losing candidate spent less than $50,000 with an average expenditure of $11,000. In the remaining 13 senate districts, the losing candidate spent more than $50,000. The average amount spent by the losing candidate in the four districts not targeted by the legislative leaders was $79,000, while the average amount spent by the losing candidate in the nine targeted districts was $256,000 (Illinois State Board of Elections 1993).

Classifying the Partisan Tendencies of Legislative Districts

Legislative districts are made up of voting precincts, each of which has a voting history. It is possible to reconstruct what the outcomes of past state and national elections would have been within a district if that district had existed at the time. These data can be used to classify districts according to their voting histories, which provide an indication of their voting tendencies. In the *Almanac of Illinois Politics—1994*, districts were classified as dominant Democratic, competitive Democratic, competitive Republican, and dominant Republican based on the vote results for the University of Illinois Board of Trustees for 1990 and 1992. The U of I trustee vote was used because it is a statewide, partisan election in which the candidates are largely unknown to the voters. The assumption is that faced with a lack of specific information voters will vote for the candidates of the party that they tend to favor. The partisan characteristics attributed to targeted legislative districts are based on the *Almanac* classifications.

Senate Leadership Election Strategies and Prospects

Strategies. The Democrats began the 1992 elections with a 31-29 majority in the senate. The Republicans had designed the new map to try to accomplish three objectives: first, concentrate Democratic voters in districts wherever possible; second, create as many safe Republican districts as possible; and third, shape districts in competitive areas to favor the Republicans. The success of the concentration strategy is evident in the 15 senate districts where Democrats ran unopposed. In contrast, there were only 5 districts where Republicans ran unopposed. Part of the decision to run a candidate involves strategic choices. There is a point where a party's dominance in a district is so overwhelming that running even a token candidate serves no purpose. There also were 9 districts in which the Democrats received more than 60 percent of the vote, while the Republicans had 15 districts in which they received more than 60 percent of the vote. Finally, there were also three senate districts where the winning Republican candidate received between 55 percent and 58 percent of the vote. In none of the districts was there any significant transfer of funds or in-kind contributions from the leadership to either of the candidates. These figures give the Democrats a base of 24 noncompetitive districts and the Republicans a base of 23.

Three senate districts fit the definition of noncompetitive, targeted districts: the 35th, 38th, and 43rd districts. On the Democratic side, two districts had incumbent senators who had been targeted by Republican leadership in previous elections: Patrick Welch in the 38th District and Thomas Dunn in the 43rd District. The senate Democratic leadership initially provided support to both incumbent senators, but the expected push by the Republican leadership did not materialize. The amount of leadership/chamber group support provided to the two Republican challengers was very low. Because of the lack of a strong challenge to the incumbents, both of these districts were counted as noncompetitive, targeted districts for the senate Democrats, raising their total base to 26.

The third of these districts, the 35th District, was an open seat created in the Rockford area. It contained much of the old district represented by Democratic incumbent senator Joyce Holmberg, including part of the city of Rockford; because of redistricting, Senator Holmberg was running in the 34th District. The Republican leadership provided substantial support for their candidate, J. Bradley Burzynski, in the 35th District, who won with 55 percent of the vote. The Democrats chose to focus on reelecting Holmberg and did not invest heavily in the 35th District. The lack of a challenge from the Democratic leadership for an open seat makes the 35th a noncompetitive, targeted district for the Republicans, raising their total base to 24.

As a result of these leadership decisions and election outcomes, there were 50 seats (26 to the Democrats and 24 to the Republicans) where the senate leaders did not contest each other. The leaders focused on the remaining nine districts as the battleground for control of the senate. These nine districts consisted of two open seats where both chamber groups strongly supported the candidates and seven districts where one chamber group strongly supported a challenger against an incumbent. Without knowing who was running and the composition of the districts, the prospects seemed fairly even. The Democrats needed to win four seats to retain control, while the Republicans needed to win six of the nine.

Prospects. Going into the election, the match-up favored the Republicans. On the basis of past election results, seven of the districts could be expected to favor Republican candidates, with three classified as dominant-Republican districts and four as competitive-Republican districts. Of those seven Republican-dominant districts, the Republicans had three incumbents and the Democrats had two incumbents and two seats open. Two districts leaned Democratic, but both were represented by longtime incumbent Republican senators.

Money in Competitive, Targeted Senate Districts

The nine competitive, targeted races in the senate in 1992 were in the 7th, 18th, 24th, 29th, 34th, 37th, 39th, 55th, and 58th districts (table 6.2, p. 153). The geographical areas where these districts lie represent the battleground areas for the 1990s under the new legislative map. Five of the districts are suburban districts located entirely or in part in Cook County. The 7th District combines territory in northwest Chicago with territory in suburban Cook County. The 18th District is in the southwestern suburbs of Cook County, while the 24th is primarily in the far western suburbs of Cook County with a little of the district extending into

DuPage County. The 29th is in the far northern Cook County suburbs with a little of the district extending into Lake County. The 39th Senate District is in the far western suburbs with half the district in Cook County and half in DuPage County.

Four of the districts are located in "downstate" Illinois (that area of the state not in Chicago and not in suburban Cook County or DuPage, Will, Kane, Lake, or McHenry counties). The 34th Senate District lies at the top of Illinois along the Wisconsin border. It contains a large portion of the city of Rockford, the city of Belvidere, and more rural areas, primarily in Boone County. The 37th District contains all or part of eight counties in far northwestern Illinois with part of the district bordering on Iowa and part bordering on Wisconsin. The 55th and 58th senate districts are in southwestern Illinois. The 55th contains all or part of six counties with the largest portion of the district lying in Madison and Marion counties. The 58th lies along the Missouri border in far southwestern Illinois. It contains all or part of four counties with the largest portions lying in Randolph and Perry counties.

Contribution Totals. Looking at the totals for the nine competitive, targeted senate districts (table 6.2, p. 153), the Republican candidates reported slightly more than $150,000 more in receipts than did the Democratic candidates. Because they had more funds available at the beginning of the general election period, the Republicans outspent the Democrats by $334,000. Within the totals, candidates from both parties received about the same percentage of their receipts from individuals and not-itemized contributions. The primary difference lies in the percentage of receipts from leaders/political sources and those from interest groups and corporations. While the Democratic candidates received approximately the same percentage of their support from leaders/political sources as from interest group sources (41 percent to 44 percent), Republican candidates received 59 percent of their financial support from leaders/political sources and only 27 percent from interest group sources. Leadership money has two distinct advantages for candidates: a candidate receiving large leadership contributions does not have to engage in the same amount of fundraising activity as a candidate who relies primarily on interest group and individuals, and leadership resources can usually be generated more quickly and deployed in a more coordinated manner than contributions from individuals or groups.

Looking at the detailed breakout of the receipts by the candidates in the nine senate races (table 6.2), while contributions from leader and chamber committees is the largest category for candidates of both parties, the Republicans received a much greater percentage of their total from leadership sources. While leadership contributions accounted for slightly more than a third of the receipts of the Democratic candidates ($709,000), the Republican candidates received more than half of their receipts from the leadership ($1.2 million). The average leadership support for Democratic candidates was $79,000 while the average for Republican candidates was $134,000.

Beyond the major difference in support from leadership, the receipts data document expected differences in interest group support. Democratic candidates received strong support from union ($427,000) and law ($115,000) groups while the support provided by these groups for Republican candidates was very limited. In contrast, Republican candidates received much stronger support from health ($101,000), business/professional ($318,000), and finance/insurance ($81,000) groups than did the Democratic candidates, although support for Democratic candidates from business/professional groups ($191,000) was still significant. While acknowledging that leadership and chamber committee support come indirectly from interest groups, the relative importance of issue group* contributions to these races is still noteworthy, exceeding the totals by union and law for Republican candidates and those by finance/insurance and health for Democratic candidates.

Only in one area were receipts approximately equal for candidates from both parties. Contributions from individuals and not-itemized contributions make up almost the same percentage of the receipts for candidates from both parties. They are tied with business/professional contributions for the second-most important source of contributions for the Republicans and are the third-most important source for Democratic candidates behind leadership and union contributions.

Contributions and Spending in Selected Individual Districts. The contribution and spending patterns and the outcomes in the 39th and 55th districts illustrate the role of money and legislative leaders in targeted senate elections in 1992.

---

* "Issue Groups" contains single issue, ideological groups such as pro-choice and pro-life proponents, NRA, and Christian Right. It also includes social service and environmental groups such as senior citizens, Sierra Club, and Vietnam vets, but these groups have very little money compared to the single-issue groups.

39th Senate District. This district is located in the far western suburbs, 60 percent in Cook County and 40 percent in DuPage County. The Republican candidate was incumbent house member Dan Cronin. The Democratic candidate was incumbent senator Ted E. Leverenz. The district contains only a small part of Leverenz's old district from the 1982 map. Based on previous voting behavior the district is classified as a dominant-Republican district. Pres. George Bush won the district by 5 percent while Republican candidates won the U of I trustee vote by 54.7 percent. Both house districts covered by the 39th Senate District elected Republicans. The Republican Cronin won with 60.7 percent of the vote.

The two candidates spent a total of $498,000, with Cronin outspending Leverenz $287,000 to $211,000 (table 6.4, p. 155). The $134,000 in support Cronin received from the Republican leadership was more than twice the $63,000 Leverenz received from the Democratic leadership. Almost half (48 percent) of Cronin's receipts came from leadership, while less than a third (31 percent) of Leverenz's support came from leadership.

In addition to receipts from political sources, Leverenz received strong support from unions, business groups, and individual/not-itemized contributions. Cronin received strong support from business and professional groups, finance and insurance groups, health groups, and individual/not-itemized contributions. Cronin, an attorney, received stronger support from lawyer groups than Leverenz.

While Leverenz was an incumbent legislator and was well funded, he was running in new territory that leaned very strongly Republican against a well-known and well-regarded member of the house. Cronin made the most of the opportunity and ran a good campaign that produced a one-sided victory.

55th Senate District. This district of small towns and rural areas is located in southwestern Illinois. It stretches from eastern Madison and St. Clair counties to western Marion County and contains parts of Clinton, Fayette, and Bond counties. The Republican candidate was Frank Watson, the incumbent senator who was first elected in 1982. The Democratic challenger was Craig Virgin, a former Olympic athlete running for public office for the first time. The district is classified as competitive Democratic. Bill Clinton won the district in the 1992 presidential election by 8 percent, and Democratic candidates for the U of I trustees carried the district with 53 percent of the vote. Of the two house districts covered by the senate district, one elected a Democrat and the other a Republican. The Republican Watson won with 55.4 percent of the vote.

Together the two candidates spent a total of $724,000, making the race the most expensive legislative race in Illinois in 1992 (table 6.5, p. 156). Watson outspent Virgin by a total of $393,000 to $331,000. Both candidates received approximately the same amount of support from leadership ($149,000 to $147,000), which accounted for almost the same portion of their total general election receipts (47 percent to 46 percent). Virgin received more in transfers from other candidates, resulting in a greater overall percentage of his support from political sources.

Besides leadership support, Virgin received strong support from unions ($83,000), issues groups (primarily pro-choice), lawyer groups, and individuals/not-itemized contributions (table 6.5). Watson received strong support from business groups ($55,000) and received individual/not-itemized contributions ($59,000) from issue groups (conservative, pro-family). In addition, Watson began the general election period with $114,000 in his campaign fund. He reported receipts of $61,000 for the primary period, June 1-June 30, which came largely from business groups, and individual/not-itemized contributions. This carryover allowed him to spend $77,000 more than he took in during the general election period.

The voters in the new 55th District had tended to vote Democratic in past elections and voted Democratic in 1992 for president and U of I trustees. But the new 55th District was quite similar to the old 55th District, and that district had elected Frank Watson to the senate three times by comfortable margins. Watson's personal strength in the district and his ability to match and exceed the large amount spent by Virgin produced another comfortable victory margin.

Outcomes and Overall Spending. Spending for the nine competitive, targeted senate races totaled $4.5 million. That is an average of $500,000 a race or $250,000 a candidate (table 6.2, p. 153). When the partisan leadership groups make a serious commitment to a legislative race, the impact on the cost of the race is dramatic. In the nine competitive, targeted races, the Republican candidate outspent the Democrat in six races, the Democratic candidate outspent the Republican in two races and the spending in one race was virtually even. In the two races where the Democrats had a spending advantage, they won one race and lost one. The Republicans won the six races where they outspent the Democrats, as well as the one race where the spending was even. The overall spending advantage for the Republicans in these nine competitive, targeted races was substantial, over $334,000 or a difference of over $37,000 per race. The difference in resources available to spend was primarily due to the greater amount of support provided for Republican candidates by the senate Republican leadership. While the senate Democratic leadership provided an average of $79,000 in support to their candidates in targeted races, the senate Republicans provided an average of $134,000, a difference of $55,000 per race (table 6.2, p. 153). The Democratic advantage in the two districts where they outspent the Republicans was $28,000 in the 29th Senate District and $44,000 in the 24th Senate District (appendix E.3, p. 195). The Republican spending advantage was the greatest in the 34th Senate District, where the Republican challenger outspent the Democratic incumbent by $145,000 (appendix E.5, 197p.). In the 39th (table 6.4, p. 155), 55th (table 6.5, p. 156), 7th, 18th, and 58th (appendix E.1, E.2, and E.7, pp. 193, 194, and 199) senate districts the Republican candidates enjoyed spending advantages between $41,000 and $76,000. In all but one of the nine competitive, targeted senate races, the Democrats were unable to overcome the Republicans' advantages of favorable districts, money, and campaign organization and delivery. The final result of 8 wins out of the 9 races gave the Republicans a total of 32 out of the 59 senate districts and control of the senate for the first time since 1972.

As noted in chapter 2, in 1993 the Senate Republican Campaign Committee reported substantial amount of expenditures that actually occurred in 1992 in support of senate candidates in the general election. The data presented here do not include those expenditures. If they were included they would make the gap even wider between the support provided by the senate Republican leadership to targeted races and the support provided by the senate Democratic leadership. This would reinforce, but not alter, the basic conclusions drawn from the data.

Looking back at the preelection projections for the senate elections, the only real surprises were the lack of strong Republican challenges in the 38th and 43rd districts. The remaining battles shaped up as expected. The Republican candidates spent more overall and had stronger leadership support than did the Democrats. Union money went overwhelmingly to Democratic candidates, business support was mixed but favored Republicans, while health and lawyer money tended to offset each other. In the end, the combination of a strong map, a spending advantage, and good campaigns resulted in the senate Republicans gaining control of the senate in a year when the national Republican ticket did very poorly in Illinois and the Democratic candidate for the U.S. Senate won. Among the nine competitive, targeted races, the Republicans won both open seats, kept four of the five Republican incumbents they were defending, and defeated two of the three Democratic incumbents where they made a strong challenge.

House Leadership Election Strategies and Prospects

Strategies. Prior to the 1992 election the Democrats held a 72-46 majority in the house. In drawing the house districts in the new map, the Republicans used the same strategic goals that were used in constructing the senate districts. This resulted, in the 1992 election, in 17 districts where the Democrats ran unopposed while only 7 Republican candidates ran unopposed. In addition there were 31 districts in which Democrats won with more than 60 percent of the votes and 27 districts where the Republican won with more than 60 percent of the votes. Finally, there were three districts where the Democrats won with between 55 percent and 59 percent of the vote and six districts in which the Republicans won with the same margin. In none of these districts were there any major transfers of funds or in-kind contributions or support provided to either candidate by leadership. These outcomes resulted in a base of 51 noncompetitive districts for the Democrats and 40 for the Republicans.

There also were six districts where the winning candidate had between 52 percent and 54 percent of the vote. In four of these districts, incumbents who were running received leadership support while the challenger did not. In all four cases the incumbent won: three Democrats and one Republican. Two districts had open seats. In one, the Democratic candidate received strong leadership support and won, while the challenger received little leadership support. In the other, the Republican candidate received strong leadership support and won, while the challenger was again on his own. All six districts qualify as noncompetitive, targeted districts. Adding these four Democratic wins to the Democratic total results in a base of 55 districts, while adding the two Republican wins produced a base of 42 districts for the Republicans.

The result of these leadership decisions and election outcomes was to reduce the battleground between the Democratic and Republican leadership from a potential of 118 districts to 21 competitive, targeted districts. These 21 districts consisted of 6 districts with open seats where both candidates received strong leadership support, 3 districts in which two incumbents were facing each other, and 12 districts in which an incumbent faced a challenger who was strongly supported by leadership of the opposition party. Without knowing the specifics of these 21 districts and the candidates, the numbers appeared to favor the Democrats. The Democrats needed to win only 5 seats to reach a total of 60 and retain their majority, while the Republicans needed to win 18 of the 21 targeted districts to gain a majority.

Prospects. Of the 21 districts in play, 9 strongly favored the Republicans on the basis of past voting behavior, while 10 leaned Republican. Only 2 of the districts leaned Democratic on the basis of previous voting patterns for statewide and federal elections. In the 9 strong Republican districts there were 3 open seats, 3 districts pitting two incumbents, 2 districts with Democratic incumbents, and 1 district with a Republican incumbent. In the 10 districts that leaned Republican, there were 4 Republican incumbents, 4 Democratic incumbents, and 2 open seats. In the 2 Democratic-leaning districts, there was 1 open seat and 1 incumbent Democrat. In all, the Democrats had 10 incumbents running in the targeted districts, 7 running against challengers, and 3 running against a Republican incumbent. The Republicans had 8 incumbents running, 5 running against a challenger and 3 running against a Democratic incumbent. Three of the open seats were in strong Republican districts, 2 were in Republican-leaning districts and 1 was in a Democratic-leaning district.

Even assuming that the Republicans would retain the 5 districts where they had an incumbent facing a challenger in districts that favored Republicans, the prospects for the Democrats picking up the five wins necessary to retain their majority seemed good because of the number of incumbents they had running.

Money in Competitive, Targeted House Districts

The 21 targeted races in the house in 1992 follow the same general geographic pattern evident in the targeted senate districts (table 6.3, p. 154). Nine of the districts are suburban districts located in the Cook County area. The 35th, 36th, 47th, and 77th house districts are all located in the western suburbs of Cook County. The 37th and 80th districts are located in southern Cook and northern Will counties. The 58th District is located in far northeastern Cook County, while the 59th and 60th districts are located in far southeastern Lake County along the border of Cook County.

Three of the districts are in northwestern Illinois. The 68th House District is located in the Rockford area, primarily in Winnebago County outside Rockford and in Boone County. The 73rd and 74th house districts make up the 37th Senate District; they are largely rural districts located in far northeastern Illinois.

Eight of the districts are located in central Illinois. The 85th District is located along the Indiana border in east-central Illinois in the Kankakee area. The 87th House District is located in Livingston and McLean counties in north-central Illinois in the Pontiac area. The 95th District is located in the Macomb area and covers nine counties. Both the 87th and 95th house districts are largely rural. The 99th District in the Springfield area and the 102nd District in the Decatur area are in central Illinois. They both contain part of a major downstate city and large areas of rural territory. The 103rd and 104th house districts in east-central Illinois contain the cities of Champaign and Urbana along with surrounding rural territory. The two remaining districts are located in southern Illinois. The 106th House District is located in far east-central Illinois along the Indiana border in the counties of Coles, Edgar, and Clark. It is a mixed district containing equal amounts of rural and urban areas. The 110th House District is located in southwestern Illinois and contains parts of Madison, St. Clair, and Clinton counties. It is a mixed district containing both urban and rural areas.

Contribution Totals. The total receipts for the 21 competitive, targeted house districts (table 6.3, p. 154) show that the Democratic candidates reported receiving slightly more than $600,000 more than Republican candidates during the general election period. Because the Republican candidates raised more money prior to the beginning of the general election period and then spent more of that money on hand during the general election period, the net Democratic advantage in expenditures for the period was $449,000. While the Republican candidates received somewhat higher percentages of their receipts from individuals and interest groups/corporations, the major difference was in support from political sources: Democratic candidates received 63 percent of their receipts from political sources compared to 42 percent for Republican candidates.

Looking at the detailed breakout of receipts, the most striking feature is the difference between leadership support of Republican and Democratic candidates. Democratic candidates received $1.58 million from leader and chamber political committees, while Republican candidates received $744,000 (table 6.3, p. 154). The average leadership support for Democratic candidates was $75,000, while the average for Republican candidates was $37,000.

As with the data on senate candidates, the detailed data on receipts show expected differences between Democratic and Republican candidates, except in the area of individual and not-itemized receipts. Contributions from individuals and small, not-itemized contributions were more significant for Republican candidates than for Democratic candidates, accounting for 21 percent of their receipts, although the actual totals for the two parties were close. Democratic candidates received significantly more from union ($285,000) and law ($96,000) groups than did Republican candidates (table 6.3). In contrast, business/professional ($298,000), health ($217,000), and finance/insurance ($69,000) groups strongly supported Republican candidates over Democratic candidates. While Republican candidates received substantially more from business/professional groups, the contributions from these groups still accounted for a significant portion of the receipts of Democratic candidates ($142,000). Issue group contributions, as in the senate race, played a secondary role but were more significant than law or union group contributions for the Republicans and more significant than finance or healthcare groups for the Democrats.

Contributions and Spending in Selected Individual Races. The contribution and spending patterns in the 58th, 60th, 77th, and 103rd house districts illustrate the role of money and the legislative leaders in targeted house races in 1992.

58th House District. The 58th House District is located along Lake Michigan in the far northeastern suburbs of Cook County. It is part of the 29th Senate District, where the incumbent Republican senator was defeated in a targeted race. The Republican candidate for the house was James D. Henderson, who was running for the first time. The Democratic candidate was Jeffrey M. Schoenberg, an incumbent house member. Although the district is classified as dominant Republican Bill Clinton won the district by 15 percent, while Republican candidates won for the U of I Board of Trustees, but with only 50.7 percent of the vote. In the companion 57th House District, Bush won the presidential vote by 2 percent and Republican candidates for U of I trustee won with 57.2

percent of the vote. The Democrat Schoenberg won with 56.6 percent of the vote.

Together the two candidates spent $366,000, making it the most expensive house race in 1992 (table 6.6, p. 157). Schoenberg outspent Henderson $201,000 to $165,000, a margin of $36,000. Schoenberg received 31 percent of his receipts from the Democratic leadership, a total of $60,000. Henderson received about half as much from the house Republican leadership, $32,000. He also received $55,000 from other political sources, primarily local party officials, making the total portion of his receipts from political sources 62 percent.

Schoenberg overcame Henderson's advantage in fundraising from political sources by raising $78,000 in contributions from individuals and not-itemized contributions, which accounted for 40 percent of his total. Schoenberg also raised significant amounts from union, lawyer, and healthcare groups. In addition to political sources, Henderson received strong support from individuals/not-itemized contributions and business groups.

In spite of the strong Republican voting history of precincts in the district, a majority of the voters in the district voted for Bill Clinton; Carol Moseley-Braun, the Democratic candidate for U.S. Senate; and for Schoenberg, who led the ticket. And the Democratic candidates for U of I Board of Trustees came within .7 percent of carrying the district. In a district that gave Gov. Jim Edgar 63 percent of the vote two years earlier, Henderson, the Republican, was clearly running against a Democratic trend. The $201,000 spent by Schoenberg also played a major role in the outcome. Being outspent by $36,000 made Henderson's task even more difficult.

60th House District. This district is located in far southeastern Lake County, bordering on Lake Michigan on the east and Cook County on the south, with a small portion actually in Cook County. The two candidates, Charles A. Cardella, the Republican, and Lauren Beth Gash, the Democrat, were both making their first runs for the legislature. The district is classified as competitive Republican. The district gave Bill Clinton a 10 percent margin of victory in the presidential election in 1992, while Republican candidates for the U of I Board of Trustees won the district with 51.1 percent of the vote. The Democratic Gash won with 60.6 percent of the vote.

The two candidates spent a total of $263,000, with Gash outspending Cardella $166,000 to $97,000 (table 6.7, p. 158). The house Democratic leadership provided $89,000 in support for Gash, accounting for 54 percent of her total receipts. Cardella received $50,000 worth of support from the house Republican leadership, which represented 48 percent of his total receipts.

The two primary sources of nonleadership support for Cardella came from individual/not-itemized contributions and business groups. Gash received strong support from individual/not-itemized contributions, labor unions, and pro-choice issue groups.

This district was initially considered a safe Republican district, and no Democrat ran in the primary. Candidates are often recruited and placed on the ballot by party officials to provide at least some opposition to otherwise unopposed candidates. In this case, an assessment by the Democrats of the district and the candidate, Cardella, who won the Republican primary, prompted a more serious effort. When Cardella's campaign appeared to be in trouble, the house Democrats shifted more resources into the race. Gash ran a strong campaign and when the polling numbers turned around, Cardella had trouble raising money. Gash's pro-choice position against Cardella's conservatism attracted pro-choice money to the race. The result was a $69,000 spending advantage for Gash (table 6.7, p. 158). As with Moseley in the 99th District (p. 125), leadership spending allowed a candidate to be competitive in a district where a Democratic candidate would have serious problems raising enough money to be competitive.

77th House District. This district is located in the far western suburbs of Cook County. It is one of the house districts contained in the 39th Senate District, where the Republican senate candidate won a targeted race with almost 61 percent of the vote. The candidates for the house district were the Republican Angelo "Skip" Saviano, a former township supervisor, and the Democrat Geoffrey S. Obrzut, an incumbent house member. The district is classified as competitive Republican. Bill Clinton carried the district in the 1992 presidential election by less than 1 percent, while the Democratic candidates for U of I trustee won with less than 1 percent of the vote. Republican Saviano captured the house seat with 54.7 percent of the vote.

Together the two candidates spent $313,000, one of only six house races where spending exceeded $300,000 (table 6.8, p. 159). Obrzut outspent Saviano $175,000 to $138,000, a margin of $37,000. The house Democratic leadership provided $102,000 in support for Obrzut, accounting for 60 percent of his receipts. Saviano received a net of

$28,000 in support from the house Republican leadership. He also received $47,000 in support from local party and candidate committees, making the total portion of his support received from political sources (58 percent) roughly the same as that for Obrzut (61 percent).

Saviano received 21 percent of his support from individual/not-itemized contributions and 21 percent from interest groups. Most of his interest group support came from business and health groups. Obrzut received only 7 percent of his support from individual/not-itemized contributions and 32 percent from interest groups. The largest sources of interest group support for Obrzut came from business groups, labor unions, law groups, and issue groups (pro-choice).

While Obrzut had a spending advantage provided by the house Democratic leadership and an incumbency advantage in part of the district, Saviano clearly had an advantage in local political support and ties to the district, both of which are reflected in his contribution data. In spite of the relatively strong showing of other Democratic candidates in the district, Saviano won by a comfortable margin.

103rd House District. This district is located in east-central Illinois. It is located primarily in Champaign County, but includes a part of Ford County to the north. The district, which contains the city of Champaign and part of Urbana and is 89 percent urban, had an open seat in 1992. Gregory D. Cozad, the Republican, faced Laurel Lunt Prussing, the Democrat, with both candidates making their first run for the state legislature. On the basis of past voting behavior the district is classified as dominant Republican. In 1992 Bill Clinton won the district by more than 12 percent, while the U of I trustee candidates for the Republicans won with 54.6 percent of the vote. Democratic Prussing won with 50.1 percent of the vote, a margin of 34 votes.

The two candidates spent a total of $345,000, making it one of six house races where total spending exceeded $300,000 (table 6.9, p. 160). Spending by the two candidates was virtually even, with Cozad outspending Prussing $174,000 to $171,000. Cozad received 30 percent from political sources, of which $28,000 was from the Republican leadership. Individual/not-itemized contributions accounted for 35 percent of his receipts for the same time period. Thirty-five percent of Cozad's general election receipts came from interest groups, with business and healthcare groups providing the largest share. Because Cozad began the general election period with a balance of $77,000 in his political committee, he was able to spend $76,000 more than he took in for the period. The money Cozad raised in the primary period came from individuals and business groups.

For the general election period, Prussing received 82 percent from political sources, of which $128,000 was from the house Democratic leadership (table 6.9, p. 160). Individual/not-itemized contributions made up another 10 percent of her receipts, leaving only 8 percent of her receipts coming from interest groups. Her largest interest group contributors were labor unions.

As a well-funded candidate in a strongly Republican district, Cozad began the race as a strong favorite. Most of the public and media attention was focused on the race in the adjoining house district, which pitted two longtime incumbent legislators against each other. As was the case in the 99th District (see p. 125), signs of strength in Prussing's campaign and weakness in Cozad's suggested an opportunity for the house Democrats. The infusion of leadership support allowed Prussing to match Cozad's spending, giving Prussing more equal exposure to voters. The result was a razor thin victory for Prussing.

Outcomes and Overall Spending. Spending for the 21 competitive, targeted house races totaled $5.3 million. That is an average of $253,000 per race and or $126,500 per candidate (table 6.3, p. 154). As with the targeted senate races, the commitment of the house legislative leadership to a race resulted in dramatically higher spending in these contests. The Democrats outspent the Republicans in 15 of the 21 contested, targeted house races: 58th (table 6.6, p. 157), 60th (table 6.7, p. 158), 77th (table 6.8, p. 159), the 35th, 36th, 37th, 47th, 59th, 68th, 74th, 85th, 87th, 95th, 104th, and 106th districts (appendix E.8-E.22, pp. 200-214). The Democrats' advantage in the 15 districts where they outspent the Republicans ranged from $3,000 to $77,000. In only two of these cases was the Democrats' advantage less than $25,000 and in seven the advantage was over $40,000. Overall the Democrats won 8 of the 15 competitive, targeted house districts where they outspent the Republicans. Of those eight victories, five were in districts where their spending advantage exceeded $40,000. In six competitive, targeted house districts the Republican outspent the Democratic candidate: 99th (table 6.1, p. 152), 103rd (table 6.9, p. 160), the 73rd, 102nd, and 110th districts (appendix E.14, E.20, and E.23, pp. 206, 212, and 215). The Republicans' spending advantage in these six districts ranged from $3,000 to $59,000, with the advantage exceeding $25,000 in three of the six house districts.

The Republicans won only two of the six house districts where they outspent the Democrats.

The overall spending advantage for Democratic candidates in the 21 competitive, targeted house races was $449,000, a difference of over $21,000 per race. The differences in resources available to spend was primarily due to the greater amount of support provided for Democratic candidates by the house Democratic leadership. While the house Republican leadership provided an average of $37,000 in support to their candidates in targeted races, the house Democrats provided an average of $75,000, a difference of $38,000 per race (table 6.3, p. 154). Most of these districts were drawn to strongly favor Republican candidates. The difference in leadership support was a major factor in the Democrats' winning 12 of the 21 competitive, targeted house races. The 12-to-9 advantage for the Democrats in these races produced an overall Democratic margin of 67 to 51 in the house, a drop of 5 seats from 1990, but still a comfortable majority.

Of the 21 districts that became competitive targets, some were considered targets by both sides almost from the moment the 1992 map was complete. These included districts where (a) two incumbents were running against each other, (b) a Democrat had been elected in 1990 from a Republican-leaning district, (c) Republican incumbents were running in Democratic-leaning districts, and (d) no incumbent was running. Not all of these potential targets became competitive, targeted districts, but all were actively considered in early strategy sessions. Some of the competitive, targeted districts that the leaders committed to early turned out to be bad investments for one side or the other.

Other districts became competitive, targeted districts as the campaigns evolved. Dominant Republican districts such as the 37th, 60th, 68th, and 99th did not seem likely Democratic targets at the beginning of 1992, but strong Democratic candidates and Democratic leadership support made them targets as the election evolved. Part of the secret of success is being able to identify opportunities as the election develops and having the available resources to take advantage of those opportunities.

Because the Republicans controlled the redistricting process, the house Republicans had a strategic advantage going into the 1992 elections. The two sides fought for control of the house on a battleground that definitely tilted toward the Republicans. While the Republicans needed to win 18 of the 21 competitive, targeted districts, that task was made easier by the fact that 9 of these were classified as dominant Republican districts and 10 were classified as competitive Republican districts. Only two were classified as leaning Democratic, and one of those districts had been drawn to help elect a former Republican representative. If the Democrats were to retain control of the house, they would have to take advantage of a lead in fundraising, a more-experienced campaign team, and more incumbents. In the end, they used their assets to win 12 of the 9 competitive, targeted races.

Some of those victories were very narrow. Eight races were decided by less than 900 votes. Of these, the Democrats won five and the Republicans won three. A shift of 1,000 votes in three districts would have given the Democrats three more seats, while a shift of 850 votes in five districts would have given the Republicans five more seats. Had the results of these close races been different, the Democrats' margin in the house could have been as small as 62-56 or as wide as 70-48. These numbers give hope and concern to both sides as they face off for a decade-long battle over control of the house. Round two went to the house Republicans in the 1994 elections. Riding a Republican trend at the national and state level, the Republicans picked up 13 house seats and took control of the house by a margin of 64 to 54. Even as the new legislature was being sworn in, speculation about the 1996 elections had already begun.

Incumbency and the 1992 Legislative Elections

In addition to the factors of money, candidates, and campaign organizations, incumbency also played a role in the 1992 elections, particularly in the house. Incumbent legislators generally have an advantage because they are well known to voters, they have experience running for office—and winning—and because they are a known quantity to special interest groups from which they need support. Incumbents also require less support and training from the legislative leaders than do new candidates. Most observers assumed that incumbency would not be as big an advantage for Democrats under the new legislative map because the Republicans had tried to force many Democratic incumbents outside of Chicago to run in substantially new districts. That assumption was not entirely correct.

All new districts contain some of a legislator's old constituents. After a new map is drawn, incumbent legislators have the option, under provisions in the Illinois Constitution, of running in the district they live in or in any district that contains part of their old district from the previous map. If an incumbent legislator is elected from a district in which he/she does not live at the time of the election, the incumbent has 18 months to establish a legal residence in the new district.

Because of their large majority from the 1990 election (72-46), the house Democrats had more incumbents to begin with. In addition, a number of Republican house members filed for senate seats being vacated by the retirement of Republican senators, who were under no pressure to run again because of the adoption of a Republican map. For example, in the 50th Senate District the longtime incumbent Republican senator John "Doc" Davidson did not run for reelection. Rep. Karen Hasara easily won the nomination and was a easy winner in the general election. In all, the Democrats had 52 incumbents seek reelection to the house (44 percent of the 118 seats), while the Republicans had only 27 (23 percent of the 118 seats). Of the 52 Democratic incumbents seeking reelection, 47 of them (90 percent) won. Of the 27 Republican incumbents seeking reelection, 23 (85 percent) won. Even with a new legislative map, incumbency has its advantages.

In the senate, incumbency was not a significant factor. Both parties had 21 incumbents running for reelection. Of those, two Democratic incumbents and one Republican incumbent were defeated. In addition, both parties had 5 senate candidates who were incumbent house members trying to move into the senate; of those 10 former house members running for the senate, only one lost.

How incumbency and events can frustrate the intentions of those who drew the legislative maps is illustrated by the race for the 100th House District, which shares Springfield with the 99th House District. This district was drawn to favor a Republican candidate and to include the home of incumbent state representative Karen Hasara (R-Springfield). While it included much of the old district represented by incumbent state representative Mike Curran (D-Springfield), it did not include his home, which was now in the new 99th District. The objective was to force Curran to run against Hasara in a district tailored to her. Even if successful in the election, Curran would then have to move into the new district after the election. His other option would be to run in the 99th District, which contained much more new territory and was also strongly Republican. When the incumbent Republican state senator from the area decided to retire, Hasara ran for the senate and won election by a landslide with 69 percent of the vote. Curran chose to run in the 100th District. Facing a challenger running for the first time, the well-known and widely respected Curran was easily reelected. Under the old map drawn by the Democrats, the Springfield area had a Republican state senator and one Democratic and one Republican state representative. With Vickie Moseley's surprise victory in the 99th District, the Springfield area in 1993 was represented by a Republican state senator and two Democratic state representatives.

The Importance of Leadership Support

The data presented on competitive, targeted districts show leadership contributions to candidates in senate races as high as $228,000 and contributions to candidates in house races as high as $128,000. For some candidates, leadership contributions accounted for more than 70 percent of their total receipts. Overall, leadership support accounted for 44 percent of the receipts of senate candidates and 48 percent of the receipts of house candidates (see appendix E, pp. 193-215).

Leadership support has a number of advantages besides being a major source of the resources necessary to be competitive in an election. First, it comes without the expenditure of time and resources of the candidate and campaign organization that are usually required to raise large sums of money. Second, such support is usually comprehensive, including polling, targeting, strategy, campaign workers and staff, and mail and media expertise; thus, the resources are applied more efficiently than those from a number of sources might be. A legislative race with strong leadership involvement is very different from one without it.

Leadership Campaign Organizations

Going into the 1992 legislative elections, the conventional wisdom was that the Democrats' campaign organization in the house gave Democratic candidates an advantage, while for senate candidates, the advantage was with the Republicans. In the house, as noted in chapter 3, Speaker Madigan's campaign organization appeared to have an advantage in experience and continuity over that of minority leader Daniels. In the 1990 house elections, the Democrats had defeated four Republican incumbents and picked up an open seat previously held by a Republican for a gain of five seats. This increased the house Democrats' majority to 72-46. Because of their strong track record and large majority, the speaker and the house Democrats had no trouble raising money in spite of a map favoring the Republicans.

In the senate, the situation seemed to favor the Republicans. The Republican leadership, headed by senate minority leader James "Pate" Philip, had been in place since 1981 and a highly regarded former chief of staff with a strong track record in running campaigns had become chief of staff for a second time in 1991.On the Democratic side, senate president Philip J. Rock announced in 1991 that he would not seek reelection and his longtime chief of staff left to become the state auditor general. In addition, four of the six assistant majority leaders also announced their retirement, making most of the senate Democratic leadership team lame ducks. Senate leaders are elected for two-year terms at the beginning of each session. Because of this, new leaders for the senate Democrats would not be elected until the new legislature convened in Springfield in January after the election. The lame-duck status of the senate president and the map favoring the Republicans made fundraising more difficult. The instability and uncertainty of the Democrats' leadership situation and the changes in staff made organizing and executing a campaign covering all 59 districts difficult, particularly in comparison to the stability and experience of the Republicans.

The Role of Interest Groups in Competitive, Targeted Races

Competitive, targeted races in the 1992 legislative elections were very expensive. In the senate, a total of $4.50 million was spent on the nine competitive, targeted races. The average expenditure per candidate was $250,000 (table 6.2, p. 153). In the house, a total of $5.31 million was spent on the 21 competitive, targeted races. The average expenditure per candidate was $126,500 (table 6.3, p. 154). The magnitude of these numbers makes it difficult for all but a few interest groups to play more than a supporting role in these types of races. A $10,000 contribution to a candidate in each of these 30 races, a total of $300,000, would exceed the total expenditures on legislative elections in 1992 of all but seven of the interest groups examined in chapter 4. While $10,000 would certainly have an impact, it represents just 4 percent of the spending by a candidate in a targeted senate race and less than 8 percent of the spending by a candidate in a targeted house race.

More important, these 30 races, while important to the leaders and critical in determining who controls the house or senate, will produce only 30 of the 177 legislators who will make up the Illinois General Assembly. The contribution patterns found in chapter 4 show that all interest groups are concerned with using campaign contributions to provide as much access to as many legislators as possible, not just those elected in competitive, targeted races. For most interest groups, access is much more important than influencing elections. So while these 30 competitive, targeted races attracted a good deal of attention and money from interest groups, races where the outcome was not in doubt also attracted the attention and even more of the money of interest groups.

Although it is difficult for a single interest group to have an impact on targeted races, coordinated contributions from businesses, health professionals, attorneys, or unions can make a difference. In some races, a particular interest group sector acts as a key player, providing a large percentage of a candidate's receipts. Finally, the legislative leaders are not printing their own money to provide contributions and support for candidates. The resources used by the leaders to influence the outcome of targeted races come primarily from interest groups and corporations. The candidate will not know specifically where the leadership money came from, but the leader and the interest group will know. Interest groups that contribute heavily to legislative leaders expect access and will lobby the leaders to influence their members, particularly those members who owe part or all of their election to the leaders.

The Impact of Political Money on the Legislative Process in Illinois

Even a casual observer of the Illinois General Assembly over the past decade will recognize the tremendous growth in the power of the legislative leaders. Their control over both the agenda and the content of the policy outcomes has become almost absolute. Many factors have contributed to this trend. Strong local and county political organizations were once critical players in the legislature; now there is only a void left by their continuing decline. Whether meaningful state political parties ever existed in relation to the General Assembly is debatable; certainly they were not a factor in the legislature of the 1980s and do not currently exist.

During the long tenure of Gov. James R. Thompson, a pattern of decision-making at the "summit" between the governor and the four legislative leaders developed, which both affirmed the growing power of the legislative leaders and contributed to it. Leadership's monopoly on the ever-growing staff resources of the General Assembly has also been an important source of their power.

But the fundraising and campaign activity of the legislative leaders has changed the nature of the legislature more than any other factor. Illinois has as wide open a campaign finance system as there is in any state. The interest group community in Illinois generally regards contributing to leaders as both a prudent and a highly efficient way of gaining influence. Smart, ambitious legislative leaders, using the power of their offices to benefit from the unrestricted campaign finance system and the willing cooperation of interest groups have created campaign organizations that raise large sums of money and assure sophisticated, highly effective campaigns for candidates running in competitive, targeted races. Candidates who are elected with substantial leadership support go to the legislature with allegiances and obligations that are not easily turned aside. Members who are elected without leadership assistance still know that the electoral performance and prospects of their party in their legislative chamber are also dependent on their leader's campaign and fundraising efforts. In the absence of any change in the dynamics of the way campaigns are financed, leadership power in the legislature and leadership power in controlling critical campaigns will continue to reinforce and intensify each other.

The probable future of the financing of legislative elections in Illinois raises questions about control of and access to the electoral process and the nature of representation. Even more important to the long-term health of the political system are the public's perceptions of a system in which it appears that money and the decisions of a few legislative leaders determine the destiny of candidates and the shape of public policy. There are alternatives to a continuation of the current campaign finance trends, but they are not without costs.

Table 6.1
99th House District - Results, Receipts, and Expenditures
1992 General Election
(June 30 - Dec. 31, 1992)
(Amounts in units of $1,000)

	DeMarco Republican		Moseley (Winner) Democrat	
Results	41.0%		59.0%	
Percent of Receipts by Source				
Individual/Not-itemized/Misc.	49		4	
Leader/Political	10		80	
Interest Group/Corporation	41		16	
Total	100		100	
Receipts by Source (Breakout of above categories)				
Individual/Not-itemized/Misc.	$34	49	$3	4
Loan from Candidate	0	0	3	4
Leader/Chamber Committee	7	10	53	76
Candidate/Local Party	3	4	3	4
Business/Professional	15	22	0	0
Financial	3	4	0	0
Union	2	3	4	6
Health	3	4	1	2
Law	1	2	3	4
Issue Group	1	2	0	0
Total	$69	100	$70	100

Net Receipts and Expenditures

DeMarco		Moseley	
Beginning Balance	$29	Beginning Balance	$2
Ending Balance	1	Ending Balance	2
Receipts	56	Receipts	50
In-kind	13	In-kind	20
Total Receipts	$69	Total Receipts	$70
Expenditures	84	Expenditures	49
In-kind	13	In-kind	20
Total Expenditures	$97	Total Expenditures	$69

Table 6.2
Targeted Senate Races 1992 General Elections
Campaign Receipts by Source and Net Expenditures

(June 30 - Dec. 31, 1992)
(7th, 18th, 24th, 29th, 34th, 37th, 39th, 55th, and 58th Districts)
(Amounts in units of $1,000)

Percent of Receipts by Source†	Republican	Democrat	Total
Individual/Not-itemized/Misc.	16	16	15
Leader/Political	59	41	50
Interest Group/Corporation	27	44	35
Total	102	101	100

Receipts by Source† (Breakout of above categories)

	Republican	%	Democrat	%	Total	%
Individual/Not-itemized/Misc.	$317	14	$323	15	$640	15
Loan from Candidate	40	2	0	0	40	1
Leader/ Chamber Committee	1,204	54	709	34	1,913	44
Candidate/Local Party	108	5	143	7	251	6
Business/Professional	318	14	191	9	509	12
Financial	81	4	68	3	149	4
Union	15	1	427	20	442	10
Health	101	5	20	1	121	3
Law	12	1	115	6	127	3
Issue Group	45	2	94	5	139	3
Total	$2,241	102	$2,090	100	$4,331	101

Net Expenditures: Total=$4.502 million		
	Republicans	$2.418 Million
	Democrats	$2.084
	Difference	+ $.334 Republicans

Average expenditures per race	= $500,000
Average expenditures per candidate	= $250,000
Average senate Republican leadership contribution	= $134,000
Average senate Democratic leadership contribution	= $ 79,000

† Percentages may not total 100 due to rounding.

Table 6.3
Targeted House Races 1992 General Elections
Campaign Receipts by Source and Net Expenditures

(June 30 - Dec. 31, 1992)
(35th, 36th, 37th, 47th, 58th, 59th, 60th, 68th, 73rd, 74th, 77th,
(80th, 85th, 87th, 95th, 99th, 102nd, 103rd, 104th, 106th and 110th Districts)
(Amounts in units of $1,000)

Percent of Receipts by Source	**Republican**	**Democrat**	**Total**
Individual/Not-itemized/Misc.	27	14	20
Leader/Political	42	63	54
Interest Group/Corporation	31	23	26
Total	100	100	100

Receipts by Source (Breakout of above categories)

	Republican		Democrat		Total	
Individual/Not-itemized/Misc.	$454	21	$382	14	$836	17
Loan from Candidate	119	6	8	0	127	3
Leader/Chamber Committee	744	35	1,584	58	2,328	48
Candidate/Local Party	144	7	132	5	276	6
Business/Professional	298	14	142	5	440	9
Financial	69	3	14	1	83	2
Union	25	1	285	10	310	6
Health	217	10	34	1	251	5
Law	19	1	96	3	115	2
Issue Group	45	2	70	3	115	2
Total	$2,134	100	$2,747	100	$4,881	100

Net Expenditures: Total=$5.313 million		
	Republicans	$2.418 Million
	Democrats	$2.867
	Difference	+ $.449 Democrats

Average expenditures per race	= $253,000
Average expenditures per candidate	= $126,500
Average senate Republican leadership contribution	= $37,000
Average senate Democratic leadership contribution	= $75,000

Table 6.4
39th Senate District - Results, Receipts, and Expenditures
1992 General Election

(June 30 - Dec. 31, 1992)
(Amounts in units of $1,000)

	Cronin (Winner) Republican		Leverenz Democrat (Incumbent)	
Results	60.7%		39.3%	
Percent of Receipts by Source†				
Individual/Not-itemized/Misc.	14		23	
Leader/Political	53		35	
Interest Group/Corporation	31		42	
Total	98		100	
Receipts by Source† (Breakout of above categories)				
Individual/Not-itemized/Misc.	$39	14	$46	23
Loan from Candidate	0	0	0	0
Leader/Chamber Committee	134	48	63	31
Candidate/Local Party	15	5	9	4
Business/Professional	44	15	35	17
Financial	14	5	1	0
Union	1	0	42	21
Health	18	6	3	2
Law	13	5	3	2
Issue Group	0	0	1	0
Total	$278	98	$203	100

Net Receipts and Expenditures

Cronin		Leverenz	
Beginning Balance	20	Beginning Balance	23
Ending Balance	16	Ending Balance	16
Receipts	174	Receipts	134
In-kind	116	In-kind	69
Give Back	-8	Total Receipts	203
Total Receipts	282		
Expenditures	179	Expenditures	142
In-kind	116	In-kind	69
Give back	-8	Total Expenditures	211
Total Expenditures	287		

† Percentages may not total 100 due to rounding.

Table 6.5
55th Senate District - Results, Receipts, and Expenditures
1992 General Election

(June 30 - Dec. 31, 1992)
(Amounts in units of $1,000)

	Watson (Winner) Republican (Incumbent)	Virgin Democrat
Results	55.4%	44.6%
Percent of Receipts by Source		
Individual/Not-itemized/Misc.	19	8
Leader/Political	50	53
Interest Group/Corporation	31	39
Total	100	100

Receipts by Source (Breakout of above categories)

	Watson $	Watson %	Virgin $	Virgin %
Individual/Not-itemized/Misc.	$59	19	$26	8
Loan from Candidate	0	0	0	0
Leader/Chamber Committee	149	47	147	46
Candidate/Local Party	8	3	23	7
Business/Professional	55	17	5	2
Financial	6	2	1	0
Union	0	0	83	26
Health	7	2	2	0
Law	2	0	14	4
Issue Group	30	10	22	7
Total	$316	100	$323	100

Net Receipts and Expenditures

Watson		Virgin	
Beginning Balance	114	Beginning Balance	7
Ending Balance	37	Ending Balance	0
Receipts	165	Receipts	156
In-kind	154	In-kind	200
Give Back	-3	Give Back	-33
Total Receipts	316	Total Receipts	323
Expenditures	242	Expenditures	164
In-kind	154	In-kind	200
Give Back	-3	Give Back	-33
Total Expenditures	393	Total Expenditures	331

Table 6.6
58th House District - Results, Receipts, and Expenditures
1992 General Election

(June 30 - Dec. 31, 1992)
(Amounts in units of $1,000)

	Henderson Republican		Schoenberg (Winner) Democrat (Incumbent)	
Results	43.4%		56.6%	
Percent of Receipts by Source†				
Individual/Not-itemized/Misc.	23		40	
Leader/Political	62		33	
Interest Group/Corporation	15		29	
Total	100		102	
Receipts by Source† (Breakout of above categories)				
Individual/Not-itemized/Misc.	$33	23	$78	40
Loan from Candidate	0	0	0	0
Leader/Chamber Committee	32	23	60	31
Candidate/Local Party	55	39	3	2
Business/Professional	14	10	6	3
Financial	6	4	2	1
Union	0	0	18	9
Health	0	0	11	6
Law	1	1	10	5
Issue Group	0	0	8	4
Total	$141	100	$196	101

Net Receipts and Expenditures

Henderson		Schoenberg	
Beginning Balance	25	Beginning Balance	6
Ending Balance	0	Ending Balance	0
Receipts	107	Receipts	127
In-kind	55	In-kind	103
Give Back	-22	Give Back	-34
Total Receipts	140	Total Receipts	196
Expenditures	132	Expenditures	132
In-kind	55	In-kind	103
Give Back	-22	Give Back	-34
Total Expenditures	165	Total Expenditures	201

† Percentages may not total 100 due to rounding.

Table 6.7
60th House District - Results, Receipts, and Expenditures
1992 General Election
(June 30 - Dec. 31, 1992)
(Amounts in units of $1,000)

	Cardella		Gash (Winner)	
	Republican		Democrat	
Results	39.4%		60.6%	
Percent of Receipts by Source				
Individual/Not-itemized/Misc.	23		23	
Leader/Political	56		56	
Interest Group/Corporation	21		21	
Total	100		100	
Receipts by Source (Breakout of above categories)				
Individual/Not-itemized/Misc.	$24	23	$38	23
Loan from Candidate	0	0	0	0
Leader/Chamber Committee	50	48	89	54
Candidate/Local Party	8	8	3	2
Business/Professional	13	12	2	1
Financial	3	3	0	0
Union	0	0	14	8
Health	1	1	1	1
Law	1	1	4	2
Issue Group	4	4	15	9
Total	$104	100	$166	100

Net Receipts and Expenditures

Cardella		**Gash**	
Beginning Balance	0	Beginning Balance	7
Ending Balance	8	Ending Balance	7
Receipts	55	Receipts	67
In-kind	50	In-kind	99
Total Receipts	105	Total Receipts	166
Expenditures	47	Expenditures	67
In-kind	50	In-kind	99
Total Expenditures	97	Total Expenditures	166

Table 6.8
77th House District - Results, Receipts, and Expenditures
1992 General Election

(June 30 - Dec. 31, 1992)
(Amounts in units of $1,000)

	Saviano (Winner) Republican		Obrzut Democrat (Incumbent)	
Results	54.7%		45.3%	
Percent of Receipts by Source				
Individual/Not-itemized/Misc.	21		7	
Leader/Political	58		61	
Interest Group/Corporation	21		32	
Total	100		100	
Receipts by Source† (Breakout of above categories)				
Individual/Not-itemized/Misc.	$25	19	12	7
Loan from Candidate	3	2	0	0
Leader/Chamber Committee	28	22	102	60
Candidate/Local Party	47	36	2	1
Business/Professional	12	9	23	13
Financial	2	2	0	0
Union	2	2	10	6
Health	10	8	2	1
Law	1	1	10	6
Issue Group	0	0	10	6
Total	$130	101	$171	100

Net Receipts and Expenditures

Saviano		**Obrzut**	
Beginning Balance	9	Beginning Balance	4
Ending Balance	1	Ending Balance	0
Receipts	93	Receipts	73
In-kind	55	In-kind	98
Give Back	-18		
Total Receipts	130	Total Receipts	171
Expenditures	101	Expenditures	77
In-kind	55	In-kind	98
Give Back	-18		
Total Expenditures	138	Total Expenditures	175

† Percentages may not total 100 due to rounding.

Table 6.9
103rd House District - Results, Receipts, and Expenditures
1992 General Election
(June 30 - Dec. 31, 1992)
(Amounts in units of $1,000)

	Cozad Republican	Prussing (Winner) Democrat
Results	49.9%	50.1%
Percent of Receipts by Source		
Individual/Not-itemized/Misc.	35	10
Leader/Political	30	82
Interest Group/Corporation	35	8
Total	100	100

Receipts by Source[†] (Breakout of above categories)	Cozad $	Cozad %	Prussing $	Prussing %
Individual/Not-itemized/Misc.	$29	30	$17	10
Loan from Candidate	5	5	0	0
Leader/Chamber Committee	28	28	128	78
Candidate/Local Party	1	1	6	4
Business/Professional	16	16	3	2
Financial	5	5	0	0
Union	3	3	5	3
Health	10	10	1	1
Law	0	0	3	2
Issue Group	1	1	2	1
Total	$98	100	$165	101

Net Receipts and Expenditures

Cozad		Prussing	
Beginning Balance	77	Beginning Balance	8
Ending Balance	1	Ending Balance	3
Receipts	56	Receipts	78
In-kind	60	In-kind	87
Give Back	-18		
Total Receipts	98	Total Receipts	165
Expenditures	132	Expenditures	84
In-kind	60	In-kind	87
Give Back	-18		
Total Expenditures	174	Total Expenditures	171

[†] Percentages may not total 100 due to rounding.

"We want completely clean elections with no tainted money, and we want full and unfettered rights of free speech and association. You cannot have both. If you're not going to tinker with the First Amendment, you have to accept the fact that you can't dam the flow of political money."

Political commentator Larry Sabato

CHAPTER 7
THE PROMISES AND PROSPECTS OF REFORM

"Politics in Illinois is a full contact sport," contends one longtime Springfield lobbyist, "Not for the faint of heart." Nor for the thin of wallet, based on the findings of this comprehensive examination of the financing of legislative elections in 1990 and 1992. The overall cost of legislative elections has risen dramatically over the past 20 years. The cost of targeted races and the level of participation by legislative leaders and interest groups has risen even more dramatically. When the reports from the 1994 elections are available and the data are analyzed, existing records for spending by candidates and legislative leaders will be broken again. Is all of this a problem? If so, are there any changes that could be adopted in the way we finance elections that are both effective and politically viable?

Concerns over the role of money in elections flow from two intertwined basic values: a desire to ensure the integrity of elections and the actions of elected officials and a desire to make running for public office as open and fair as possible. The health of our political system depends on public confidence that the electoral process is open and fair, that elected public officials are honest and really care about their constituents, and that individuals count and can make a difference. If elections can be bought, or if most citizens believe they can, the faith of the general public in the legitimacy and fairness of the political system will be destroyed. If candidates for office can be bought, or if most citizens believe they can, then the integrity and sincerity of all elected public officials is called into question. If elections are so expensive that only incumbents or rich, famous, or unscrupulous challengers can get elected, or if the citizens believe they are, the belief that individuals count and that they can make a difference will be lost.

While the basic values invoked by those concerned about the role of money in elections are universally shared, no such agreement exists as to the actual dangers posed by the role of money in elections. Even a general agreement that the role money plays in elections creates problems usually fails to survive a discussion of what the specific problems are. And agreement on the problems seldom extends to agreement on the best way to attack the problem.

For example, are most legislative elections uncompetitive because they are too expensive? Or is the ever-growing cost of elections the result of challengers trying to make them more competitive? How the problem is defined will largely determine what solutions seem appropriate. If the problem is how to ensure that challengers raise enough money to be competitive with incumbents, then the limits and restrictions making it more difficult to raise money that are aimed at reducing the costs of elections overall could also make elections less competitive by increasing the difficulty for challengers to compete with incumbents. If the problem is how to make challengers more competitive in legislative elections, then a system of voluntary spending limits and generous public funding would make all challengers more competitive. But it would also greatly increase the total cost of legislative elections, primarily through the expenditure of public funds.

Campaign Finance Regulation and Legislative Elections

In addition to the general problems inherent in designing a system of campaign finance regulation, designing a system for legislative elections presents some unique problems if the goal is to level the playing field for challengers. The first problem is that of frivolous candidates winning primary elections for the minority party in noncompetitive districts. Unlike the election of a chief executive, the chances are good that some challengers who are not responsible, serious candidates will win official party nominations for seats in the legislature. The prospect of these fringe candidates being eligible for universal benefits, such as free mailings or public financing, makes public acceptance or legislative approval of these types of reforms less likely and, if enacted, more difficult to administer. Second, the size of legislative bodies can quickly make the cost of any public financing system very expensive, again making it harder to sell. Finally, legislatures have both leadership systems and members who run from uncompetitive districts. If legislative leaders and members can raise money and then transfer funds to other legislative candidates, they have the ability to concentrate campaign funds in specific districts, greatly increasing the cost of these races and making some candidates competitive who would not have been so without leadership support. Legislative leaders who have considerable power over the outcome of legislative elections are unlikely to voluntarily give it up. Implementing a campaign finance system is complicated by the nature of legislatures and legislative elections. Furthermore, concerns over implementation further dim the already unlikely prospect that legislatures will adopt measures that provide more resources for challengers.

In contrast, placing limits on who can contribute to a candidate and how much and placing limits on the transfer of money from one campaign to another is no more complicated to implement for legislative elections than for presidential or gubernatorial elections. Getting legislatures to adopt these types of restrictions is still difficult, but the implementation for legislative elections does not present any unique problems.

Options for Change

The alternative futures for regulating the financing of legislative elections in Illinois are variations on four themes: a status quo option, a restriction option, an augmentation option, or a sunshine option. The appeal of a particular option depends on how a person feels about the particular objectives that underlie the option. Most everyone agrees that money should not corrupt or appear to corrupt either legislative elections or the legislative process. Similarly, most everyone believes in open and fair legislative elections. In pursuit of those values, most everyone agrees that the role of money on the outcome of legislative elections should not be totally unregulated, without limits, disclosure, or reporting. Howcvcr, that is about all on which there is agreement. Disagreements over controlling the influence of money and to what end are varied and deep.

Status Quo Option. The current system of regulating the influence of money in legislative elections in Illinois has operated largely unchanged for the past 20 years. The result is a wide-open system with no restrictions on who can contribute or how much they can contribute, no system of voluntary limits and public financing, and no restrictions on how contribution funds can be spent. The consequences of this system are not surprising. Legislative campaigns have become more and more expensive. There has been a corresponding increase in the influence of groups that contribute large sums of money to political campaigns and in the influence of the legislative leaders who control much of the fundraising and spending in key legislative races. Also, funds raised from campaign contributions are routinely spent for purposes that have little or nothing to do with winning elections.

This absence of restraint and regulation is combined with a disclosure and reporting system that has produced little public awareness or understanding of who is contributing to legislative candidates, how much they are contributing, or what the money is being spent on. Continuing the status quo option guarantees more of the same: more costly elections, more concentration of power in interest groups and legislative leaders, and a growing number of scandals over nonelection spending waiting to happen or be revealed.

Restriction Option. If change were to come to the campaign finance system in Illinois, it might come through the adoption of a comprehensive set of restrictions on the flow of money. Setting legal limits and prohibitions on who can contribute and how much they can contribute would make it more difficult for groups and individuals with money to influence campaigns and the legislative process. The same limits, if applied to legislative leaders and party officials who direct the flow of money to campaigns, would also lessen the influence leaders have over campaigns and the legislative process.

Restrictions and limits could also be adopted on the expenditure of funds from campaign committees and on the use of funds after an elected official leaves office. Expenditures that are either clearly proper or clearly improper are easy to define and specify through examples. But some expenditures fall into a gray area where agreement over what is proper or improper does not come easily. Administration of this type of law is difficult and often controversial.

These types of changes would make it more difficult, but clearly not impossible, for those who control the flow of money to dominate the electoral and legislative process. Such restrictions might also slow down the growth of campaign costs. Experience at the federal and state levels with limits on contributions is not encouraging. And given the U.S. Supreme Court decision in *Buckley v. Valeo*, there is no way to limit independent or personal expenditures. In practice, attempts to hold back the flow of money in politics seem as successful as trying to hold back the tide. One analyst compared political money to the liquid-metal robot in *Terminator 2*, "Just when you think you have dealt with it, it rises from the floor behind your back" (Gurwitt 1992).

Augmentation Option. In an effort to make challengers more competitive or to reduce the influence of interest groups, proposals could be adopted to provide some form of a system of public financing. Money could be given directly to candidates or funneled through political parties. Nonmonetary resources could be provided to candidates or political parties in the form of publicly funded mailings, TV, or radio time. These resources could be provided without restriction. If public funding were combined with voluntary spending limits, the change would both augment and restrict the existing campaign finance system. But there is no certainty that these types of changes would achieve either the goal of making elections more competitive or the goal of lessening the cost of campaigns. Again, the federal and state experiences are not encouraging. And there is no certainty what indirect effects these changes would produce in the electoral system.

Sunshine Option. Change might also come to Illinois through adopting and implementing a comprehensive reporting program that make both the raw contribution and expenditure data and summaries and analysis of that data readily available to the news media and the general public. Letting the sun shine on the campaign finance activities of candidates, legislative and party committees, and interest groups and corporations would not *require* any change in behavior. But certain knowledge, such as the sources of a candidate's money and what that money was spent on, would become widely disseminated; public knowledge would certainly cause reflection and modification of present and future behavior by some candidates. The basic assumption of the sunshine option is that the campaign finance process can become self regulating if the candidates realize that voters will know who contributes to the candidate's campaign, how much was contributed, and how much the candidate is spending to get elected.

While the goals of the sunshine option are simple and clear, full implementation would be difficult and costly. The dual keys to the success of a sunshine approach are complete information and timely information. The major difficulty comes in trying to ensure that information is timely. Most of the spending and much of the fundraising take place in the last month before an election. Providing preelection data to the general public that accurately reflect the sources and the magnitude of the contributions and expenditures would be a daunting task. It would require electronic filing by candidates using a standard format and software program and a huge investment by the State Board of Elections in hardware, software, and additional staff. The exact magnitude of the cost would depend on whether data were to be available through summary written reports provided by the state board, electronic copies of candidate's reports, or on-line access to a database for all candidates, or all of the above.

Without some kind of coding or interpretation, the significance of much of the raw data on contributions and expenditures would be lost on most people who examine candidate reports, but providing coding or interpretation would require more staff time. And much of the information would come from uncontested races and therefore of little interest or use to voters or the news media.

The cost of providing preelection data in a form other than public access to a general database or copies of candidates' reports on a disk in a standard format would probably be prohibitive. One intermediate step would be to adopt the requirement that records of all contributions from individuals contain the occupation or employer of the contributor. This requirement is used by a number of states. The problem is that if information about contributions and expenditures is not available in any comprehensive form until after the election, then the preventive, self-regulating impact of having to report receipts and expenditures is lessened. It is not eliminated, however, because most candidates expect to run again. With an eye toward the next election, they will be careful about both appearances and real conflicts. The requirement to disclose sources of funds and objects of expenditures through (1) comprehensive post-election reporting; (2) easy access to the data for news organizations and the general public; and (3) comprehensive coding, sorting, and interpreting of the data will affect candidate behavior before the election.

Adopting some form of the restriction or the augmentation options does not exclude also adopting the reporting requirements of the sunshine option. Proponents of restrictions or augmentation usually include full disclosure and reporting as part of an overall approach to regulating campaign finance. But they regard reporting as only supportive of their primary goal of changing the campaign finance system by either restricting the flow of private money or substituting public resources for private resources. However, proponents of the sunshine option see it as a comprehensive solution. As Kent Cooper of the Federal Election Commission put it, "You've got to let the voters see what's going on and then let them make their own decision. If they want to reelect a guy who's representing a cash constituency more than them, fine: If they make an informed choice, the system's not corrupt" (Gurwitt 1992).

Monitoring and enforcing contribution limits, providing public funding for campaigns, monitoring and enforcing expenditure restrictions, providing mailing or media for candidates, and processing and reporting contribution and expenditure data in a timely manner all cost money. Any one of these reforms would require additional staff, equipment, and funding for the State Board of Elections. The total bill for any comprehensive change in the campaign finance system would be substantial.

Reforming Campaign Finance in Illinois

Historically, Illinois has not been in the vanguard of political reform. It is not an accident that two of the seminal U.S. Supreme Court decisions limiting political patronage originated in Illinois. The most recent, *Rutan v. The Republican Party of Illinois*, was decided in 1990. Perhaps the most-often quoted statement on political reform comes from Finley Peter Dunne's fictional character Mr. Dooley, who offered political commentary during the late 1800s. When the municipal reform-good government movement was sweeping the country, Mr. Dooley asserted that "Chicago ain't ready for reform." When it comes to campaign finance reform, Illinois probably ain't ready for that either.

The adoption of the lobbyist registration law is illustrative of how reform usually comes to Illinois. Until 1993 Illinois had one of the weakest lobbyist registration and reporting laws in the nation. During the push in 1991 and 1992 for riverboat or casino gambling in Chicago, there were claims that lobbyists for gambling interests were spending more than $1 million dollars to insure passage. Press examinations of lobbyist expenditure reports yielded little information because the reporting requirements were weak and easily circumvented. This provided the impetus for putting legislation to tighten the registration and reporting requirements on the public agenda. Long an agenda item for reform/good government groups like Common Cause, the idea would have been doomed without a powerful political sponsor. That came in the form of the secretary of state, George Ryan, who took up the issue for reasons having as much to do with running for reelection as with a commitment to reform. Ryan's sponsorship and the fact that the changes did not involve limits of behavior or disclosure of fees helped to allay the fears of lobbyists. Scandal or the threat of scandal are generally necessary for the serious consideration of reform in Illinois, although they are rarely sufficient in and of themselves.

Serious consideration may lead to the adoption of reform, but adoption does not always guarantee success. Early experience with the new lobbying registration law is again illustrative. The new law places no restrictions on the behavior of lobbyists, but it does require that lobbyists register and report expenditures. Preliminary examinations of the reports indicate that there is little going on worth noting. While the requirement to report expenditures may have tempered the behavior of both lobbyists and legislators, there is a better explanation for the lack of large expenditures on legislators. Gifts, trips, meals, and honoraria from lobbyists have generally been problems in states with restrictive campaign finance laws. There is little reason in Illinois for a group to organize a dinner and pay a legislator a large honorarium for a speech, when they can just write a check in any amount and contribute it to the legislator's campaign committee.

The record of campaign finance reform legislation in Illinois over the past 20 years is a sorry one. As noted earlier, the Democratic-controlled legislature passed public funding plans for the office of governor, knowing that the governor would veto them. Which is exactly what happened. Beyond that there is nothing. No limits, no restrictions, no controls, no augmentation, no increased reporting.

Barring a major scandal, a major restructuring of the Illinois campaign finance system is very unlikely. Legislators and their leaders are not going to vote for limits on contributions or transfers, and few incumbents will vote for programs that put resources in the hands of candidates who might challenge them in the next election.

But some modest proposals in the areas of reporting and regulating nonelection expenditures are worth advancing. Five specific changes are offered for consideration.

Disclosure: Expanding Who Has to File. In addition to candidates, all groups and entities, but not individuals, that contribute more than a certain amount to campaigns in Illinois should be required to file disclosure reports (appendix A, pp. 175-83). Some labor unions file reports, some do not. Some Illinois-based corporations file reports, most do not. Some national corporations file reports, most do not. Some issue groups file reports, some do not. In many cases, forming a political committee with officers would be unnecessary or redundant. A simple, itemized report would be sufficient. A higher threshold, $10,000, for example, would exempt most who contribute, particularly local groups and companies. This requirement would provide comprehensive information on the activities of groups across campaigns. It would also provide information that could be crosschecked against candidate reports, allowing for verification of what was being reported by both the candidates and the contributors.

Disclosure: Truth in Labeling. Individuals who contribute more than $500 to a candidate's political committee should be required to list their occupation and the name of the company that employs them. This might have a chilling effect on some contributions, but it would make it much more difficult to hide contributions on behalf of a particular interest group by fragmenting them among the individual members of the group.

Groups should continue to be able to name their political committees anything they choose. If the association for hazardous waste disposal sites wants to call its political committee the Environmental Conservation League, it should have that right. But the information filed with the State Board of Elections when a committee is organized should clearly state who the committee represents. There are times when reading the D-1 form filed for a committee organization merely marks the beginning of the hunt to discover the group's composition or membership.

Reporting: Creating a Database and Making It Accessible. As a first step, campaigns and political committees that exceed a given spending or contribution threshold should be required to file their reports on computer disk in a standard format using a universally compatible software program. Any campaign or political committee of any size has computerized record keeping, or should have. The State Board of Elections staff would be overwhelmed if required to create a database for all of the contribution and expenditure records of all of the campaigns in Illinois. If campaigns are required to do what most of them are already doing, put records of campaign contributions and expenditure on an electronic spreadsheet or in a database and then share that information with the state board, the task becomes much more manageable.

Once the database has been created, the next step is to make it accessible. The law requiring a person to complete a D-3 form and send a copy to each committee examined is a dinosaur law whose only purpose is to make access to campaign records more troublesome. It should be eliminated in the name of good sense and fair play. As a practical matter, once the state board creates a database of campaign records, the D-3 form requirement will have to be eliminated. Otherwise, every time a citizen wants to search the database, he/she will be required to fill out over 300 D-3s. A more reasonable approach would be to require anyone examining disclosure reports to identify themselves in writing and sign a form acknowledging the penalties for misuse of the information, but to eliminate the requirement that information be sent to the committee being examined.

Access to the database should be as open as possible, allowing individuals to search and examine records in the offices of the state board and/or to purchase parts or all of the database at a reasonable cost.

Reporting: Expanding the Reporting and Analysis Function of the State Board. While media organizations, academic researchers, political parties, public officeholders, and interest groups will all take advantage of access to the database, their collective efforts will not ensure that the raw contribution and expenditure data will be translated into information that systematically describes and explains what the numbers and the trends mean. The State Board of Elections should be the source of comprehensive analysis and objective reporting of campaign finance data in Illinois. Providing the board with the staff and resources to accomplish this responsibility ensures that detailed analysis and reporting will take place on a continuing basis.

Regulation: Restricting Nonelection Expenditures. In the spring of 1993 the contributors to Rep. Robert LeFlore's political committee got to do what many voters only dream about: bury a politician. Following his death, both his funeral and his burial plot were paid for with funds from his political committee. While that may have been the ultimate non-electoral expenditure, it does not rank all that far below the expenditures of campaign funds on cars, sporting event tickets, trips, no-interest loans, country club dues, meals, flowers, gifts, and booze that exceed hundreds of thousands of dollars each election cycle. As one longtime association lobbyist put it, "Only about a third of my contributions go to contested elections, the rest just support politicians lifestyles." Definitions of what are proper expenditures of campaign funds and what are improper, and therefore illegal, expenditures of campaign funds should be written into the law. Limitations or prohibitions on former elected officials using campaign funds after they leave office should also be adopted. To make this work, the State Board of Elections should be given the resources and the authority to administer and enforce these restrictions.

The Prospects for Reform

The chances for adoption of even these modest reforms are problematic. The current system works well for legislative leaders, members of the General Assembly, and organized interest groups. From the perspective of the legislative leaders, and most of their members, and most interest groups, no change is better than some change. But those who benefit from the system as it stands, if pushed to make changes, will want to choose those changes that have the least impact on the achievement of their goals. The only recent initiatives in the area of campaign finance reform to attract much support in the General Assembly are proposals to ban legislators from holding fundraisers in Springfield during the last month of the legislative session, except for the legislative leaders. Only in Illinois would such a proposal be considered serious campaign finance reform. Faced with pressure for change generated by some major scandal or some external political event like Watergate in the early 1970s, the natural response of those in control of the political system in Illinois would be to look for one that was entirely symbolic or at least minimal in its actual impact. From this perspective, enhanced reporting and adoption of regulations on nonelection expenditures could be seized upon as a way of doing something while forestalling attempts to push for more comprehensive or restrictive changes in Illinois' campaign finance system.

The Paradox of Sunshine-based Reform

The benefits from putting restrictions on nonelection expenditures of campaign funds would be immediate and positive. It would alter the behavior of candidates and elected officials and remove one source of the cynicism that citizens and the news media hold toward the role of money in politics. Dramatically increasing the amount of information available on who is contributing, how much they are contributing, and how much is being spent on political campaigns could also have a positive impact on the behavior of candidates and the perceptions of citizens, but the results would not be immediate. In fact, the public reaction to the disclosures that would follow from making Illinois' campaign finance law a true sunshine law would probably be strongly negative.

Detailed, comprehensive information about the amount, sources, and impact of money would tend to confirm the belief that the political system in Illinois is a marketplace, but not a marketplace of ideas as envisioned by the proponents of democracy. Calls for drastic action or increased cynicism about the role of money in the political process would be the likely short-term response. The alienated and the disaffected would use the information as an excuse for becoming more cynical and more withdrawn from the political process. Increased information about who is paying for elections in Illinois and what they cost would also be met with calls for restrictions on who could contribute and with severe limits on the amount of money an individual or group could contribute. Merely overlaying a system of controls on the Illinois political system without trying to fundamentally change the nature of how we define and play politics is not likely to produce the desired results. The politics of reaction are tempting, but "do something, anything" is a tried and true formula for producing a public policy disaster. An even stronger temptation would be to blame the individuals in office for the state of the political system and call for their defeat at the polls. Some of this would be sincere and some would be pure opportunism. Whatever the motivation, somehow "throwing the rascals out" never seems to lead to fundamental change.

Given time, complete sunshine in disclosing and reporting campaign contributions and expenditures will cause both politicians and interest groups to significantly modify their behavior. The question is: will the change be toward obscuring the relationships and linkages between candidates for public office and those who contribute to their campaigns with new and more complex ways of circumventing the spirit and the letter of the law, or will the change be toward a more restrained, open system of financing elections based on the conscience of the candidates and the watchful eye of voters determined to hold candidates accountable at the ballot box and in office for the relationship between their actions and those who finance their campaigns? A mature dialogue between citizens, candidates, elected officials, and the news media about the role of money in politics sounds both trite and unrealistic in the face of the way we finance campaigns in Illinois and the alienation and mistrust that dominates the monologues of what currently passes for public discourse on politics. But change must start somewhere. And a few modest steps toward restoring public confidence by providing the basis for an informed conversation are a beginning.

Appendix A - State Board of Elections Campaign Disclosure Forms

FORM **D-1**

STATEMENT OF ORGANIZATION

PLEASE TYPE OR PRINT IN BLACK INK

Full name and complete mailing address of Political Committee

FOR OFFICE USE ONLY
IDENTIFICATION NO.

☐ CHECK IF ADDRESS CHANGE

SEE GUIDE TO CAMPAIGN DISCLOSURE FOR INSTRUCTIONS

1. DATE COMMITTEE CREATED ____________

2. AMOUNT OF FUNDS AVAILABLE FOR CAMPAIGN EXPENDITURES AS OF THE DATE THE COMMITTEE WAS CREATED $ ____________

3. ☐ NEW COMMITTEE ☐ AMENDMENT (MUST BE FILED WITHIN 10 DAYS OF ANY CHANGES)

4. POLITICAL COMMITTEE'S AREA OF ACTIVITY, SCOPE AND PARTY AFFILIATION

A — ☐ STATE POLITICAL COMMITTEE ☐ STATE & LOCAL POLITICAL COMMITTEE
☐ LOCAL POLITICAL COMMITTEE

B — IF THIS IS A LOCAL OR A STATE AND LOCAL POLITICAL COMMITTEE, PLEASE LIST THE COUNTY OR COUNTIES IN WHICH IT WILL OPERATE:

C — THIS COMMITTEE WILL PRIMARILY ☐ SUPPORT ☐ OPPOSE CANDIDATES FOR LOCAL OR STATE OFFICE

D — THIS COMMITTEE WILL ☐ SUPPORT ☐ OPPOSE QUESTIONS OF PUBLIC POLICY

E — POLITICAL PARTY AFFILIATION ____________

F — COUNTY OF RESIDENCE OF CANDIDATE ____________

5. PURPOSE(S) OF THE POLITICAL COMMITTEE: *

6. CANDIDATE(S) THE COMMITTEE IS SUPPORTING OR OPPOSING *

NAME AND STREET ADDRESS	SUPPORT	OPPOSE	OFFICE	PARTY AFFILIATION

* IF MORE SPACE FOR INFORMATION IS REQUIRED, PLEASE ATTACH ADDITIONAL SHEETS

(THIS FORM MAY BE REPRODUCED)

Appendix A, continued

NAME OF POLITICAL COMMITTEE	IDENTIFICATION NUMBER

7. REQUIRED COMMITTEE OFFICERS *

POSITION	NAME	STREET ADDRESS AND PHONE NUMBER
CHAIRMAN		
TREASURER		

8. POSITION, NAME AND ADDRESS OF EACH CUSTODIAN OF THE COMMITTEE'S BOOKS AND ACCOUNTS *

POSITION	NAME	STREET ADDRESS

9. LIST OF ALL FINANCIAL INSTITUTIONS AND OTHER REPOSITORIES OF COMMITTEE FUNDS *
(IF AMENDING, LIST ALL AS OF TODAY'S DATE) *

NAME	ADDRESS

10. DISPOSITION OF RESIDUAL FUNDS IN THE EVENT OF DISSOLUTION OR TERMINATION OF THE COMMITTEE

- ☐ RETURN TO CONTRIBUTORS IN AMOUNTS NOT TO EXCEED THEIR INDIVIDUAL CONTRIBUTION
- ☐ TRANSFER TO ANOTHER POLITICAL COMMITTEE ____________________
- ☐ TRANSFER TO A CHARITABLE ORGANIZATION ____________________

VERIFICATION

I DECLARE THAT THIS STATEMENT OF ORGANIZATION HAS BEEN EXAMINED BY ME AND TO THE BEST OF MY KNOWLEDGE IS A TRUE, CORRECT AND COMPLETE STATEMENT OF ORGANIZATION AS REQUIRED BY ARTICLE 9 OF THE ELECTION CODE. I UNDERSTAND THAT THE PENALTY FOR WILLFULLY FILING A FALSE STATEMENT SHALL BE A FINE NOT TO EXCEED $500 OR IMPRISONMENT IN A PENAL INSTITUTION OTHER THAN THE PENITENTIARY NOT TO EXCEED 6 MONTHS, OR BOTH FINE AND IMPRISONMENT.

SIGNATURE OF TREASURER OR CANDIDATE ____________________ DATE

THE ILLINOIS STATE BOARD OF ELECTIONS IS REQUESTING DISCLOSURE OF INFORMATION THAT IS NECESSARY IF YOU QUALIFY AS A POLITICAL COMMITTEE AS OUTLINED UNDER PUBLIC ACT 78–1183. DISCLOSURE OF THIS INFORMATION IS REQUIRED. FAILURE TO PROVIDE ANY INFORMATION COULD RESULT IN A FINE UP TO $1,000.00. THIS FORM IS IN COMPLIANCE WITH THE FORMS MANAGEMENT PROGRAM ACT.

STATE POLITICAL COMMITTEE
RETURN TO:
STATE BOARD OF ELECTIONS
1020 SOUTH SPRING STREET
P.O. BOX 4187
SPRINGFIELD, IL 62708

LOCAL POLITICAL COMMITTEES AND
STATE AND LOCAL POLITICAL COMMITTEES
RETURN ORIGINAL TO:
STATE BOARD OF ELECTIONS
AND COPY TO:
APPROPRIATE COUNTY CLERK

REVISED JULY 1, 1990

Appendix A, continued

FORM D-2	REPORT OF CAMPAIGN CONTRIBUTIONS AND EXPENDITURES
	(CHECK APPROPRIATE BOXES) (PLEASE TYPE OR PRINT IN BLACK INK)
	☐ Pre-Election Report — Election Date ______________
	☐ Semi-Annual Report
	☐ Non-Participation — Election Date ______________
	☐ FINAL REPORT
	☐ Amendment of Report indicated above

Full name and complete mailing address of Political Committee

FOR OFFICE USE ONLY
IDENTIFICATION NO.

☐ CHECK IF ADDRESS CHANGE

REPORTING PERIOD	FUNDS AVAILABLE AT THE BEGINNING OF THE REPORTING PERIOD	STATE POLITICAL COMMITTEES RETURN TO:	LOCAL POLITICAL COMMITTEES AND STATE AND LOCAL POLITICAL COMMITTEES
FROM ______ THRU ______	$	STATE BOARD OF ELECTIONS 1020 SOUTH SPRING STREET P.O. BOX 4187 SPRINGFIELD, IL 62708	RETURN ORIGINAL TO: STATE BOARD OF ELECTIONS AND COPY TO: APPROPRIATE COUNTY CLERK

SEE GUIDE TO CAMPAIGN DISCLOSURE FOR INSTRUCTIONS

COMPLETE 1-7 FOR PRE-ELECTION REPORTS

COMPLETE ALL SECTIONS FOR SEMI-ANNUAL AND FINAL REPORTS

SECTION A — RECEIPTS

1. Individual Contributions:
   a. Itemized (from Schedule A) . . $ ______________(1a)
   b. Not-Itemized . . . . $ ______________(1b)

2. Transfers In:
   a. Itemized (from Schedule A) . . $ ______________(2a)
   b. Not-Itemized . . . . $ ______________(2b)

3. Loans Received:
   a. Itemized (from Schedule A) . . $ ______________(3a)
   b. Not-Itemized . . . . $ ______________(3b)

4. Other Receipts:
   a. Itemized (from Schedule A) . . $ ______________(4a)
   b. Not-Itemized . . . . $ ______________(4b)
   TOTAL RECEIPTS (1-4) . . . . . . $ ______________

★★★★★★★★★★

5. In-kind Contributions:
   a. Itemized (from Schedule I) . . $ ______________(5a)
   b. Not-Itemized . . . . $ ______________(5b)
   TOTAL IN-KIND . . . . $ ______________

SECTION B — EXPENDITURES

6. Transfers Out:
   a. Itemized (from Schedule B) . . $ ______________(6a)
   b. Not-Itemized . . . . $ ______________(6b)
7. Loans Made:
   a. Itemized (from Schedule B) . . $ ______________(7a)
   b. Not-Itemized . . . . $ ______________(7b)
8. Expenditures:
   a. Itemized (from Schedule B) . . $ ______________(8a)
   b. Not-Itemized . . . . $ ______________(8b)
   TOTAL EXPENDITURES (6-8) . $ ______________

SECTION C — DEBTS AND OBLIGATIONS

(Include previously reported unpaid debts)

9. a. Itemized (from Schedule C) . $ ______________(9a)
   b. Not-Itemized . . . . $ ______________(9b)
   TOTAL DEBTS & OBLIGATIONS $ ______________

SECTION D — FUNDS BALANCE

Funds available at the beginning of the reporting period . . . . . . $ ______________(A)
Total Receipts (Section A) . . . . . $ ______________(B)
Subtotal . . . . $ ______________(C)
Total Expenditures (Section B) . . $ ______________(D)
Funds available at the close of the reporting period . . . . . . $ ______________(E)

VERIFICATION

I DECLARE THAT THIS REPORT OF CAMPAIGN CONTRIBUTIONS OR THIS SEMI-ANNUAL REPORT OF CAMPAIGN CONTRIBUTIONS AND EXPENDITURES (INCLUDING ACCOMPANYING SCHEDULES AND STATEMENTS) HAS BEEN EXAMINED BY ME AND TO THE BEST OF MY KNOWLEDGE AND BELIEF IS A TRUE, CORRECT AND COMPLETE REPORT AS REQUIRED BY ARTICLE 9 OF THE ELECTION CODE. I UNDERSTAND THAT THE PENALTY FOR WILLFULLY FILING A FALSE STATEMENT SHALL BE A FINE NOT TO EXCEED $500 OR IMPRISONMENT IN A PENAL INSTITUTION OTHER THAN THE PENITENTIARY NOT TO EXCEED 6 MONTHS, OR BOTH FINE AND IMPRISONMENT.

SIGNATURE OF TREASURER OR CANDIDATE ________________ DATE

(THIS FORM MAY BE REPRODUCED)

Printed on Recycled Paper

Appendix A, continued

NAME OF POLITICAL COMMITTEE:

REPORTING PERIOD

FROM THRU

SCHEDULE A

INDICATE THE PART OF FORM D-2 BEING ITEMIZED:

☐ PART 1 — INDIVIDUAL CONTRIBUTIONS INCLUDING TICKET AND RAFFLE SALES

☐ PART 2 — TRANSFERS IN POLITICAL COMMITTEE CONTRIBUTIONS INCLUDING TICKET AND RAFFLE SALES

☐ PART 3 — LOANS RECEIVED INCLUDING ENDORSER

☐ PART 4 — OTHER RECEIPTS

FOR OFFICE USE ONLY
IDENTIFICATION NO.

SEE GUIDE TO CAMPAIGN DISCLOSURE FOR INSTRUCTIONS

ITEMIZED RECEIPTS FULL NAME, MAILING ADDRESS, AND ZIP CODE	DATE RECEIVED	AMOUNT OF EACH RECEIPT	AGGREGATE AMOUNT FOR THIS REPORTING PERIOD

USE SEPARATE PAGE(S) FOR EACH NUMBERED PART

TOTAL THIS PERIOD $ ____________
(LAST PAGE OF THIS PART ONLY)

(THIS FORM MAY BE REPRODUCED)

PAGE ______

Printed on Recycled Paper

Appendix A, continued

SCHEDULE A–1

REPORT OF CAMPAIGN CONTRIBUTIONS OF $500 OR MORE

THIS FORM MAY BE TRANSMITTED BY FAX. THE ORIGINAL MUST BE FORWARDED ON THE DAY OF FAX TRANSMITTAL.

Full name and complete mailing address of Political Committee

FOR OFFICE USE ONLY
IDENTIFICATION NO.

INSTRUCTIONS

ANY CONTRIBUTION IN AN AGGREGATE OF $500.00 OR MORE RECEIVED IN THE THIRTY DAY PERIOD PRECEDING ANY ELECTION MUST BE REPORTED WITHIN TWO BUSINESS DAYS OF RECEIPT.

CONTRIBUTIONS MUST ALSO BE REPORTED ON THE NEXT REGULAR CAMPAIGN CONTRIBUTIONS REPORT — FORM D-2 — SCHEDULE A.

RECEIVED FROM. FULL NAME, MAILING ADDRESS, AND ZIP CODE	DATE	AMOUNT
		$
		$
		$
		$
		$
		$
		$

SIGNATURE OF TREASURER OR CANDIDATE DATE

THE ILLINOIS STATE BOARD OF ELECTIONS IS REQUESTING DISCLOSURE OF INFORMATION THAT IS NECESSARY IF YOU QUALIFY AS A POLITICAL COMMITTEE AS OUTLINED UNDER PUBLIC ACT 78–1183. DISCLOSURE OF THIS INFORMATION IS REQUIRED. FAILURE TO PROVIDE ANY INFORMATION COULD RESULT IN A FINE UP TO $1,000.00. THIS FORM IS IN COMPLIANCE WITH THE FORMS MANAGEMENT PROGRAM ACT.

STATE POLITICAL COMMITTEE
RETURN TO:
STATE BOARD OF ELECTIONS
1020 SOUTH SPRING STREET
P.O. BOX 4187
SPRINGFIELD, IL 62708

LOCAL POLITICAL COMMITTEES AND
STATE AND LOCAL POLITICAL COMMITTEES
RETURN ORIGINAL TO:
STATE BOARD OF ELECTIONS
AND COPY TO:
APPROPRIATE COUNTY CLERK

(THIS FORM MAY BE REPRODUCED)

Printed on Recycled Paper

Appendix A, continued

NAME OF POLITICAL COMMITTEE:

REPORTING PERIOD

FROM THRU

SCHEDULE I
IN-KIND CONTRIBUTIONS

FOR OFFICE USE ONLY
IDENTIFICATION NO.

SEE GUIDE TO CAMPAIGN DISCLOSURE FOR INSTRUCTIONS

FULL NAME, MAILING ADDRESS, AND ZIP CODE	DATE INCURRED	DESCRIPTION OF IN-KIND	AMOUNT OF EACH RECEIPT	AGGREGATE AMOUNT FOR THIS REPORTING PERIOD

TOTAL THIS PERIOD $ ____________

(THIS FORM MAY BE REPRODUCED)

PAGE ________

Printed on Recycled Paper

Appendix A, continued

NAME OF POLITICAL COMMITTEE:

REPORTING PERIOD

FROM THRU

SCHEDULE B

INDICATE THE PART OF FORM D-2 BEING ITEMIZED:

☐ PART 6 — TRANSFERS OUT
EXPENDITURES TO POLITICAL COMMITTEES — INCLUDING TICKET & RAFFLE PURCHASES

☐ PART 7 — LOANS MADE

☐ PART 8 — EXPENDITURES

FOR OFFICE USE ONLY
IDENTIFICATION NO.

SEE GUIDE TO CAMPAIGN DISCLOSURE FOR INSTRUCTIONS

ITEMIZED EXPENDITURES FULL NAME, MAILING ADDRESS, AND ZIP CODE	DATE OF EXPENDITURE	PURPOSE	BENEFICIARY	AMOUNT OF EACH EXPENDITURE THIS REPORTING PERIOD	AGGREGATE AMOUNT THIS REPORTING PERIOD

USE SEPARATE PAGE(S) FOR EACH NUMBERED PART

TOTAL THIS PERIOD $ ________
(LAST PAGE OF THIS PART ONLY)

(THIS FORM MAY BE REPRODUCED)

PAGE ______

Printed on Recycled Paper

Appendix A, continued

NAME OF POLITICAL COMMITTEE:

REPORTING PERIOD

FROM THRU

FOR OFFICE USE ONLY

IDENTIFICATION NO.

SCHEDULE C

DEBTS AND OBLIGATIONS

SEE GUIDE TO CAMPAIGN DISCLOSURE FOR INSTRUCTIONS

FULL NAME, MAILING ADDRESS, AND ZIP CODE	DATE INCURRED	ORIGINAL AMOUNT	CUMULATIVE PAYMENT TO DATE ON DEBT	OUTSTANDING BALANCE AT THE CLOSE OF THIS PERIOD

TOTAL THIS PERIOD $ ______________

(THIS FORM MAY BE REPRODUCED) PAGE ________ *Printed on Recycled Paper*

Appendix A, continued

FORM D–3 | **REQUEST FOR INSPECTION OF CAMPAIGN DISCLOSURE DOCUMENTS**

Pursuant to Chapter 46, Article 9, Section 9–17, Illinois Revised Statutes, every "person examining a statement or report must first fill out a form prepared by the Board identifying the examiner by name, occupation, address and telephone number, and listing the date of examination and reason for such examination."

A duplicate copy of the Form D–3 will be forwarded to the political committee whose statements and/or reports have been inspected.

PLEASE PRINT

Committee Number ______________________

Committee Name & Mailing Address:

____

____

____

____

Name & Mailing Address of Person Making Inspection:

____

____

____

____

Telephone Number ______________________

Occupation & Name of Employer

____

____

MAKE CHECK PAYABLE TO STATE OF ILLINOIS

______________________ DATE

______________________________________ SIGNATURE

Reason(s) for Inspection:

____

____

WARNING — CLASS B MISDEMEANOR FOR VIOLATION: Any information copied from a committee's file shall not be sold or utilized by any person for the purpose of soliciting contributions or for any commercial purpose. It is unlawful to alter or falsify information on a copy of a committee's report for the purpose of publishing or distributing such reports with the intent to misrepresent contributions or expenditures. (For statutory reference, see Chapter 46, Section 9–17, Illinois Revised Statutes.)

The Illinois State Board of Elections is requesting disclosure of information that is necessary to accomplish the statutory purpose as outlined under Public Act 78–1183. Disclosure of this information is required. Failure to provide any information could result in a fine up to $500. This form is in compliance with the Forms Management Program Act.

**** TO BE COMPLETED FOR MAIL REQUESTS ****

I hereby certify that the information supplied in this request is true and accurate under penalty of perjury.

______________________________________ SIGNATURE

DISTRIBUTION:

White — File
Canary — Political Committee
Pink — Person Making Inspection

FOR OFFICE USE ONLY

No. of Pages ____________

Duplication Cost ____________

Postage ____________

TOTAL ____________

Date ____________

Initial ____________

Appendix B
Description of Contribution Sectors

Sources of Candidate Receipts

For this study, receipts from individuals, corporations, associations, and political sources were combined into the following categories.

Individual, Not-itemized, and Miscellaneous Contributions: Contributions from individuals who could not be identified as acting on behalf of, or in support of, a specific interest group or corporation are classified as individual contributions. Most of the itemized receipts listed under individual contributions are small ($250 or less), although the figures presented do include some very large contributions from individuals who are not linked to any particular interest. Loans from individuals other than the candidate or the candidate's family are also included in this category. Finally, all candidates are required to disclose total contributions under $150, but they are not required to itemize them or disclose the sources. These not-itemized receipts generally reflect both checks from individual citizens and ticket sales from fundraising events.

Receipts from individuals and not-itemized contributions generally represent grassroots fundraising within the district. Because such receipts represent local fundraising efforts, the total amount of individual contributions and their percentage of a candidate's total receipts provide insight into the nature of a candidate's fundraising activities.

Leadership and Chamber Committee Support: This category represents both direct transfers of funds from leader and chamber political committees and in-kind contributions. A few candidates in targeted districts may receive large transfers of money from leadership sources, but the bulk of the support that candidates receive for leadership comes in the form of in-kind contributions. The services and support expended on behalf of a candidate by leadership usually include polling and targeting information, consulting services, campaign staff, printing and mailing of direct-mail brochures, and the preparation and broadcast of media advertisements.

As noted in chapters 3 and 5, the house and senate Republican leadership transferred money to the state Republican Party, which in turn paid for printing and mailing of direct-mail brochures for Republican candidates, which had a value equal to the money transferred to the party from the leadership. Therefore, in-kind contributions for the state Republican Party to house and senate legislative candidates were included in the leadership totals.

The totals reported here are net contributions from leadership. In a number of campaigns, candidate reports will show in-kind contributions from legislative leaders in the receipts section and then transfers of funds from the candidate's committee to the chamber committee in amounts equal to a large portion of the value of the in-kind services received. A candidate may list an in-kind contribution from the chamber committee for the cost of printing and mailing a direct-mail brochure and then list a transfer of funds to the chamber committee equal to the value of the mailing. In such a case the leadership is acting as a vender of campaign services rather than as a source of in-kind campaign support. In calculating the support provided by leadership to a candidate, transfers of funds from candidates to chamber committees were subtracted from the value of any in-kind contribution from leadership. The amounts reported as receipts from leadership and chamber committees are net receipts.

Business/Professional: Receipts in this category come from businesses and manufacturing associations, individual business and manufacturing corporations, and professional associations other than lawyers or providers of financial services.

Financial: Receipts in this category come from financial and insurance associations, individual finance and insurance corporations, and professional associations such as those for accountants, underwriters, and independent insurance agents.

Union: Receipts in this category come from individual union locals, regional groupings of locals, statewide labor organizations, and national union groups and associations.

Health Professionals and Facilities: Receipts in this category come from associations of health professionals such as doctors and dentists, associations representing health facilities such as hospitals and nursing homes, and individual facilities and clinics.

Law: Receipts in this category come from associations representing attorneys, individual law firms, and individuals identified as attorneys who made large contributions.

Issue Groups: Receipts in this category come from groups such as pro-choice and pro-life groups, the National Rifle Association, groups supporting women candidates, and groups representing various conservative causes.

Loans from Candidates: Loans to the campaign from the candidate or the candidate's family are listed as receipts in this category.

Appendix C
Top 20 Interest Group Contributors to Legislative Campaigns

American Federation of State, County, and Municipal Employees (AFSCME)
Associated Beer Distributors of Illinois
Cable TV and Communication Association of Illinois
Illinois Association of Realtors
Illinois Bankers Association
Illinois CPA Society
Illinois Education Association (IEA)
Illinois Hospital and Healthsystems Association
Illinois Manufacturers' Association
Illinois New Car/Truck Dealers Association
Illinois State Dental Society
Illinois State Medical Society
Illinois State AFL-CIO
Illinois State Bar Association
Illinois Trial Lawyers Association
Personal PAC
Philip Morris, Inc.
Professional Independent Insurance Agents of Illinois
Teamsters Joint Council No. 25
United Auto Workers (UAW)

Appendix D.1
Overview of Interest Group and Corporation Campaign Contributions for the 1992 Election Cycle
January 1, 1991 through December 31, 1992
Amounts in units of $1,000

Name & ID Number	Total Expend.	Election Expend.	Legis. Elect. Expend.	$ to Democr. Leader/ Chamber	$ to Repub. Leader/ Chamber	$ to Incumb. Democr. Legis.	$ to Incumb. Repub. Legis.	$ to Democr. Challeng.	$ to Repub. Challeng.
AFL-CIO-IL PAC (S-2633) (COPE)	270	144	115	28	3	42	2	40	1
AFSCME-IL PAC (S-3348)	235	182	153	35	9	46	8	47	9
Bankers Association PAC (S-1625)	406	340	311	47	45	113	60	17	29
Beer Distributors PAC (S-3623) (ABDI)	370	365	345	56	44	118	75	25	27
Cable Association PAC (S-3482)	188	185	153	43	26	50	21	7	6
Caterpillar	52	52	52	2	22	3	16	0	9
Central Illinois Public Service (S-1678)	65	64	64	8	9	22	15	4	7
Chicago Assoc. of Commerce & Industry PAC (S-3120) (ACI)	74	66	64	5	6	23	13	6	10
Chicago Federation of Labor (S-2538)	196	132	53	23	5	14	1	9	1
Chicago Firefighters Association (S-2141)	101	58	47	10	5	19	8	6	0
Chicago Teachers Union (S-564)	179	89	61	23	0	23	1	13	1
Chicago Title Staff PAC (S-1335)	61	60	38	16	13	4	3	1	1
Community Bankers Association PAC (S-1556)	130	99	88	6	8	44	17	8	5
Construction Industry PAC (S-0316)	66	66	66	5	15	16	18	1	12
Continental Corporation PAC (S-4320)	72	65	36	8	13	12	4	1	0
CNA PAC (S-2551)	114	96	77	7	21	20	19	3	8
CPA Association PAC (S-1884)	254	248	231	27	26	92	58	11	17
Currency Exchange PAC (S-1762)	117	117	53	17	11	16	7	2	0
Credit Union League PAC (S-0879)	219	119	113	6	11	44	29	7	17
Dentist Association PAC (S-1791) (LICD)	243	191	181	32	39	53	38	7	12
Employers PAC (S-2543) (Management Assoc. of IL)	80	66	64	0	16	7	22	0	20
Ist Chicago Corporation PAC (S-3457)	262	182	108	27	32	27	14	4	4
Food Distributors Association PAC (S-2545)	90	66	65	4	6	17	18	4	16
General Contractors Association PAC (S-1182)	52	52	52	5	11	11	13	0	11
GTE-IL PAC (S-1108)	50	50	48	4	9	12	18	0	5
Harness Horseracing Association PAC (S-3389) (IHHA PAC)	60	50	41	11	10	12	4	3	2

Appendix D.1, continued

Name & ID Number	Total Expend.	Election Expend.	Legis. Elect. Expend.	$ to Democr. Leader/ Chamber	$ to Repub. Leader/ Chamber	$ to Incumb. Democr. Legis.	$ to Incumb. Repub. Legis.	$ to Democr. Challeng.	$ to Repub. Challeng.
Health Care Assoc. PAC (S-0908) (Nurs. Homes/Long)	97	57	55	3	8	26	16	0	2
Home Builders Association PAC (S-0479)	52	51	47	4	0	26	11	3	3
Hospital Association PAC (HOPE) (S-1674)	363	286	267	62	28	90	56	16	15
Hotel and Restaurant Employees Union PAC (TIP) (S-3189)	238	222	100	50	11	32	0	7	0
Household International PAC	78	78	78	26	27	9	10	4	3
IBEW 701 PAC (S-3076)	134	67	55	23	4	15	2	11	0
Illinois Amoco PAC (S-2041)	98	97	91	10	11	28	21	3	17
Illinois AT&T PAC (S-3519)	102	100	85	18	21	22	14	4	8
Illinois Bell PAC	80	80	80	27	29	4	10	1	8
Illinois Education Association (S-0478) (IPACE)	1426	679	639	4	1	328	40	224	41
Illinois Federation of Teachers (S-1692)	81	54	48	15	1	22	1	9	1
Illinois Firefighters Association (S-1804)	104	101	92	16	12	45	10	6	3
Illinois Power (S-2606) (Employee Pol. Enrollment Comm.)	113	108	100	16	18	25	23	3	16
Illinois State Bar PAC (S-2120) (Illinois Lawyers PAC)	212	152	152	25	9	63	21	22	13
Illinois State Chamber of Commerce (S-1096) (IPAC)	101	80	79	3	17	15	28	1	14
Independent Insurance Agents PAC (S-1619)	166	147	146	5	31	20	32	2	56
IUOE #143 PAC (S-3648)	58	52	42	12	6	14	5	5	1
IUOE #150 PAC (S-2759)	202	158	70	5	7	28	6	19	6
IUOE #399 PAC (S-2283)	171	96	65	26	7	21	4	7	1
Life Underwriters PAC (S-0021) (LUPAC)	86	70	70	12	10	14	14	4	24
Manufacturers' Association PAC (S-1228) (IMPAC)	572	471	452	22	86	79	135	4	127
Medical Society PAC (S-0512)	1701	1654	1483	43	279	229	304	225	401
Mid-Central Carpenters Union (S-2912)	165	77	39	3	0	19	0	17	0
New Car/Truck Dealers Assoc. PAC (S-0348) (Car of Illinois)	143	132	120	10	15	45	33	5	13
Northern Illinois Gas PAC (S-2790)	59	58	55	4	18	7	17	1	8
Nurses Association PAC (S-1623) (SCAPI)	82	48	46	5	2	21	5	6	7
Optometric Association PAC (S-3668)	89	83	81	7	15	23	18	7	10

Appendix D.1, continued

Name & ID Number	Total Expend.	Election Expend.	Legis. Elect. Expend.	$ to Democr. Leader/ Chamber	$ to Repub. Leader/ Chamber	$ to Incumb. Democr. Legis.	$ to Incumb. Repub. Legis.	$ to Democr. Challeng.	$ to Repub. Challeng.
Ophthalmologist Assoc. PAC (S-3615) (Medical Eye PAC)	62	61	60	2	1	21	22	4	10
Personal PAC (Pro Choice) (S-2622) (Pro Choice)	622	204	204	0	0	48	22	114	18
Pharmacy PAC (S-1017)	98	83	69	16	9	22	15	4	2
Philip Morris	164	164	164	61	41	33	9	18	2
Realtors Association PAC (S-410)	586	440	387	63	58	126	81	15	44
Retail Merchants Assoc. PAC (S-1604) (IL Merchants Team)	102	102	94	10	13	26	19	6	19
Savings and Loan Association PAC (S-0484)	66	59	50	10	9	15	12	3	2
Sears PAC	81	81	81	18	34	11	10	2	7
Teamsters Volunteers in Politics PAC	196	196	196	128	17	34	1	16	1
Trial Lawyers Association PAC (S-2125)	596	566	503	45	3	244	52	127	32
Troopers PAC (S-2985)	58	38	32	10	9	10	2	0	1
United Auto Workers - Illinois PAC	218	218	218	49	0	90	0	79	0
United Republican Fund PAC (S-0722)	1270	513	47	0	1	0	31	0	16
Waste Management PAC	58	58	58	28	23	2	3	1	2

Appendix D.2
Breakdown of 1992 Interest Group and Corporation Campaign Contributions for Legislative Elections
January 1, 1991 through December 31, 1992
Amounts in units of $1,000

Name & ID Number	$ to Hse. Dem. Ldr./Chm.	$ to Hse. Rep. Ldr./Chm.	$ to Sen. Dem. Ldr./Chm.	$ to Sen. Rep. Ldr./Chm.	$ to Hse. Dem. Incumb.	$ to Hse. Rep. Incumb.	$ to Sen. Dem. Incumb.	$ to Sen. Rep. Incumb.	$ to Hse. Dem. Challeng.	$ to Hse. Rep. Challeng.	$ to Sen. Dem. Challeng.	$ to Sen. Rep. Ldr./Chm.
AFL-CIO-IL PAC	22	1	6	2	27	1	14	1	16	1	24	0
AFSCME-IL PAC	15	8	20	1	33	5	13	3	16	6	31	3
Bankers Association PAC	25	28	23	18	80	35	34	25	5	11	12	18
Beer Distributors PAC	30	24	26	20	75	42	43	33	8	13	17	14
Cable Association PAC	33	12	11	14	30	11	20	11	2	3	5	3
Caterpillar	1	10	1	12	3	9	0	7	0	8	0	1
Central Illinois Public Service	6	4	2	5	16	8	6	8	2	2	2	4
Chicago Assoc. of Comm./Ind. PAC	5	3	0	4	17	7	7	6	4	8	2	3
Chicago Federation of Labor	14	3	10	2	5	0	9	0	2	1	8	0
Chicago Firefighters Association	6	1	5	4	14	2	6	7	3	0	3	0
Chicago Teachers Union	13	0	10	0	14	1	9	0	4	1	10	0
Chicago Title Staff PAC	10	5	6	8	2	1	2	1	0	0	1	1
Community Bankers Assoc. PAC	3	3	3	5	30	6	14	11	1	3	8	3
Construction Industry PAC	3	7	2	8	10	9	6	9	0	6	0	6
Continental Corporation PAC	4	4	4	8	8	1	4	3	0	0	1	0
CNA PAC	4	9	3	12	12	10	8	9	0	2	3	6
CPA Association PAC	16	13	11	13	61	34	32	24	5	10	6	8
Currency Exchange PAC	11	2	6	9	6	2	11	5	0	0	3	0
Credit Union League PAC	4	4	2	6	27	15	16	14	3	8	4	9
Dentist Association PAC	18	23	14	16	35	25	18	12	1	5	6	7
Employers PAC	0	7	0	9	4	11	3	11	0	9	0	11
1st Chicago Corporation PAC	14	14	13	18	15	6	12	7	2	2	3	2
Food Distributors Association PAC	3	3	1	3	13	11	4	7	2	9	2	7
General Contractors Association PAC	3	4	2	7	7	6	4	8	0	3	0	8
GTE-IL PAC	2	4	2	5	8	10	4	9	0	2	0	3
Harness Horseracing Assoc. PAC	6	5	5	6	6	2	6	2	0	0	3	2

Appendix D.2, continued

Name & ID Number	$ to Hse. Dem. Ldr./Chm.	$ to Hse. Rep. Ldr./Chm.	$ to Sen. Dem. Ldr./Chm.	$ to Sen. Rep. Ldr./Chm.	$ to Hse. Dem. Incumb.	$ to Hse. Rep. Incumb.	$ to Sen. Dem. Incumb.	$ to Sen. Rep. Incumb.	$ to Hse. Dem. Challeng.	$ to Hse. Rep. Challeng.	$ to Sen. Dem. Challeng.	$ to Sen. Rep. Ldr./Chm.
Health Care Assoc. PAC	2	3	1	5	16	8	9	8	0	0	1	2
Home Builders Association PAC	2	0	2	0	19	5	7	6	0	0	2	2
Hospital Association PAC (HOPE)	30	19	32	9	61	22	29	34	4	6	12	10
Hotel/Restaurant Employees Union	20	0	30	11	29	0	4	0	0	0	7	0
Household International PAC	20	16	6	11	7	3	2	7	1	1	3	2
IBEW 701 PAC	14	0	10	4	7	1	9	0	0	0	11	0
Illinois Amoco PAC	10	4	0	7	20	13	8	8	1	9	2	9
Illinois AT&T PAC	13	10	5	11	14	4	8	10	1	2	3	6
Illinois Bell PAC	16	15	11	15	2	5	1	6	1	5	1	4
Illinois Education Association	3	1	1	0	183	32	146	9	71	34	154	7
Illinois Federation of Teachers	8	1	7	0	12	1	10	0	3	1	5	0
Illinois Firefighters Association	11	9	6	4	27	4	18	6	2	1	4	1
Illinois Power	11	10	5	8	17	15	7	8	2	10	1	7
Illinois State Bar PAC	21	4	4	4	49	16	14	5	10	5	12	8
Illinois State Chamber of Commerce	2	8	2	10	13	17	2	12	0	5	1	9
Independent Insurance Agents PAC	5	12	0	19	17	23	4	9	0	35	2	21
IUOE #143 PAC	9	1	3	5	10	1	4	4	1	0	5	1
IUOE #150 PAC	5	3	0	5	21	5	6	1	9	0	9	6
IUOE #399 PAC	23	1	3	5	14	2	7	3	2	0	6	0
Life Underwriters PAC	7	7	5	3	10	9	4	5	2	16	2	8
Manufacturers' Association PAC	10	43	13	43	62	79	18	56	2	67	2	59
Medical Society PAC	25	181	18	98	181	201	48	104	175	278	50	124
Mid-Central Carpenters Union	1	0	2	0	16	0	3	0	12	0	5	0
New Car/Truck Dealers Assoc. PAC	7	10	3	5	29	18	16	15	1	6	4	7
Northern Illinois Gas PAC	3	9	2	9	4	10	3	7	0	3	1	5
Nurses Association PAC	4	1	2	1	15	3	6	2	3	5	3	2
Optometric Association PAC	5	5	2	10	15	10	8	8	3	6	4	4

Appendix D.2, continued

Name & ID Number	$ to Hse. Dem. Ldr./Chm.	$ to Hse. Rep. Ldr./Chm.	$ to Sen. Dem. Ldr./Chm.	$ to Sen. Rep. Ldr./Chm.	$ to Hse. Dem. Incumb.	$ to Hse. Rep. Incumb.	$ to Sen. Dem. Incumb.	$ to Sen. Rep. Incumb.	$ to Hse. Dem. Challeng.	$ to Hse. Rep. Challeng.	$ to Sen. Dem. Challeng.	$ to Sen. Rep. Ldr./Chm.
Ophthalmologist Assoc. PAC	1	1	1	0	14	13	6	10	2	4	3	6
Personal PAC (Pro Choice)	0	0	0	0	41	22	7	0	29	18	85	0
Pharmacy PAC	14	4	2	6	16	6	6	9	1	2	3	0
Philip Morris	30	31	31	11	26	6	7	3	12	0	6	2
Realtors Association PAC	33	34	30	24	79	44	46	37	6	18	10	25
Retail Merchants Assoc. PAC	6	7	4	6	21	10	5	10	5	11	2	9
Savings and Loan Association PAC	6	5	4	4	7	6	8	6	0	0	3	2
Sears PAC	13	20	5	14	7	6	3	4	1	4	1	3
Teamsters Volunteers in Politics PAC	76	7	53	10	23	0	11	1	12	1	5	0
Trial Lawyers Association PAC	22	3	23	0	161	40	83	12	68	13	60	19
Troopers PAC	6	2	5	7	5	0	5	1	0	1	0	0
United Auto Workers - Illinois PAC	16	0	33	0	62	0	29	0	29	0	50	0
United Republican Fund PAC	0	1	0	0	0	6	0	25	0	10	0	6
Waste Management PAC	19	12	9	11	1	1	1	3	1	2	0	0

Appendix E.1
7th Senate District - Results, Receipts, and Expenditures
1992 General Election
(June 30 - Dec. 31, 1992)
(Amounts in units of $1,000)

	Dudycz (Winner) Republican (Incumbent)	McGing Democrat
Results	51.6%	48.4%
Percent of Receipts by Source		
Individual/Not-itemized/Misc.	9	16
Leader/Political	71	13
Interest Group/Corporation	20	71
Total	100	100

Receipts by Source (Breakout of above categories)

	Dudycz $	Dudycz %	McGing $	McGing %
Individual/Not-itemized/Misc.	$25	9	$38	16
Loan from Candidate	0	0	0	0
Leader/Chamber Committee	200	70	21	9
Candidate/Local Party	3	1	10	4
Business/Professional	34	12	48	20
Financial	5	2	32	13
Union	4	1	50	20
Health	9	3	0	0
Law	2	1	25	10
Issue Group	4	1	20	8
Total	$285	100	$244	100

Net Receipts and Expenditures

Dudycz		McGing	
Beginning Balance	4	Beginning Balance	1
Ending Balance	4	Ending Balance	5
Receipts	130	Receipts	220
In-kind	156	In-kind	56
		Give Back	- 32
Total Receipts	286	Total Receipts	244
Expenditures	130	Expenditures	217
In-kind	156	In-kind	56
		Give Back	- 32
Total Expenditures	286	Total Expenditures	241

Appendix E.2
18th Senate District - Results, Receipts, and Expenditures
1992 General Election
(June 30 - Dec. 31, 1992)
(Amounts in units of $1,000)

	O'Malley (Winner) Republican	McNamara Democrat (Incumbent)
Results	58%	42%
Percent of Receipts by Source		
Individual/Not-itemized/Misc.	27	12
Leader/Political	52	43
Interest Group/Corporation	21	45
Total	100	100

Receipts by Source (Breakout of above categories)

	O'Malley $	O'Malley %	McNamara $	McNamara %
Individual/Not-itemized/Misc.	$27	13	$29	12
Loan from Candidate	29	14	0	0
Leader/Chamber Committee	102	50	77	33
Candidate/Local Party	5	2	23	10
Business/Professional	29	14	16	7
Financial	6	3	5	2
Union	0	0	72	31
Health	3	2	3	1
Law	3	2	10	4
Issue Group	0	0	0	0
Total	$204	100	$235	100

Net Receipts and Expenditures

O'Malley		McNamara	
Beginning Balance	72	Beginning Balance	12
Ending Balance	4	Ending Balance	14
Receipts	118	Receipts	133
In-kind	86	In-kind	143
		Give Back	- 41
Total Receipts	204	Total Receipts	235
Expenditures	190	Expenditures	133
In-kind	86	In-kind	143
		Give Back	- 41
Total Expenditures	276	Total Expenditures	235

Appendix E.3
24th Senate District - Results, Receipts, and Expenditures
1992 General Election
(June 30 - Dec. 31, 1992)
(Amounts in units of $1,000)

	Raica (Winner) Republican (Incumbent)	Cummings Democrat
Results	51.9%	48.1%
Percent of Receipts by Source[†]		
Individual/Not-itemized/Misc.	8	17
Leader/Political	63	18
Interest Group/Corporation	29	64
Total	100	99

Receipts by Source (Breakout of above categories)

	Raica $	Raica %	Cummings $	Cummings %
Individual/Not-itemized/Misc.	$9	8	$35	17
Loan from Candidate	0	0	0	0
Leader/Chamber Committee	75	62	25	12
Candidate/Local Party	1	1	12	6
Business/Professional	20	17	59	30
Financial	3	2	17	8
Union	6	5	31	15
Health	5	4	0	0
Law	1	1	23	11
Issue Group	0	0	0	0
Total	$120	100	$202	100

Net Receipts and Expenditures

Raica		Cummings	
Beginning Balance	17	Beginning Balance	1
Ending Balance	16	Ending Balance	38
Receipts	44	Receipts	189
In-kind	76	In-kind	47
		Give Back	- 34
Total Receipts	120	Total Receipts	202
Expenditures	44	Expenditures	151
In-kind	76	In-kind	47
		Give Back	- 34
Total Expenditures	120	Total Expenditures	164

[†] Percentages may not total 100 due to rounding.

Appendix E.4
29th Senate District - Results, Receipts, and Expenditures
1992 General Election
(June 30 - Dec. 31, 1992)
(Amounts in units of $1,000)

	Keats Republican (Incumbent)	Stern (Winner) Democrat
Results	47.7%	52.3%
Percent of Receipts by Source[†]		
Individual/Not-itemized/Misc.	12	30
Leader/Political	48	38
Interest Group/Corporation	39	34
Total	99	102

Receipts by Source[†] (Breakout of above categories)

	Keats $	Keats %	Stern $	Stern %
Individual/Not-itemized/Misc.	$28	12	$73	30
Loan from Candidate	0	0	0	0
Leader/Chamber Committee	55	24	90	36
Candidate/Local Party	54	24	4	2
Business/Professional	44	19	6	2
Financial	37	16	4	2
Union	2	1	30	12
Health	6	3	9	4
Law	0	0	22	9
Issue Group	0	0	13	5
Total	$226	99	$251	102

Net Receipts and Expenditures

Keats		Stern	
Beginning Balance	11	Beginning Balance	34
Ending Balance	0	Ending Balance	31
Receipts	173	Receipts	145
In-kind	65	In-kind	179
Give Back	- 11	Give Back	- 77
Total Receipts	227	Total Receipts	247
Expenditures	157	Expenditures	148
In-kind	65	In-kind	179
Give back	- 11	Give Back	- 77
Total Expenditures	212	Total Expenditures	250

† Percentages may not total 100 due to rounding.

Appendix E.5
34th Senate District - Results, Receipts, and Expenditures
1992 General Election
(June 30 - Dec. 31, 1992)
(Amounts in units of $1,000)

	Syverson (Winner) Republican	Holmberg Democrat (Incumbent)
Results	53.6%	46.4%

Percent of Receipts by Source		
Individual/Not-itemized/Misc.	24	19
Leader/Political	55	39
Interest Group/Corporation	21	42
Total	100	100

Receipts by Source (Breakout of above categories)

	Syverson $	Syverson %	Holmberg $	Holmberg %
Individual/Not-itemized/Misc.	$63	19	$32	19
Loan from Candidate	15	5	0	0
Leader/Chamber Committee	172	52	42	25
Candidate/Local Party	10	3	24	14
Business/Professional	33	10	8	4
Financial	4	1	3	2
Union	1	0	44	26
Health	24	7	3	2
Law	1	0	6	4
Issue Group	10	3	7	4
Total	$333	100	$169	100

Net Receipts and Contributions

Syverson		Holmberg	
Beginning Balance	7	Beginning Balance	34
Ending Balance	18	Ending Balance	26
Receipts	205	Receipts	112
In-kind	128	In-kind	60
		Give Back	-3
Total Receipts	333	Total Receipts	169
Expenditures	194	Expenditures	120
In-kind	128	In-kind	60
		Give Back	-3
Total Expenditures	322	Total Expenditures	177

Appendix E.6
37th Senate District - Results, Receipts, and Expenditures
1992 General Election
(June 30 - Dec. 31, 1992)
(Amounts in units of $1,000)

	Sieben (Winner) Republican	Gubelman Democrat
Results	54.5%	45.5%
Percent of Receipts by Source†		
Individual/Not-itemized/Misc.	16	6
Leader/Political	63	71
Interest Group/Corporation	22	23
Total	101	100

Receipts by Source† (Breakout of above categories)

	Sieben $	Sieben %	Gubelman $	Gubelman %
Individual/Not-itemized/Misc.	$25	16	$10	6
Loan from Candidate	0	0	0	0
Leader/Chamber Committee	90	57	102	59
Candidate/Local Party	9	6	21	12
Business/Professional	27	17	3	2
Financial	3	2	0	0
Union	0	0	26	15
Health	5	3	0	0
Law	0	0	3	2
Issue Group	0	0	7	4
Total	$159	101	$172	100

Net Receipts and Expenditures

Sieben		Gubelman	
Beginning Balance	25	Beginning Balance	7
Ending Balance	5	Ending Balance	1
Receipts	111	Receipts	100
In-kind	48	In-kind	77
		Give Back	-5
Total Receipts	159	Total Receipts	172
Expenditures	131	Expenditures	106
In-kind	48	In-kind	77
		Give Back	-5
Total Expenditures	179	Total Expenditures	178

† Percentages may not total 100 due to rounding.

Appendix E.7
58th Senate District - Results, Receipts, and Expenditures
1992 General Election
(June 30 - Dec. 31, 1992)
(Amounts in units of $1,000)

	R. Dunn (Winner) Republican (Incumbent)	Buzbee Democrat
Results	51.7%	48.3%

Percent of Receipts by Source

	R. Dunn	Buzbee
Individual/Not-itemized/Misc.	13	12
Leader/Political	69	55
Interest Group/Corporation	18	35
Total	100	100

Receipts by Source[†] (Breakout of above categories)

	R. Dunn $	R. Dunn %	Buzbee $	Buzbee %
Individual/Not-itemized/Misc.	$42	13	$34	12
Loan from Candidate	0	0	0	0
Leader/Chamber Committee	228	68	142	49
Candidate/Local Party	3	1	17	6
Business/Professional	31	10	11	4
Financial	3	1	5	2
Union	1	0	51	18
Health	24	7	0	0
Law	0	0	9	3
Issue Group	1	0	24	8
Total	$333	100	$293	102

Net Receipts and Expenditures

R. Dunn		Buzbee	
Beginning Balance	14	Beginning Balance	6
Ending Balance	4	Ending Balance	0
Receipts	184	Receipts	146
In-kind	149	In-kind	163
		Give Back	- 16
Total Receipts	333	Total Receipts	293
Expenditures	194	Expenditures	150
In-kind	149	In-kind	163
		Give Back	- 16
Total Expenditures	343	Total Expenditures	297

† Percentages may not total 100 due to rounding.

Appendix E.8
35th House District - Results, Receipts, and Expenditures
1992 General Election
(June 30 - Dec. 31, 1992)
(Amounts in units of $1,000)

	Barnes Republican	Steczo (Winner) Democrat (Incumbent)
Results	43.5%	56.5%
Percent of Receipts by Source		
Individual/Not-itemized/Misc.	14	17
Leader/Political	61	46
Interest Group/Corporation	25	37
Total	100	100

Receipts by Source† (Breakout of above categories)

	Barnes $	Barnes %	Steczo $	Steczo %
Individual/Not-itemized/Misc.	$18	14	$25	17
Loan from Candidate	0	0	0	0
Leader/Chamber Committee	80	60	67	45
Candidate/Local Party	1	1	1	1
Business/Professional	16	12	21	14
Financial	2	2	1	1
Union	1	1	19	13
Health	11	8	5	3
Law	3	2	5	3
Issue Group	4	3	6	4
Total	$133	101	$150	101

Net Receipts and Expenditures

Barnes		Steczo	
Beginning Balance	19	Beginning Balance	77
Ending Balance	34	Ending Balance	34
Receipts	51	Receipts	70
In-kind	91	In-kind	80
Give Back	-9		
Total Reciepts	133	Total Receipts	150
Expenditures	36	Expenditures	113
In-kind	91	In-kind	80
Give Back	-9		
Total Expenditures	116	Total Expenditures	193

† Percentages may not total 100 due to rounding.

Appendix E.9
36th House District - Results, Receipts, and Expenditures
1992 General Election
(June 30 - Dec. 31, 1992)
(Amounts in units of $1,000)

	Murphy (Winner) Republican		McGann Democrat (Incumbent)	
Results	55.8%		44.2%	
Percent of Receipts by Source†				
Individual/Not-itemized/Misc.	22		14	
Leader/Political	59		57	
Interest Group/Corporation	19		30	
Total	100		101	
Receipts by Source† (Breakout of above categories)				
Individual/Not-itemized/Misc.	$19	22	$17	14
Loan from Candidate	0	0	0	0
Leader/Chamber Committee	51	58	68	55
Candidate/Local Party	1	1	2	2
Business/Professional	6	7	13	11
Financial	2	2	2	2
Union	0	0	14	11
Health	8	9	1	1
Law	0	0	6	5
Issue Group	1	1	0	0
Total	$88	100	$123	101

Net Receipts and Expenditures

Murphy		McGann	
Beginning Balance	3	Beginning Balance	19
Ending Balance	10	Ending Balance	16
Receipts	40	Receipts	55
In-kind	56	In-kind	68
Give Back	- 8		
Total Receipts	88	Total Receipts	123
Expenditures	33	Expenditures	58
In-kind	56	In-kind	68
Give Back	- 8		
Total Expenditures	81	Total Expenditures	126

† Percentages may not total 100 due to rounding.

Appendix E.10
37th House District - Results, Receipts, and Expenditures
1992 General Election
(June 30 - Dec. 31, 1992)
(Amounts in units of $1,000)

	Vandenberg Republican	Sheehy (Winner) Democrat
Results	49.8%	50.2%
Percent of Receipts by Source†		
Individual/Not-itemized/Misc.	24	13
Leader/Political	57	70
Interest Group/Corporation	19	16
Total	100	99

Receipts by Source† (Breakout of above categories)

	Vandenberg $	Vandenberg %	Sheehy $	Sheehy %
Individual/Not-itemized/Misc.	$13	24	$12	13
Loan from Candidate	0	0	0	0
Leader/Chamber Committee	31	57	66	70
Candidate/Local Party	0	0	0	0
Business/Professional	6	11	7	7
Financial	2	4	0	0
Union	0	0	6	6
Health	2	4	0	0
Law	0	0	3	3
Issue Group	0	0	0	0
Total	$54	100	$94	99

Net Receipts and Expenditures

Vandenberg		Sheehy	
Beginning Balance	19	Beginning Balance	15
Ending Balance	0	Ending Balance	9
Receipts	30	Receipts	30
In-kind	32	In-kind	64
Give Back	- 8		
Total Receipts	54	Total Receipts	94
Expenditures	48	Expenditures	38
In-kind	32	In-kind	64
Give Back	- 8		
Total Expenditures	72	Total Expenditures	102

† Percentages may not total 100 due to rounding.

Appendix E.11
47th House District - Results, Receipts, and Expenditures
1992 General Election
(June 30 - Dec. 31, 1992)
(Amounts in units of $1,000)

	Donoval Republican		McAfee (Winner) Democrat (Incumbent)	
Results	46.4%		53.6%	
Percent of Receipts by Source				
Individual/Not-itemized/Misc.	10		10	
Leader/Political	64		50	
Interest Group/Corporation	26		40	
Total	100		100	
Receipts by Source[†] (Breakout of above categories)				
Individual/Not-itemized/Misc.	$10	10	$12	10
Loan from Candidate	13	13	0	0
Leader/Chamber Committee	64	64	62	50
Candidate/Local Party	0	0	0	0
Business/Professional	12	12	8	7
Financial	0	0	2	2
Union	0	0	13	11
Health	0	0	2	2
Law	0	0	15	12
Issue Group	0	0	9	7
Total	$99	99	$123	101

Net Receipts and Expenditures

Donoval		McAfee	
Beginning Balance	2	Beginning Balance	20
Ending Balance	0	Ending Balance	0
Receipts	36	Receipts	52
In-kind	67	In-kind	71
Give Back	-4		
Total Receipts	99	Total Receipts	123
Expenditures	37	Expenditures	72
In-kind	67	In-kind	71
Give Back	-4		
Total Expenditures	100	Total Expenditures	143

[†] Percentages may not total 100 due to rounding.

Appendix E.12
59th House District - Results, Receipts, and Expenditures
1992 General Election
(June 30 - Dec. 31, 1992)
(Amounts in units of $1,000)

	Frederick (Winner) Republican (Incumbent)	**Matijevich** Democrat (Incumbent)
Results	54.4%	45.6%
Percent of Receipts by Source		
Individual/Not-itemized/Misc.	12	15
Leader/Political	15	63
Interest Group/Corporation	73	22
Total	100	100

Receipts by Source (Breakout of above categories)

	Frederick $	Frederick %	Matijevich $	Matijevich %
Individual/Not-itemized/Misc.	$12	12	$14	15
Loan from Candidate	0	0	0	0
Leader/Chamber Committee	12	12	58	60
Candidate/Local Party	3	3	3	3
Business/Professional	20	19	4	4
Financial	6	6	1	1
Union	0	0	12	13
Health	33	32	1	1
Law	0	0	3	3
Issue Group	17	16	0	0
Total	$103	100	$96	100

Net Receipts and Expenditures

Frederick		**Matijevich**	
Beginning Balance	30	Beginning Balance	41
Ending Balance	37	Ending Balance	16
Receipts	50	Receipts	36
In-kind	57	In-kind	60
Give Back	-4		
Total Receipts	103	Total Receipts	96
Expenditures	42	Expenditures	62
In-kind	57	In-kind	60
Give Back	-4		
Total Expenditures	95	Total Expenditures	122

Appendix E.13
68th House District - Results, Receipts, and Expenditures
1992 General Election
(June 30 - Dec. 31, 1992)
(Amounts in units of $1,000)

	Wait Republican	Giolitto (Winner) Democrat
Results	49.6%	50.4%
Percent of Receipts by Source†		
Individual/Not-itemized/Misc.	71	11
Leader/Political	9	65
Interest Group/Corporation	20	25
Total	100	101

Receipts by Source† (Breakout of above categories)

	Wait $	Wait %	Giolitto $	Giolitto %
Individual/Not-itemized/Misc.	$15	13	$8	8
Loan from Candidate	70	58	3	3
Leader/Chamber Committee	10	8	59	56
Candidate/Local Party	1	1	9	9
Business/Professional	11	9	5	5
Financial	1	1	0	0
Union	0	0	15	14
Health	10	8	0	0
Law	1	1	3	3
Issue Group	1	1	3	3
Total	$120	101	$105	101

Net Receipts and Expenditures

Wait		Giolitto	
Beginning Balance	9	Beginning Balance	2
Ending Balance	31	Ending Balance	6
Receipts	109	Receipts	67
In-kind	35	In-kind	38
Give Back	- 24		
Total Receipts	120	Total Receipts	105
Expenditures	87	Expenditures	63
In-kind	35	In-kind	38
Give Back	- 24		
Total Expenditures	98	Total Expenditures	101

† Percentages may not total 100 due to rounding.

Appendix E.14
73rd House District - Results, Receipts, and Expenditures
1992 General Election
(June 30 - Dec. 31, 1992)
(Amounts in units of $1,000)

	Deets	von Bergen Wessels (Winner)
	Republican (Incumbent)	Democrat
Results	49.6%	50.4%
Percent of Receipts by Source		
Individual/Not-itemized/Misc.	11	7
Leader/Political	31	81
Interest Group/Corporation	58	12
Total	100	100

Receipts by Source† (Breakout of above categories)	Deets $	Deets %	von Bergen Wessels $	von Bergen Wessels %
Individual/Not-itemized/Misc.	$20	11	$10	7
Loan from Candidate	0	0	0	0
Leader/Chamber Committee	54	29	96	68
Candidate/Local Party	4	2	19	13
Business/Professional	11	6	0	0
Financial	2	1	0	0
Union	1	1	13	9
Health	91	49	0	0
Law	1	1	2	1
Issue Group	1	1	1	1
Total	$185	101	$141	99

Net Receipts and Expenditures

Deets		**von Bergen Wessels**	
Beginning Balance	22	Beginning Balance	5
Ending Balance	5	Ending Balance	3
Receipts	44	Receipts	70
In-kind	141	In-kind	71
Total Receipts	185	Total Receipts	141
Expenditures	61	Expenditures	72
In-kind	141	In-kind	71
Total Expenditures	202	Total Expenditures	143

† Percentages may not total 100 due to rounding.

Appendix E.15
74th House District - Results, Receipts, and Expenditures
1992 General Election
(June 30 - Dec. 31, 1992)
(Amounts in units of $1,000)

	Lawfer (Winner) Republican	**Mulcahey** Democrat (Incumbent)
Results	51.0%	49.0%
Percent of Receipts by Source		
Individual/Not-itemized/Misc.	16	9
Leader/Political	75	63
Interest Group/Corporation	9	28
Total	100	100

Receipts by Source[†] (Breakout of above categories)	Lawfer $	Lawfer %	Mulcahey $	Mulcahey %
Individual/Not-itemized/Misc.	$7	16	$9	9
Loan from Candidate	0	0	0	0
Leader/Chamber Committee	33	73	51	53
Candidate/Local Party	1	2	10	10
Business/Professional	2	4	5	5
Financial	0	0	1	1
Union	0	0	17	18
Health	0	0	0	0
Law	1	2	4	4
Issue Group	1	2	0	0
Total	$45	99	$97	100

Net Receipts and Expenditures

Lawfer		**Mulcahey**	
Beginning Balance	1	Beginning Balance	1
Ending Balance	3	Ending Balance	27
Receipts	15	Receipts	61
In-kind	30	In-kind	36
Total Receipts	45	Total Receipts	97
Expenditures	14	Expenditures	36
In-kind	30	In-kind	36
Total Expenditures	44	Total Expenditures	72

[†] Percentages may not total 100 due to rounding.

Appendix E.16
80th House District - Results, Receipts, and Expenditures
1992 General Election
(June 30 - Dec. 31, 1992)
(Amounts in units of $1,000)

	Regan Republican (Incumbent)	Ostenburg (Winner) Democrat
Results	46.0%	54.0%

Percent of Receipts by Source

	Regan	Ostenburg
Individual/Not-itemized/Misc.	12	12
Leader/Political	56	67
Interest Group/Corporation	32	21
Total	100	100

Receipts by Source[†] (Breakout of above categories)

	Regan $	Regan %	Ostenburg $	Ostenburg %
Individual/Not-itemized/Misc.	$17	12	$12	10
Loan from Candidate	0	0	2	2
Leader/Chamber Committee	77	55	77	64
Candidate/Local Party	1	1	4	3
Business/Professional	22	16	1	1
Financial	9	6	0	0
Union	0	0	19	16
Health	9	6	1	1
Law	1	1	2	2
Issue Group	5	4	3	2
Total	$141	101	$121	101

Net Receipts and Expenditures

Regan		Ostenburg	
Beginning Balance	13	Beginning Balance	1
Ending Balance	4	Ending Balance	1
Receipts	67	Receipts	47
In-kind	87	In-kind	74
Give Back	- 13		
Total Receipts	141	Total Receipts	121
Expenditures	76	Expenditures	47
In-kind	87	In-kind	74
Give Back	- 13		
Total Expenditures	150	Total Expenditures	121

[†] Percentages may not total 100 due to rounding.

Appendix E.17
85th House District - Results, Receipts, and Expenditures
1992 General Election
(June 30 - Dec. 31, 1992)
(Amounts in units of $1,000)

	Clark Republican	Novak (Winner) Democrat (Incumbent)
Results	42.4%	57.6%
Percent of Receipts by Source		
Individual/Not-itemized/Misc.	29	13
Leader/Political	58	49
Interest Group/Corporation	13	38
Total	100	100

Receipts by Source† Breakout of above categories)

	Clark $	Clark %	Novak $	Novak %
Individual/Not-itemized/Misc.	$25	29	$18	13
Loan from Candidate	0	0	0	0
Leader/Chamber Committee	44	52	60	42
Candidate/Local Party	5	6	10	7
Business/Professional	7	8	26	18
Financial	0	0	3	2
Union	0	0	16	11
Health	2	2	4	3
Law	2	2	5	4
Issue Group	0	0	0	0
Total	$85	99	$142	100

Net Receipts and Expenditures

Clark		Novak	
Beginning Balance	23	Beginning Balance	12
Ending Balance	1	Ending Balance	14
Receipts	35	Receipts	87
In-kind	50	In-kind	55
Total Receipts	85	Total Receipts	142
Expenditures	57	Expenditures	85
In-kind	50	In-kind	55
Total Expenditures	107	Total Expenditures	140

† Percentages may not total 100 due to rounding.

Appendix E.18
87th House District - Results, Receipts, and Expenditures
1992 General Election
(June 30 - Dec. 31, 1992)
(Amounts in units of $1,000)

	Rutherford (Winner) Republican		Rolinski Democrat	
Results	50.9%		49.1%	
Percent of Receipts by Source				
Individual/Not-itemized/Misc.	62		17	
Leader/Political	14		69	
Interest Group/Corporation	24		14	
Total	100		100	
Receipts by Source[†] (Breakout of above categories)				
Individual/Not-itemized/Misc.	$49	41	$22	17
Loan from Candidate	25	21	0	0
Leader/Chamber Committee	16	13	85	64
Candidate/Local Party	1	1	7	5
Business/Professional	22	18	6	5
Financial	2	2	0	0
Union	2	2	8	6
Health	2	2	1	1
Law	1	1	3	2
Issue Group	0	0	0	0
Total	$125	101	$132	100

Net Receipts and Expenditures

Rutherford		Rolinski	
Beginning Balance	1	Beginning Balance	12
Ending Balance	0	Ending Balance	0
Receipts	103	Receipts	56
In-kind	22	In-kind	76
Total Receipts	125	Total Receipts	132
Expenditures	103	Expenditures	68
In-kind	22	In-kind	76
Total Expenditures	125	Total Expenditures	144

† Percentages may not total 100 due to rounding.

Appendix E.19
95th House District - Results, Receipts, and Expenditures
1992 General Election
(June 30 - Dec. 31, 1992)
(Amounts in units of $1,000)

	Bond Republican		Edley (Winner) Democrat (Incumbent)	
Results	49.1%		50.9%	
Percent of Receipts by Source				
Individual/Not-itemized/Misc.	25		11	
Leader/Political	55		62	
Interest Group/Corporation	20		27	
Total	100		100	
Receipts by Source[†] (Breakout of above categories)				
Individual/Not-itemized/Misc.	$17	22	$14	11
Loan from Candidate	3	4	0	0
Leader/Chamber Committee	39	49	64	51
Candidate/Local Parties	7	9	14	11
Business/Professional	6	8	5	4
Financial	1	1	1	1
Union	1	1	21	17
Health	5	6	2	2
Law	0	0	5	4
Issue Group	0	0	0	0
Total	$79	100	$126	101

Net Receipts and Expenditures

Bond		Edley	
Beginning Balance	4	Beginning Balance	6
Ending Balance	1	Ending Balance	0
Receipts	47	Receipts	61
In-kind	32	In-kind	65
Total Receipts	79	Total Receipts	126
Expenditures	52	Expenditures	67
In-kind	32	In-kind	65
Total Expenditures	84	Total Expenditures	132

† Percentages may not total 100 due to rounding.

Appendix E.20
102nd House District - Results, Receipts, and Expenditures
1992 General Election
(June 30 - Dec. 31, 1992)
(Amounts in units of $1,000)

	Noland (Winner) Republican (Incumbent)	Wolfe Democrat
Results	55.6%	44.4%
Percent of Receipts by Source		
Individual/Not-itemized/Misc.	36	12
Leader/Political	14	75
Interest Group/Corporation	50	13
Total	100	100

Receipts by Source (Breakout of above categories)

	Noland $	Noland %	Wolfe $	Wolfe %
Individual/Not-itemized/Misc.	$36	36	$15	12
Loan from Candidate	0	0	0	0
Leader/Chamber Committee	13	13	84	68
Candidate/Local Party	1	1	9	7
Business/Professional	35	35	0	0
Financial	8	8	0	0
Union	4	4	10	8
Health	3	3	0	0
Law	0	0	3	2
Issue Group	1	1	2	2
Total	$101	100	$123	100

Net Receipts and Expenditures

Noland		Wolfe	
Beginning Balance	52	Beginning Balance	8
Ending Balance	14	Ending Balance	2
Receipts	86	Receipts	63
In-kind	36	In-kind	60
Give Back	-21		
Total Receipts	101	Total Receipts	123
Expenditures	124	Expenditures	68
In-kind	36	In-kind	60
Give Back	-21		
Total Expenditures	139	Total Expenditures	128

Appendix E.21
104th House District - Results, Receipts, and Expenditures
1992 General Election
(June 30 - Dec. 31, 1992)
(Amounts in units of $1,000)

	T. Johnson (Winner) Republican (Incumbent)		Satterthwaite Democrat (Incumbent)	
Results	60.7%		39.3%	
Percent of Receipts by Source				
Individual/Not-itemized/Misc.	14		10	
Leader/Political	9		76	
Interest Group/Corporation	77		14	
Total	100		100	
Receipts by Source[†] (Breakout of above categories)				
Individual/Not-itemized/Misc.	$10	14	$17	10
Loan from Candidate	0	0	0	0
Leader/Chamber Committee	6	9	123	75
Candidate/Local Party	0	0	1	1
Business/Professional	22	31	4	2
Financial	6	9	1	1
Union	4	6	14	9
Health	12	17	1	1
Law	7	10	0	0
Issue Group	3	4	3	2
Total	$70	100	$164	101

Net Receipts and Expenditures

T. Johnson		Satterthwaite	
Beginning Balance	73	Beginning Balance	30
Ending Balance	7	Ending Balance	23
Receipts	55	Receipts	73
In-kind	25	In-kind	95
Give Back	- 10	Give Back	- 4
Total Receipts	70	Total Receipts	164
Expenditures	121	Expenditures	80
In-kind	25	In-kind	95
Give Back	- 10	Give Back	- 4
Total Expenditures	136	Total Expenditures	171

[†] Percentages may not total 100 due to rounding.

Appendix E.22
106th House District - Results, Receipts, and Expenditures
1992 General Election
(June 30 - Dec. 31, 1992)
(Amounts in units of $1,000)

	Weaver (Winner) Republican (Incumbent)	**Hodge** Democrat
Results	53.5%	46.5%
Percent of Receipts by Source		
Individual/Not-itemized/Misc.	42	15
Leader/Political	11	68
Interest Group/Corporation	47	17
Total	100	100

Receipts by Source[†] (Breakout of above categories)	Weaver $	Weaver %	Hodge $	Hodge %
Individual/Not-itemized/Misc.	$16	42	$16	15
Loan from Candidate	0	0	0	0
Leader/Chamber Committee	4	11	65	61
Candidate/Local Party	0	0	7	7
Business/Professional	10	26	0	0
Financial	1	3	0	0
Union	3	8	11	10
Health	3	8	0	0
Law	1	3	3	3
Issue Group	0	0	4	4
Total	$38	101	$106	100

Net Receipts and Expenditures

Weaver		**Hodge**	
Beginning Balance	57	Beginning Balance	6
Ending Balance	21	Ending Balance	0
Receipts	32	Receipts	59
In-kind	6	In-kind	47
Total Receipts	38	Total Receipts	106
Expenditures	68	Expenditures	66
In-kind	6	In-kind	47
Total Expenditures	74	Total Expenditures	113

[†] Percentages may not total 100 due to rounding.

Appendix E.23
110th House District - Results, Receipts, and Expenditures
1992 General Election
(June 30 - Dec. 31, 1992)
(Amounts in units of $1,000)

	Stephens (Winner) Republican (Incumbent)	Daiber Democrat
Results	50.3%	49.7%
Percent of Receipts by Source		
Individual/Not-itemized/Misc.	19	10
Leader/Political	53	63
Interest Group/Corporation	28	27
Total	100	100

Receipts by Source (Breakout of above categories)

	Stephens $	Stephens %	Daiber $	Daiber %
Individual/Not-itemized/Misc.	$25	19	$13	10
Loan from Candidate	0	0	0	0
Leader/Chamber Committee	65	50	67	49
Candidate/Local Party	4	3	19	14
Business/Professional	20	15	3	2
Financial	8	6	0	0
Union	1	1	26	19
Health	2	2	0	0
Law	0	0	4	3
Issue Group	5	4	4	3
Total	$130	100	$136	100

Net Receipts and Expenditures

Stephens		Daiber	
Beginning Balance	20	Beginning Balance	2
Ending Balance	0	Ending Balance	4
Receipts	73	Receipts	62
In-kind	57	In-kind	74
Total Receipts	130	Total Receipts	136
Expenditures	93	Expenditures	60
In-kind	57	In-kind	74
Total Expenditures	150	Total Expenditures	134

Bibliography

Alexander, Herbert E. *Reform and Reality: The Financing of State and Local Campaigns*. St. Fredrick, Md.: Twentieth Century Fund Press, 1991.

Breaux, David, and Anthony Gierzynski. "'It's Money that Matters': Campaign Expenditures and State Legislative Primaries." *Legislative Studies Quarterly* 16 (August 1991): 429-43.

Buckley v. Valeo, 424 U.S. 1 (1976).

Burroughs v. U.S., 290 U.S. 534 (1934).

Conway, M. Margaret. "PACs, the New Politics, and Congressional Campaigns." In *Interest Group Politics*, ed. Allan J. Cigler and Burdett A. Loomis, 126-44. Washington, D.C.: Congressional Quarterly Inc., 1983.

Council of Governmental Ethics Laws. *COGEL Blue Book: Campaign Finance, Ethics, Lobby Law and Judicial Conduct.* Lexington, Ky.: Council of State Governments, 1993.

Dunne, Peter F. *Observations by Mr. Dooley*. New York: Harber & Bros., 1906.

Ehrenhalt, Alan. *The United States of Ambition: Politicians, Power and the Pursuit of Office.* New York: Times Books, 1991.

Evans, Diana. "Oil PACs and Aggressive Contribution Strategies." *Journal of Politics* 50 (November 1988): 1047-56.

Farr, Jr., Fletcher. "Bribery with More Subtlety." Springfield *Illinois Times*, 22 August 1980.

———. "Commentary: Wanda was Wronged." Springfield *Illinois Times*, 29 August 1980.

Federal Election Commission v. Massachusetts Citizens for Life, 107 S.Ct. 616 (1986).

First National Bank of Boston v. Bellotti, 435 U.S. 765 (1978).

Gherardini, Caroline. "Budget Put Together, Once All Side Deals Settled." *Illinois Issues* (August/September 1993): 48-49.

Gierzynski, Anthony. *Legislative Party Campaign Committees in the American States.* Lexington, Ky.: The University Press of Kentucky, 1992.

Gierzynski, Anthony, and David Breaux. "Money and Votes in State Legislative Elections." *Legislative Studies Quarterly* 16 (May 1991): 203-17.

Gopoian, J. David. "What Makes PACs Tick? An Analysis of the Allocation Patterns of Economic Interest Groups." *American Journal of Political Science* 28 (1984): 259-81.

Graff, Steve. "High-Tech Tools for Campaigners." *State Legislatures* (May 1992): 24-27.

Grenzke, Janet M. "PACs and the Congressional Supermarket: The Currency is Complex." *American Journal of Political Science* 33 (1989): 1-24.

Gurwitt, Rob. "The Mirage of Campaign Reform." *Governing* (August 1992): 48-55.

Hall, Richard L., and Frank W. Wayman. "Buying Time: Moneyed Interests and the Mobilization of Bias in Congressional Committees." *American Political Science Review* 84 (September 1990): 797-820.

Herndon, James F. "Access, Record, and Competition as Influences on Interest Group Contributions to Congressional Campaigns." *Journal of Politics* 44 (1982): 996-1019.

Illinois General Assembly. House. *House Debates.* Illinois General Assembly, 1974.

Illinois General Assembly. Senate. *Senate Debates*. Illinois General Assembly, 1974.

Illinois Governmental Ethics Act, 5 ILCS 420/4A 101-7.

Illinois State Board of Elections. *Illinois Money and Elections in 1990*. Springfield: Illinois State Board of Elections, 1992.

Illinois State Board of Elections. *Money and Elections in Illinois: 1992*. Springfield: Illinois State Board of Elections, 1993.

Jacobson, Gary C. *The Politics of Congressional Elections*. 2nd ed. Boston: Little, Brown & Co., Inc., 1987.

Jewell, Malcolm E., and David M. Olson. *Political Parties and Elections in American States*. 3rd ed. Chicago: Dorsey Press, 1988.

Johnson, Richard R. "Partisan Legislative Campaign Committees: New Power, New Problems." *Illinois Issues* (July 1987): 16-18.

Jones, Ruth A. "Financing State Elections." In *Money and Politics in the United States*, ed. Michael J. Malbin, Chatham, N.J.: Chatham House, 1984.

Kenney, David, and Barbara L. Brown. *Basic Illinois Government: A Systematic Explanation*. Carbondale: Southern Illinois University Press, 1993.

Loftus, Tom. *The Act of Legislative Politics*. Washington, D.C.: Congressional Quarterly Inc., 1994.

McDermott, Kevin, Jay Fitzgerald, Doug Finke, Bernard Schoenburg. "Gambling Lobby Flexes its Political Muscles." Springfield (Ill.) *State Journal-Register*, 24 October 1993.

———. "Cash Transactions: The Highest Bidder." Springfield (Ill.) *State Journal-Register*, 22-25 May 1994.

Michaelson, Ronald D. "The PAC Man Cometh in Illinois." *Illinois Issues* (May 1987): 10-12.

Neal, Tommy. "The Sky-High Cost of Campaigns." *State Legislatures* (May 1992): 16-23.

Olson, Mancur. *The Logic of Collective Action: Public Goods and the Theory of Groups*. Cambridge: Harvard University Press, 1965.

Poole, Keith T., Thomas Romer, and Howard Rosenthal. "The Revealed Preferences of Political Action Committees." *American Economic Review* 77 (1987): 298-302.

Redfield, Kent D. "Financing Legislative Elections in Illinois: The Role of Legislative Leaders." *Illinois Issues* (December 1991): 10-16.

———. "Limited Role of State Political Parties in Financing Illinois Campaigns." *Illinois Issues* (November 1992): 16-19.

———. "Candidates, Campaigns and Cash: How Madigan Beat the Map in the '92 Illinois House Elections." *Illinois Issues* (June 1993): 17-21.

———. "Investing in the Illinois General Assembly: Interest Group Campaign Contribution Strategies in the 1992 Legislative Elections." In *Almanac of Illinois Politics—1994,* ed. Jack R. Van Der Slik, 1-26. Springfield, Ill.: Institute for Public Affairs, Sangamon State University (University of Illinois at Springfield as of July 1, 1995), 1994.

Rosenthal, Alan. *The Third House: Lobbyists and Lobbying in the States*. Washington, D.C.: Congressional Quarterly Inc., 1993.

Rutan v. Republican Party of Illinois, 110 S.Ct. 2734 (1990).

Sabato, Larry J. *The Rise of the Political Consultants: New Ways of Winning Elections.* New York: Basic Books, 1981.

———. *PAC Power: Inside the World of Political Action Committees.* New York: W.W. Norton, 1985.

———. *Paying for Elections: The Campaign Political Thicket.* New York: Priority

Press Publications, 1989.

Schoenburg, Bernard. "GOP, Democrats Improperly Used Mailing Permit." Springfield (Ill.) *State Journal-Register*, 11 August 1993.

———. "Political Campaign Funds in Illinois Lack Tight Restrictions." Springfield (Ill.) *State Journal-Register*, 18 December 1994.

Sorauf, Frank J. *Money in American Elections.* Glenview, Ill.: Scott Foresman and Company, 1988.

Thayer, George. *Who Shakes the Money Tree?* New York: Simon and Schuster, 1973.

Troy v. State Board of Elections, Ill. App. 406 N.E.2nd 562 (1980).

Van Der Slik, Jack R., ed. *Almanac of Illinois Politics 1990.* Springfield, Ill.: Illinois Issues, 1990.

———. *Almanac of Illinois Politics—1992.* Springfield, Ill.: Illinois Issues, 1992.

———. *Almanac of Illinois Politics—1994.* Springfield, Ill.: Institute for Public Affairs, Sangamon State University (University of Illinois at Springfield as of July 1, 1995), 1994.

Van Der Slik, Jack R., and Kent D. Redfield. *Lawmaking in Illinois*. 2nd printing. Springfield, Ill.: Office of Public Affairs Communication, Sangamon State University (University of Illinois at Springfield as of July 1, 1995), 1989.

Wade, Rick. "The Prickly Politics of Health Care." *Illinois Issues* (January 1994): 22-25.

Walker v. State Board of Elections, 391 N.E.2nd 507 (1979).

Wright, John R. "PACs, Contributions and Roll Calls: An Organizational Perspective." *American Political Science Review* 79 (1985): 400-414.

———. "Contributions, Lobbying, and Committee Voting in the U.S. House of Representatives." *American Political Science Review* 84 (1990): 417-38.

Index